MOBILIZING *for the* COMMON GOOD

Places where I read this book : (H) = home

BOI : p. 216 - Mission Mississippi
Video. p. XVIII - Perkin's biography
p. 159 The Wisdom of Stability: Rooting Faith in
   a Mobile Culture
p. 159 To Live In Peace? Biblical Faith &
the Changing Inner City   Adds a
4th "R" = repentance.

# MOBILIZING *for the* COMMON GOOD

## The Lived Theology of John M. Perkins

✝

Edited by Peter Slade, Charles Marsh, and
Peter Goodwin Heltzel

UNIVERSITY PRESS OF MISSISSIPPI / JACKSON

www.upress.state.ms.us

The University Press of Mississippi is a member of the Association of American
University Presses.

First printing 2013

∞

Library of Congress Cataloging-in-Publication Data

Mobilizing for the common good : the lived theology of John M. Perkins / edited by
Peter Slade, Charles Marsh, and Peter Goodwin Heltzel.
    pages cm
    Includes index.
ISBN 978-1-61703-858-7 (cloth : alk. paper) — ISBN 978-1-61703-859-4 (pbk. : alk.
paper) — ISBN 978-1-61703-860-0 (ebook) 1. Christianity and justice—United
States. 2. Church and social problems—United States. 3. Perkins, John, 1930– I. Slade,
Peter, 1970– II. Marsh, Charles, 1958– III. Heltzel, Peter.
    BR115.J8M64 2013
261.8092—dc23                                                2013004416

British Library Cataloging-in-Publication Data available

# CONTENTS

# FOREWORD

## Ronald J. Sider

I FIRST MET JOHN PERKINS AT THE THANKSGIVING WORKSHOP IN CHI-
cago in 1973 when a diverse group of evangelical leaders wrote "The Chicago
Declaration of Evangelical Social Concern." The majority of the participants
were white evangelicals. But the gripping story of this daring, innovative
black Christian—he and his wife, Vera Mae, had already developed a major ministry of evangelism, education, health care, and promotion of civil
rights in rural Mississippi that just two years earlier, in 1970, had gotten
John beaten almost to the point of death by a local white police officer—had
already begun to circulate in white evangelical circles.

From that first meeting, I have counted John Perkins as a colleague, a
partner on the same journey, and a friend. We have never spent long peri-
ods of time together, although repeatedly over four decades we have found
ourselves together at the same conferences, speaking engagements, and
board meetings. John has a wonderful way of embracing you as a friend
and brother. And from the beginning, it was clear that we shared the same
vision: a passion to follow Jesus Christ; a commitment to combine evangelism and social action; and a resolve to battle racism in church and society.

As I have listened to John Perkins speak and read his books over the
years, I have noticed a number of key ideas or themes. I want to discuss
four: holistic ministry; the three Rs; indigenous leadership; and empowerment, not welfare.

Combining evangelism and social ministry has been at the heart of
John's passion for as long as I have known him. He has, ever since his conversion, been deeply committed to inviting people to accept Jesus Christ as
their personal Lord and Savior. But ministering to the physical and material
needs of people has been an equally vigorous commitment. He knows people need Jesus and health care, Jesus and economic resources. Both in his
preaching and teaching and in his personal example, John has championed
holistic ministry that combines word and deed. His example and witness

stand as a reminder to the next generations of evangelical social activists not to lose the passion for evangelism.

John Perkins is rightly famous for his three Rs: relocation, reconciliation, and redistribution.

The emphasis on relocation is both pragmatic and theological. The Perkinses' original move back to rural, impoverished black Mississippi may have flowed from a mixture of calling and intuition. But they quickly learned by experience that the most effective transformative leaders of poor communities live in the community, sharing the problems and struggles and then working together to solve the problems that are not "their" but "our" problems.

Theologically, John Perkins's call for relocation is clearly grounded in the incarnation. For God's fullest revelation, God did not send a book. The only Son became flesh and dwelled among us. It is the model of the incarnation that Perkins summons us to follow in his ringing appeal for more people to relocate and live in the midst of poor, broken neighbors, becoming "poor" that they may become "rich."

John knows that reconciliation has a double focus. He knows that human relationships (especially black-white relationships in the United States) are far too deeply broken for any merely human solution. The starting point must be a transformed relationship with God. The experience of unmerited forgiveness through the cross and the indwelling presence of the Holy Spirit is the best way to transform wounded people enough so they can begin to work at reconciliation between classes and races. It is because Perkins knew, taught, and lived in that divine grace that he and his circle of followers have been able to be such powerful leaders in racial reconciliation.

His own example is stunning. It took many months, but John came to forgive the white racist sheriff who almost beat him to death. It was God's grace in Perkins's life that made that possible. And his example has encouraged untold thousands to follow his example in working for racial reconciliation.

Everywhere the Perkins family lived, they began to model a reconciled community of black and white Christians. It was always a hard struggle. Racist attitudes and the other effects of a long racist history do not quickly disappear. But the Perkinses persisted. And again and again, black and white Christians were drawn together to walk the hard road toward genuine racial reconciliation in the body of Christ. That John and Vera Mae's oldest son, Spencer, became an articulate, nationally known Christian leader in racial reconciliation is a powerful witness to their vision of reconciliation.[1]

John Perkins also knew that genuine reconciliation involves a lot more than blacks and whites holding hands and singing together "We Shall Overcome." True reconciliation involves justice—economic justice. Perkins knows that true racial reconciliation must be built on the foundation of economic justice for black Americans. He also knows that will require redistribution of economic resources so that black Americans have genuine access to the land, education, and capital that will enable them to create wealth and enjoy economic independence. So with a warm smile and friendly embrace, he persuaded wealthy (conservative!) white Americans to part with some of their wealth to empower poor African Americans. One of the most amazing things about John Perkins is that he can make redistribution (*economic* redistribution!) one of his central ideas and still win the friendship and support of wealthy whites.

Indigenous leadership has been another central part of Perkins's vision. In every major place where he lived and developed holistic ministries of community development—Mendenhall and Jackson, Mississippi, and Pasadena, California—he nurtured and developed a core of younger community leaders who were able to take over when he and Vera Mae moved on. He knew that the lack of gifted, trained leadership was one of the most serious deficiencies of impoverished communities, and he learned how to identify, encourage, and train potential young leaders. Sometimes, after these young folk had gone off to college for a good education, they were just as reluctant to return to their poor home communities as John and Vera Mae were when God called them to leave their comfortable life in California and return to rural Mississippi.[2] But the Perkinses' example and teaching regularly managed to raise up new indigenous leaders.

Finally, empowerment, not welfare. John has no interest in a grand welfare system. He wants poor people to be empowered so they can earn their own way. He was an early, harsh critic of the American welfare system, which he believed destroyed initiative and created dependency. That, in part, is why he can talk about redistribution to wealthy conservative Christians. They know he has no interest in handouts. He wants the resources to produce programs that will empower poor communities to create wealth and become self-sufficient.

John Perkins has had an enormous impact on the Christian church in the United States and around the world. His honorary doctorate from Wheaton College is a vivid reminder of that. (Wheaton does not award very many doctorates to people who dropped out of school in second grade!) His impact, I believe, has been most powerful and lasting in two areas: holistic community development among the poor and racial reconciliation.

In the 1960s when John and Vera Mae started combining evangelism and social action among the very poor in rural Mississippi, most white evangelical leaders thought and taught that evangelism was the primary mission of the church. If you had a little money and time left over from your primary work in evangelism, you could do a little social ministry. Today, forty-plus years later, almost every evangelical leader agrees that biblical Christians must do both evangelism and social action.

Many people, of course, have contributed to this dramatic change. But one of the very important factors has been John Perkins's example, preaching, and writing. The story of how the Perkinses successfully combined evangelism and social action in Mendenhall and then elsewhere slowly spread in the church, especially in the white evangelical community. Everywhere John preached (and he has preached almost everywhere) he told his story of holistic ministry. And then he wrote books that told the story.

Slowly but steadily, the vision of holistic ministry in community development spread. More and more people began to develop local ministries among the poor and broken modeled on what the Perkins family was doing. Eventually, John and others organized the Christian Community Development Association (CCDA). Today, the CCDA's large annual conference—with its myriad of speeches and workshops on how to do community development in poor neighborhoods—is the very best annual conference to learn about how to truly implement holistic ministry combining evangelism and social action.

John Perkins's own modeling and his speaking, writing, and organizing have played a major role in helping not just the American church but the global church move much closer to a biblically balanced combination of word and deed.

A second major area of impact has been in the area of racial reconciliation—especially with the white evangelical community. John uses language that white evangelicals understand. His own personal story of oppression, anger, and then forgiveness is powerful. His theological grounding of reconciliation is biblically compelling. And John's warm personality is almost irresistible. His numerous appearances on boards and committees and at conferences and other events have been a steady contribution to racial understanding. His unusual combination of warmth and honesty has helped tens of thousands of white evangelicals make progress toward racial understanding and reconciliation.

Why has John Perkins been so successful? I certainly do not know anything like the complete answer to that question. But I want to reflect on some of the reasons.

First and most important is John Perkins's desire to make Jesus the center of all he does. Jesus provides both the power and the path for John. Everybody who meets John Perkins soon discovers that his overriding goal is to follow Christ and obey the Scriptures. They also see that he embraces a solidly evangelical theology. Even those who disagree with some of his ideas respect that and therefore listen carefully.

Second, Perkins's passion for evangelism wins him a hearing in places that might otherwise not listen to a black preacher talking about redistribution! In the conservative evangelical world, a strong commitment to evangelism and a solid track record of actually leading people to Christ go a long way in winning a hearing for a discussion of economic and racial justice. John's commitment to evangelism is not a tool or strategy to win supporters. It is central to his heart and theology. But it certainly does open doors and makes him more effective in evangelical circles.

Third, John is a great storyteller. Anyone who has listened to him speak knows how he weaves his own personal story into a call to empower the marginalized and overcome racism. That his own story is so powerful and compelling certainly helps. But he tells it in a way that wins hearts and minds—even donors to a great ministry.

Fourth, his life has integrity. Over many decades, he has lived what he preached. In his marriage and family and in his ministry's finances, he has been faithful. A life of consistent integrity and faithful discipleship that stretches over many decades adds power to his words. So does the humility that pervades all he does.

Perkins's warm, disarming personality has also enhanced his impact. It is very hard not to like him. He is a delightful person to be with. I suspect even Scrooge would have found him irresistible.

Finally, John Perkins was wise enough and confident enough to seek strong partners and colleagues. One thinks of H. P. Spees, who collaborated with Perkins in some of his important writing, or Wayne Gordon, who played a key role with him in establishing the CCDA. It takes a wise, confident person to be able to attract gifted persons to come on board as real partners.

John Perkins and his wonderful wife and partner in ministry, Vera Mae, have been a marvelous gift to the church in the twentieth century. They have played a key role in shaping the evangelical world, and they have blessed the lives of many thousands of hurting people. Thank you, dear brother and sister, for your faithful lives.

## NOTES

1. Spencer Perkins and Chris Rice, *More Than Equals: Racial Healing for the Sake of the Gospel* (Downers Grove, Ill.: InterVarsity Press, 1993).

2. See Dolphus Weary and William Hendricks, *I Ain't Comin' Back* (Wheaton, Ill.: Tyndale, 1990).

# INTRODUCTION

*Peter Slade*

JOHN M. PERKINS IS A TRULY EXTRAORDINARY MAN WHOSE HISTORY AND influence defy easy categorization. An African American fundamentalist Bible teacher and preacher, a third grade dropout, a recipient of honorary doctorates from numerous universities and colleges, an adviser to presidents, an author, public speaker, entrepreneur, provocateur, and community developer, he is the founding organizer and spiritual leader of the Christian Community Development Association (CCDA)—a coalition of over 200 churches and community projects working in economically depressed neighborhoods. Perhaps surprisingly, despite receiving honorary doctorates, Perkins's life, work, and influence have received surprisingly little attention from the academy.[1] The conviction of the contributors to this volume is that this situation needs to be rectified. Perkins is a significant figure in the history of the evangelical and American church. Furthermore, the lived theology implicit in his life, ministry, and the faith communities he has established and the theology explicit in his preaching and writing are important resources for critical reflection.

Consider this scene. It is nine o'clock on a bright Mississippi spring morning in West Jackson. Thirty students—the T-shirts read Wheaton, Duke, Eastern Nazarene, and Ashland—sit along both sides of a long line of white folding tables. With notepads and Bibles at the ready, they listen with rapt attention to John Perkins—the short animated figure with huge hands preaching from the end of the room.

He has placed the treasure of His love in these earthen vessels.
This is the most difficult place he could put it.
Because the idea is those vessels have got to be cracked.
They've got to take pain because they've got to enter into other
people's pain.
And because they have been broken in humility and cracked, now
they can let the light shine out!

This is not empty rhetoric, and the students know it—that is why they are here. Perkins's history and his body carry the scars of a lifetime of entering into the pain of others. "That's the most difficult task because we run away from brokenness," Perkins continues. "We run away from pain in life." The students respond to the authenticity of this man's witness and to his apparent humility: they want to choose costly discipleship; they want to be broken earthen vessels.

These students are participants in a well-established evangelical pilgrimage to Mississippi. Since the early 1970s thousands of earnest young Christians—mostly white and mostly evangelical—have traveled to Mendenhall and Jackson to Voice of Calvary and John Perkins. It is here in Mississippi—the scene of the crime—that these students from across America come to learn the truths of the gospel. "And so what is this central truth in Christianity?" Perkins asks.

> The central truth to Christianity then is that we have a leader.
> He's alive.
> He comes back to live in us with the Holy Spirit.
> He comes back to live among us when we gather together.
> And where two or three are gathered together in his name he is there
>     and there is the possibility of goodness.

This is the heart of Perkins's theology: the church, constituted by Christ, is a community that can make a unique and essential difference to our neighborhoods and to society. That this is a new message to so many American evangelicals and that it is brought to them by such an unlikely prophet is startling and worth consideration. At eighty years of age, Perkins is still passionate about this mission and communicating it to others.

Caught by the power of his own rhetoric, Perkins pauses:

> Man, that makes me want to cry.
> That we can do good!
> I really desire to do something for God.
> I think most people want to do something for God.
> I think that is why you are here.[2]

Why are they there? What significance does this man's remarkable life and work have for understanding the evangelical church in America at the beginning of the twenty-first century? What does Perkins's theology of racial reconciliation and his ecclesiology of community development and urban renewal have to say to a new generation of American Christians faced with the problems of a postindustrial society in the grips of the great recession and the challenges of immigration and globalization?

That morning in Mississippi with Perkins and the students surely points to the places any serious assessment of Perkins's lived theology must begin. It must consider the importance of *location*: this meeting is taking place in a poor black neighborhood in Jackson, the state capital of Mississippi. It must consider *history*, both Perkins's own history and the history of the church: this morning his words draw power from his own experiences of torture and brutality at the hands of white Mississippi police officers. It must consider his *audience*: this group of students who had traveled thousands of miles to meet with Perkins points to his appeal to a certain segment of the white evangelical church—an appeal that continues to grow in his ninth decade. Finally, it must consider and evaluate his *message*: "The central truth to Christianity," he told the students "[is] where two or three are gathered together in his name he is there and there is the possibility of goodness." Considering his location, his history, his audience, and his message, this is a bold, perhaps foolish claim.

In April 2009 John Perkins joined scholars and activists who assembled at the University of Virginia to take part in the Project on Lived Theology's three-day spring institute, "American Evangelicalism and the Practices of Peace: The Lived Theology of John M. Perkins." The conversations and excitement generated that spring in Virginia gave rise to this volume.

This book explores Perkins's life and legacy. Taking its shape and commitments from the Project on Lived Theology, this is an unusual book in that its contributors are a collection of historians, theologians, community workers, and activists. Some of the contributors have known Perkins for years and have worked closely with him (Chris Rice, Lowell Noble), while others consider him from a greater distance. Lived Theology is an approach to the study of Christian theology that takes social location, cultural context, and historical background seriously because, as liberation theologian Gustavo Gutiérrez contends, theology should be a "critical reflection on praxis."[3] Lived Theology provides a contextual theological paradigm to engage with the performative character of people and faith communities that interpret Scripture and work for social justice. We need to pay attention to these theological dramas; through them we can discern God's gracious activity of reconciliation and redemption in the people and places of history.[4]

The book, organized into three sections, begins with four chapters written by historians seeking to contextualize Perkins's ministry in the broader history of African American spirituality, politics, racial reconciliation movements, and the evangelical church in America. In the opening chapter Albert G. Miller shows how a pragmatic secular spirituality with a long history in African American communities influenced Perkins's Christian conversion and subsequent ministry. The second chapter considers Perkins's involvement in Ronald Reagan's Task Force on Food Assistance. Historian Lauren Winner shows how Perkins's emphasis on self-reliance made him such a fierce critic of the welfare system and an advocate for churches as the agents of change in America's poor communities. The family is the most important building block of society, and welfare is, for Perkins, the latest enemy threatening the black family. Christ's church is the new family that can redeem and heal disintegrating families and communities. The family of the church ultimately replaces human families, making possible the reconciliation of its members, even between former enemies. The third chapter examines Perkins's use of the term "brotherhood" in his public reconciliation with former Klansman Thomas Tarrants. The last chapter in this section shows how Perkins's call to act like family has both challenged and played a part in transforming white evangelical churches. A new generation of white evangelicals is embracing a theology of the social gospel and appropriating the legacy of the civil rights movement despite evangelicals' history of rejecting both.

The second section brings together essays by theologians exploring the ways that Perkins's lived theology of Christian community development, particularly his call to churches to relocate themselves and their resources into poor communities and redistribute these resources, constructively challenges existing theologies of church and ministry. Three of the chapters make explicit the theological resources Perkins brings to bear against a white church that has eviscerated its gospel from a holistic message of salvation: a church that is in lock step with consumerism. Peter Goodwin Heltzel and Christian T. Collins Winn identify Perkins's challenge to the evangelical church as being similar to Dietrich Bonhoeffer's call for a religionless Christianity. Kelly West Figueroa-Ray, using as a case study Perkins's account of community development through his reading of the story of Jesus's encounter with the woman at the well (John 4:1–42), offers a literal-realistic and community-situated way of reading Scripture. This African American biblical hermeneutic employed by Perkins offers postliberal theology a living example of scriptural reading habits that embody faithful and public engagement. In the following chapter, an edited transcript of an address given at the Spring Institute for Lived Theology, minister and theologian Cheryl J. Sanders picks up on Perkins's reading of John 4 and reminds us that his message presents a different type of challenge for African American churches than it does to either white evangelicals or the academy. In her lecture and her answers to questions, Sanders considers the implications of Perkins's prophetic call for relocation and racial reconciliation for her African American congregation in Washington, D.C., as it experiences the gentrification of its neighborhood.

The third section, containing essays by theologian/activists, looks beyond Perkins to the way forward for the church in a broken world: how his life and work point us to continue the journey whose goal is reconciliation. It starts with the chapter by Chris Rice who, taking his perspective from his global work with the Duke Divinity School's Center for Reconciliation as well as the years spent with Voice of Calvary in Jackson, again picks up on the importance of Perkins's themes of family and church—communities of resurrection—that lie beyond justice. Essential to these communities, the gospel remind us, is the love of Christ. The next two chapters show us that this is not a trite Sunday school (or Beatles song) answer to every question. Perkins reminds us how love demands that we enter into the pain of others. Lisa Sharon Harper, a community organizer working for Sojourners in Washington, D.C., argues that Perkins's model for Christian community development concentrates on "personal, interpersonal, and communal transformation" because of the political realities faced by black communities in Mississippi in the early 1970s. The solidarity of pain that love demands, Harper contends, means that the time has come to mobilize these resurrection communities for the "civic transformation of policies and systems." The final chapter by Soong-Chan Rah sees in Perkins and the CCDA a prophetic, intercultural model of ministry that challenges the white American evangelical church to recognize the multiethnic and global character of Christianity in the twenty-first century.

This volume does not offer the reader a neat biographical sketch of Perkins's life—that has been done elsewhere—nor is it an exhaustive, comprehensive, or systematic examination of the subject.[5] Instead, the editors hope this book is the beginning of a conversation in the academy: a conversation that will continue to appreciate and explore the significance of the lived theology of John M. Perkins.

## NOTES

1. Recent exceptions to this are chapters in two books written by editors of this volume: Charles Marsh, "Unfinished Business: John Perkins and the Radical Roots of Faith-Based Community Building," in *The Beloved Community: How Faith Shapes Social Justice, from the Civil Rights Movement to Today* (New York: Basic Books, 2005), 153–188; Peter Goodwin Heltzel, "The Christian Community Development Association: A Quiet Revolution," in *Jesus and Justice: Evangelicals, Race, and American Politics* (New Haven, Conn.: Yale University Press, 2009), 160–177.

2. John Perkins, Morning Devotions, The John M. Perkins Foundation for Reconciliation & Development, Jackson, Mississippi, March 10, 2011. Transcribed by Michael Good from a recording made by Lindsey Jo Bailey.

3. Gustavo Gutiérrez, *A Theology of Liberation: History, Politics, and Salvation*, rev. ed., trans. Sister Caridad Inda and John Eagleson (Maryknoll, N.Y.: Orbis, 1988), 5.

4. See Charles Marsh, "The Civil Rights Movement as Theological Drama—Interpretation and Application," *Modern Theology* 18, no. 2 (April 2002), 231–250.

5. Readers unfamiliar with the details of John M. Perkins life should start by reading "Let Justice Roll Down: A Conversation with John Perkins" in this book's appendix. For more details, see Perkins's autobiography, *Let Justice Roll Down* (Ventura, Calif.: Regal Books, 1976), which was republished in 2006 with a foreword by Shane Claiborne; and Marsh, *Beloved Community*, 153–188. Readers should also watch the documentary film *Let Justice Roll On: The Life and Legacy of John M. Perkins* (2011), directed by Michael Eaton.

Part I

# RELOCATION

*Considering the Journey*

✝

# The Black Apostle to White Evangelicals

*Albert G. Miller*

FOR JOHN PERKINS, THE APOSTLE PAUL HAS ALWAYS BEEN CENTRAL TO
his theological core. In this essay I argue that as the apostle Paul was called
to preach the gospel of reconciliation to the Gentile community in the first
century, so, too, Perkins's call has been to preach the Christian gospel of
reconciliation, redistribution, and relocation to the white evangelical community of the United States on behalf of the poor, black, brown, and white
communities. Paul was the major Christian theological influence upon
the Christian life and faith of Perkins, including his conversion as a young
adult. Before his conversion, Perkins saw himself as a secular and nonreligious person, raised in a black secular world. The impact of this worldview
profoundly shaped his later understanding of his Christian concern for the
black poor in Mississippi and spread to reinforce his Christian call for reconciliation.

There are similarities between the early life of Paul of Tarsus and that of
John Perkins of Mendenhall, Mississippi. Both were steeped in their religious tradition or spiritual worldview, yet from very different perspectives.
In Philippians 3:5–7 Paul discusses his impressive pedigree, as he indicates
that he was "circumcised the eighth day, of the nation of Israel, of the tribe
of Benjamin, a Hebrew of Hebrews; as to the Law, a Pharisee; as to zeal, a
persecutor of the church; as to the righteousness which is in the Law, found
blameless. But whatever things were gain to me, those things I have counted
as loss for the sake of Christ." Paul clearly lays out for the churches at Philip-
pi his right to call himself the son of the soil of the Jewish tradition and to
claim his legitimacy as a Hebrew. He was truly a son of legalistic tradition
within the Jewish nation. Yet following his conversion, God calls him to
place Jesus before his allegiance to his Hebrew tradition. Paul's conversion
leads him to become the voice of Christ-centered reconciliation.

John Perkins, too, can be called the son of the soil of black Mississippi.
Unlike Paul, Perkins could not call up a deeply holy and pious religious tradition. In fact, Perkins is quick to say in his personal testimony of his early

3

life that he and his family were not religious at all. They, at best, ignored Christianity and, at worst, despised it. Perkins states that his family lacked any religious upbringing: "As I look back at my family history, I am the first person I know of in the Perkins family to receive Jesus Christ as personal Savior. My people in Mississippi were bootleggers and gamblers as far back as I can go."[1] Perkins further elaborates on his family lifestyle and his perspective on religion:

> Since we were bootleggers, we did a pretty good business with a lot of the church people, both white and black. Since I had never heard the central message of the gospel, I did not see the black church as relevant to my needs. I always looked at things economically, and it was hard to see how the shouting and turning over benches in black churches at the time was giving any kind of incentive to people to develop. In fact, I always looked at these black Christians as sort of inferior people whose religion was keeping them oppressed by making them submissive to an oppressive structure.[2]

Clearly, Perkins was raised in a nonreligious family and one that lived the tough life outside of the law. In his writing, he also expresses a rather pragmatic rational view of the world, one that worked inside or outside of the law to build a sense of self-determination and economic independence. In the Deep South in the 1930s, 1940s, and 1950s, many black people were relegated to menial farm work and sharecropping for survival. In many cases, this work was not enough to survive financially, and some workers turned to illegal operations such as bootlegging. Vera Mae Perkins, John's wife, says of the Perkins family financial status, "But sharecroppers almost always came out in the red. And as soon as he was done cropping, a sharecropper had to scramble to do something else just to keep things going. That's one of the reasons why Aunt Babe, Toop's grandma, sold whiskey [Perkins was called "Toop" by his family]."[3]

For Perkins and his family, religion was not practical and relied too much on emotion to be useful in the illegal world of gamblers and bootleggers, who always had to be rational and clear-minded to stay ahead of the white power structure and its law enforcement. A secularist Marxian-like view of religion also undergirded this pragmatic self-determination hewed out of the experience of centuries of southern white oppression of black people who understood the nature of racial oppression.[4] Perkins viewed religion as just another opiate of the oppressed. Vera Mae's reflection on how religion encouraged black people to accept their own oppression reflects this Marxian way of thinking:

> It seems funny now how some of the people most oppressed by the system were some of the greatest defenders of it, just in order to protect their little piece of the action. But it was also something in the people that made them feel inferior. Religion played a part in the whole way that the society would make black people feel inferior and coward. Religion was just the melody to the beat that everybody walked by.[5]

Perkins and many within black southern life saw the church as less a religious institution and more of a place for social gatherings. Many within the Perkins clan had little or no respect for the church or religion. Referencing an incident where another of John Perkins's uncles was killed on a church ground, Vera Mae summed up this feeling about the Perkins family's view of the church when she states:

> One of the things that really made the Perkins different was that they were almost against religion. I guess they had to be, the way the religious people would talk about them. But it made them different, because the religion in the churches made you a coward. All my folks were religious back in those days. And I saw again and again how their religion made them humble down to the white structure, with all of its injustice. The Perkins were not like that.[6]

In spite of this cynical and irreligious view of religion, I maintain that underlying this seeming secular and, at best, agnostic view of black and white southern life was a deeper "secular" spirituality that would come to shape John Perkins's evangelical understanding in profound ways. Much of the scholarship on the history of black religious life in the United States has been significantly shaped by a dominant Christian worldview. This Christian spiritual understanding emerged over time in African Americans' encounter with slavery and in the postslavery experience through the efforts of both black and white churches and through black independent and white-controlled evangelistic enterprises. Thus nineteenth-century black Christianity emerged out of a give-and-take between African traditional religions (which survived to a lesser degree), folk religious traditions, and evangelistic outreach from both African American and white evangelists. This fledgling development of a black Christian religious experience emerged in both the North and South. As Albert Raboteau argues in his groundbreaking work, *Slave Religion: The "Invisible Institution" in the Antebellum South*:

> Even as the gods of Africa gave way to the God of Christianity, the African heritage of singing, dancing, spirit possession, and magic continued to influence Afro-American spirituals, ring shouts, and folk beliefs. That this was so is evidence of the slaves' ability not only to adapt to new contexts but to do so creatively.[7]

It is in this sense of "creativity" that we see the emergence of the black church Christian experience in the North and the South. What emerged were varied African American Christian worship experiences, some of which John Perkins saw as emotional excess in southern black Christianity.

However, this creativity was not limited to the black church experience. Much of the research on religion in the African American experience has tended to ignore other creative trends and traditions of spirituality and secular views in black life. The ranges of these other traditions are wide but little explored. Yet some scholars of the African American religious experience have explored these neglected expressions of the black religious spirituality. The research of Yvonne Chireau, Stephanie Mitchem, and others has suggested that African Americans were not solely wedded to the Christian experience. Some and maybe many were able to explore multiple religious traditions, in some cases supplementing their Christian worldview with folk traditions, remnants from the almost forgotten African religions of the past. Others left these Christian traditions for the spiritualist tradition and other forms of thurmaturgical or magical religious movements.[8] Stephanie Mitchem has persuasively argued that folk healing and folk cultural traditions continue to have significant influence in the African American spiritual worldview.[9]

One of the ways these folk traditions have been expressed is through the blues. The blues represent African American folk art and poetry, but also express an alternative black worldview to the dominant white American culture. As Amiri Baraka argued: "Cool meant non-participation; soul means a 'new' establishment. It is an attempt to reverse the social roles within the society by re-defining the canons of value. . . . White is then not 'right,' as the old blues had it, but a liability, since the culture of white precludes the possession of Negro 'soul.'"[10]

Much of Mississippi black culture in which John Perkins grew up was a world in which blacks were redefining their worldview against the prevailing white and Christian values. The blues reflected the black counterculture within which Perkins identified himself (gamblers, bootleggers, and law-breakers)—those folk who were not afraid of southern white people and struggled to control their own destiny. Perkins's wife, Vera Mae, reflects upon the family and culture that he was raised in, who were known for drinking and living the tough life and did not fear blacks or whites. In describing the early experiences of meeting Perkins at a funeral of his sister, who was killed by her boyfriend, she said:

> Sensitivity wasn't what the Perkins family was known for. They were one of the toughest families around. Everybody was afraid of the Perkins, even some of the white folks. The Perkins just wouldn't take nothing off of nobody. They were bootleggers and gamblers, known to fight and carry on incidents on the church grounds.[11]

In his book *Black Culture and Black Consciousness: Afro-American Folk Thought from Slavery to Freedom*, Lawrence W. Levine argues persuasively that it is wrong to see the sacred and secular expressions of the black folk-loric tradition (trickster stories, blues, tales, humor, gospel, and spirituals) as wholly separate. They are in fact two sides of the same coin. Even the secular blues had elements that had "ritual significance."[12] Drawing upon earlier anthropological observers of early black folk culture such as Charles Keil and John Szwed, Levine writes:

> [The blues] has definite sacred overtones in that it combines the elements of charisma, catharsis, and solidarity in the same manner a church service does: common problems are enunciated, understood, shared and frequently the seeds of a solution to them are suggested. Similarly, John Szwed has argued that the bluesman is something of a shaman: "He presents difficult experiences for the group, and the effectiveness of his performance depends upon a mutual sharing of experience.... Church music is directed collectively to God blues are directed individually to the collective."[13]

Levine goes on to state that the "blues performed some of the functions for the secularized masses that religion did; it spoke out of a group experience; it made many individual problems—dislocations, loneliness, broken families, economic difficulties—seem more common and converted them into shared experiences."[14]

The irreverence for organized religion and the lack of fear of white authority, power, or domination that was prevalent in the Perkins family speaks to another understanding of worldview that scholar Anthony Pinn called secular humanism. This understanding of the black life challenged the prevailing traditional Christian black religious worldview. Pinn's book *Why, Lord?: Suffering and Evil in Black Theology* tackles the thorny problem of theodicy within black theological thinking. His work challenges the notion of human redemptive suffering found within African American Christian theology historically. What is important for our discussion is his argument that not all of historical and contemporary black worldviews was limited to the Christian perspective. He argues that there was, embedded within the African worldview, a more secular perspective that reflects what he calls a "strong humanism." Pinn indicates that it was wrong to argue that "strong humanism rests outside 'Black Traditional' thought and was therefore of limited use by the Black religious community. . . . Strong humanism is in keeping with Black tradition (although it is not Christian), when one recognizes the breadth of Black religious expression—which includes the full spectrum of theism and humanism."[15] Thus Pinn argues for recognition of humanism as a legitimate expression of African American spirituality. He suggests that this form of humanistic worldview was also reflected among the multiple spiritual perspectives in the African American slavery experience and emerged in black spirituals, in folktales, and later in the blues. Of this humanism, Pinn contends:

> The alternative nontheistic position of strong humanism first emerges in antebellum slave communities' cynicism toward God, and has these characteristics: (1) it gives historical reign to humans; (2) it makes humanity the measure for all proofs; (3) it signifies or denies God's existence; (4) it operates according to an ethic of risk and is pragmatic in nature; and, (5) it provides an ultimate concern related to community or human life. These points are essential because they mark the defining character of strong humanism: that it entails an atheistic outlook which places humanity at the center of interest and activity.[16]

Clearly, John Perkins and his family, before his conversion to Christianity, held this broad humanist worldview, and it profoundly shaped his thinking about religion and spirituality. Perkins always viewed life from a practical and economic perspective and could not see any value to the emotionalism of the black church. From his view, black Christians were "cowards and Uncle Toms," and "I did not see the black Church as relevant to me and my needs."[17] Similarly, Perkins held the white church with the same cynical contempt. "To me [the white church] was part of that whole system that helped dehumanize and destroy black people; that system which identified me as a nigger. So how could the white Church really be concerned about me?"[18]

It must be stated here that even with the so-called hardcore strong humanist tradition one must heed the warning of Mircea Eliade regarding the notion of a purely secular person. Eliade made this argument during the early stages of the twentieth century in the midst of the rise of secularism, yet it still holds true today. He contended that

> what matters for our purpose is the experience of space known to nonreligious man—that is, to a man who rejects the sacrality of the world, who accepts only a profane existence, divested of all religious presuppositions.
>
> It must be added at once that such a profane existence is never found in the pure state. To whatever degree he may have desacralized the world, the man who has made his choice in favor of a profane life never succeeds in completely doing away with religious behavior. . . . It will appear that even the most desacralized existence still preserves traces of a religious valorization of the world.[19]

Thus even with the most vigorous protest of Perkins that his family had little room for religion, especially southern black Christianity, he found himself on a search for spiritual meaning.

Perkins's openness to the exploration of faith came in stages after he left the South, joined the army, and eventually settled in the Los Angeles area after his discharge from the military. Perkins's conversion to Christianity was not an immediate process. He had to leave the South and its extreme environment, racial hatred, prejudice, and oppression in order to find enough mental and physical safe space to explore more social and spiritual matters. As Vera Mae put it, "Those years in California gave us a unique time to be developed and prepared by God without the pressure of hatred and malice. It also gave us exposure to a world much bigger than the one we grew up in."[20] During his 1947 transition to California, Perkins married his wife, Vera Mae, and they began to have children. This entire geographical and mental shift provided the stage for his spiritual evolution to the Christian faith. Even then, it was in exploratory stages with other new religious movements. Given his suspicions of southern Christianity, black or white, it is not surprising that Perkins's road to faith would route him through an exploration of various black new religious movements or "cults."

Given his disdain for emotionalism in the black church, Perkins was initially drawn to new religious movements that had a more cerebral focus, such as the New Thought tradition of Father Divine, Christian Science, Science of the Mind, and the Nation of Islam.[21]

The New Thought tradition argued for a notion of spirituality that claimed that God was within the individual. Father Divine claimed to be God and that his followers had a piece of God within them. Like the humanist tradition, this black New Thought tradition maintained that each human controlled his or her own destiny by activating the "god" within himself or herself. This theology seemed to fit well with Perkins's humanist temperament of self-determination (one's ability to control and determine one's destiny) and financial success. Perkins later stated, "I even became involved in Science of the Mind. And with this, I began to associate religion with success. Success and money and 'making it' were my religion, but I was not happy. I had no peace inside."[22]

Before his conversion to Christianity in California, Perkins also flirted with the homegrown African American variety of Islam, the Nation of Islam (Black Muslims). The Nation of Islam had a major impact upon Perkins. He would state, "I was trying everything. I know one thing. If I hadn't become a Christian, I would have become a Black Muslim. Their strict devotion and discipline have always appealed to me."[23] Vera Mae echoed Perkins's strong interest in the Nation of Islam, "In recent years he had worked side-by-side with men who were black Muslims and I have often thought if he had never become a Christian, he would have been a Muslim, with their strict devotion and discipline and he would have risen right to the top."[24] By the early 1950s the Black Muslims were gaining ascendancy in the African American community with the rise of the influence of Malcolm X on the movement. Beyond their focus on discipline (to which Perkins was attracted), their focus on building independent black wealth and nationhood surely must have titillated Perkins's senses. The Nation of Islam's black nationalist philosophy and theology fit well within this humanist tradition. It challenged blacks to stop being dependent upon whites and to establish an economic base for their liberation and nation building. Scholar Lawrence Mamiya has suggested that ever since Elijah Muhammad took over the mantle of leadership of the Nation when Master Farrad mysteriously disappeared in 1934, his message of black nationalism tinged with a strong dose of economic uplift, "do for yourself," was directed at the black masses. Like all black mass movements the Black Muslims attempted to capitalize on the lower class Black Man's despair and reservations about the white man.[25]

Perkins's conversion to Christianity came slowly, first through the influence of his son, Spencer, who was attending a small black Holiness church's children's Bible classes. Spencer invited his father to visit church with him.[26] Perkins's friend Calvin Bourne invited him to attend his church, Bethlehem Church of Christ Holiness. The fact that it was a church affiliated with the Church of Christ (Holiness) USA denomination is important. This denomination was founded by Charles Price Jones, who broke with Charles Harrison Mason, the founder of the Church of God in Christ.[27] Jones broke with Mason over their disagreement about the issue of the Pentecostal experience of tongues and the ecstatic worship experience, which was similar to the emotionalism that Perkins criticized in the black churches he had known in Mississippi. It was in this holiness milieu of rational theological reflection on righteous living that Perkins was introduced to the theology of the apostle Paul. As Perkins began to attend a Bible study at the church, he was introduced to the theology of Paul, which began to challenge his humanist and rational worldview:

> The thing that really hit me about Paul was this motivation he had. By this time in life, I was pretty super-motivated myself, but I was motivated for my own economic betterment. As I read and studied the life of Paul, I saw that he was super-motivated, too. But his motivation was unselfish. And it was a religious motivation
>
> A religious motivation! That really got to me. How could religion mean so much to anyone, even Paul? The question hounded me all summer long.[28]

This was the beginning of Perkins's transformation to Christianity. What is important here is the recognition that Perkins's conversion to the Christian faith was through mentoring relationships with several black and white Christian men of a rational and conservative, even fundamentalist persuasion.[29] It is important also to note that these relationships were almost wholly void of emotionalism and any remnants of the southern black ecstatic worldview that Perkins had grown up seeing. After flirting with the various black and white versions of new religious movements, which had a more rational bent to them, finally it was a more rational version of the Christian faith that began to sink in. Recollecting their early ministry involvement with the Child Evangelism Fellowship, which they used as an evangelistic tool,[30] Perkins would ponder, "Yet when I look at it, I saw what I had seen in the adult class that had helped to bring me to God: an emphasis on learning, on getting something solid. This was way different from the emotionalism of the black Church I had rejected years before."[31]

Even with this strong conservative Christian influence on his early Christian development, Perkins's earlier life experience of humanism helped to shape his theological orientation toward a continuing commitment to serve poor black southerners. In part, what attracted Perkins to this conservative version of Christianity was its focus on a more rational understanding of spirituality rather than an appeal to the emotions. Perkins's attraction to conservative fundamentalist Christianity was also driven by his humanist understanding of rationality. "There were churches for black folk all around, but the religion they got there was not for learning; it was just for getting emotional and for socializing. I wanted to catch their hearts with the truth that had caught my heart—that the Bible was for learning, real learning about God."[32]

Perkins's growing interest in the civil rights movement in Mississippi reflected at least in part this earlier humanist orientation. His Christian faith transformed his humanism, but still the appeal of self-help as human initiative was an aspect of the civil rights movement that proved attractive. While understanding the difficulties implementing this concept within an oppressed community, nevertheless Perkins came to advocate this strategy within his Christian efforts at organizing poor southern black people. Perkins explained:

> In most discussions about working with the poor, self-help is usually lifted up as a key to success. And it is. Yet in the black community where ingrained economic and psychological dependence and unstable family and social structures have been a way of life for all the generations of black people in America, self-help becomes a difficult reality to grab hold of....
>
> For a real movement of Christians to affect a community it needs the power and motivation of God, it demands a biblical strategy, it

requires an economic base. But most important, the movement must have people who have invested their lives in making real their beliefs.[33]

While it is clear that Perkins's ministry has had as one of its foci racial reconciliation and that this has helped to build his stature within the larger American evangelical community, it is also clear that Perkins has always maintained his commitment to serve the community out of which he emerged. Much of his outreach is driven by his commitment to a Christ-centered notion of self-help that has in part been influenced by his earlier life background of rational and practical theology. In explaining to his evangelical constituency his growing involvement and leadership within the civil rights movement in Mississippi in the late 1960s, Perkins stated:

> At this point the deep needs of black people were my primary concern. Our whole ministry was focused on the black community. It would be several years before God would give me a burden for the deep needs among people in the white community, needs for reconciliation and love. . . . No, at this point in our ministry, we had come to know the depth of the problem and were now looking for a strategy through which to attack and dismantle the whole, unwieldy cycle that was destroying our people.[34]

The apostle Paul's encounter with Jesus transformed his Jewish reality and what it meant for him to be a Jew. Even as Paul broadened his understanding of the gospel to include reconciliation with gentiles (Gal. 3:28), the account of his missionary journeys in Acts makes it clear that he never lost his desire to minister to the Jewish communities in the towns in which he preached. In like manner, Perkins's call to preach reconciliation—to be a black apostle to white evangelicals—has not diminished his original commitment to serve and minister to poor black southerners.

## NOTES

1. John Perkins, *A Quiet Revolution: Meeting Human Needs Today: A Biblical Challenge to Christians*, rev. ed. (Pasadena, Calif.: Urban Family Publications with Network Unlimited International, 1976), 15.

2. Perkins, *Quiet Revolution*, 17.

3. Vera Mae Perkins quoted in Perkins, *Quiet Revolution*, 27.

4. For Marx's view of religion, see Robert C. Tucker, ed., *The Marx-Engels Reader*, 2nd ed. (New York: W. W. Norton, 1978), 53–55. See also a review of Marx's perspective on

religion in Klaus Bockmuehl, *The Challenge of Marxism: A Christian Response* (Madison, Wis.: InterVarsity Press, 1980).

5. Vera Mae Perkins quoted in Perkins, *Quiet Revolution*, 29.

6. Vera Mae Perkins quoted in Perkins, *Quiet Revolution*, 25.

7. Albert J. Raboteau, *Slave Religion: The "Invisible Institution" in the Antebellum South* (New York: Oxford University Press, 2004), 92.

8. For a discussion of these folk, spiritualist, and thurmaturgical traditions, see Yvonne Chireau, *Black Magic: Religion and the African American Conjuring Tradition* (Berkeley: University of California Press, 2003). See also Hans A. Baer and Merrill Singer, eds., *African-American Religion in the Twentieth Century: Varieties of Protest and Accommodation* (Knoxville: University of Tennessee Press, 1992); and Hans A Baer, *The Black Spiritual Movement: A Religious Response to Racism* (Knoxville: University of Tennessee Press, 1984). What is also clear is that some African Americans left the Christian tradition altogether for African American variations of Judaism and Islam. See chapters 7 and 8 of Gayraud S. Wilmore, *Black Religion and Black Radicalism: An Interpretation of the Religious History of African Americans*, 3rd ed. (Maryknoll, N.Y.: Orbis Books, 2002).

9. Stephanie Y. Mitchem, *African American Folk Healing* (New York: New York University Press, 2007).

10. Imamu Amiri Baraka, *Blues People: Negro Music in White America* (New York: W. Morrow, 1963), 219, quoted in Ron Gruver, "The Blues as a Secular Religion," in *Write Me a Few of Your Lines: A Blues Reader*, ed. Steven C. Tracy (Amherst: University of Massachusetts Press, 1999), 222.

11. Vera Mae Perkins quoted in Perkins, *Quiet Revolution*, 24–25.

12. Lawrence W. Levine, *Black Culture and Black Consciousness: Afro-American Folk Thought from Slavery to Freedom* (New York: Oxford University Press, 1977), 234.

13. Levine, *Black Culture and Black Consciousness*, 234–235.

14. Levine, *Black Culture and Black Consciousness*, 235.

15. Anthony B. Pinn, *Why, Lord?: Suffering and Evil in Black Theology* (New York: Continuum Publishing, 1995), 18–19.

16. Pinn, *Why, Lord?* 148.

17. John Perkins, *Let Justice Roll Down* (Ventura, Calif.: Regal Books, 1976), 56.

18. Perkins, *Let Justice Roll Down*, 57.

19. Mircea Eliade, *The Sacred and the Profane: The Nature of Religion* (Orlando: Harcourt, 1987), 23.

20. Vera Mae Perkins quoted in Perkins, *Quiet Revolution*, 29.

21. For a discussion of Father Divine's religious connections to the New Thought tradition, Unity School of Christianity, and its legacy within the African American religious experience, see Jill Watts, *God, Harlem U.S.A.: The Father Divine Story* (Berkeley: University of California Press, 1992). For a look at the social and civil rights dimensions of Father Divine's International Peace Mission movement, see Robert Weisbrot, *Father Divine and the Struggle for Racial Equality* (Boston: Beacon Press, 1984). For a discussion of the Nation of Islam, see Edward E. Curtis IV, *Black Muslim Religion in the Nation of Islam, 1960–1975* (Chapel Hill: University of North Carolina Press, 2006). See also C. Eric Lincoln, *The*

*Black Muslims in America*, foreword by Gordon W. Allport (1973; repr., Westport, Conn.: Greenwood Press, 1982).

22. Perkins, *Let Justice Roll Down*, 65.

23. Perkins, *Let Justice Roll Down*, 67.

24. Vera Mae Perkins quoted in Perkins, *Quiet Revolution*, 29.

25. Lawrence H. Mamiya, "From Black Muslim to Bilalian: The Evolution of a Movement," *Journal for the Scientific Study of Religion* 21 (1982): 146.

26. Perkins, *Let Justice Roll Down*, 65–66.

27. For a discussion about the holiness movement of Charles Price Jones, see David Douglas Daniels III, "The Cultural Renewal of Slave Religion: Charles Price Jones and the Emergence of the Holiness Movement in Mississippi" (Ph.D. diss., Union Theological Seminary, 1992).

28. Perkins, *Let Justice Roll Down*, 67.

29. For a discussion of several black conservative Christian men and women who mentored him in the area of person-to-person evangelism, including people like Rev. Curry Brown, Rev. George Moore, Elizabeth Wilson, and Jim Winston, see Perkins, *Let Justice Roll Down*, 72. For a discussion of the influence of white conservative Christians, see Perkins, *Let Justice Roll Down*, 72. Among the most significant white people to influence and support John Perkins's ministry in the early days was Rev. Jack MacArthur, the pastor of Calvary Bible Church in Burbank, California. MacArthur, and by extension Calvary Bible Church, was thoroughly Calvinistic and fundamentalist in his outlook. Perkins was so influenced by MacArthur that he named his ministry in Mendenhall Mississippi after the radio broadcast sponsored by MacArthur in California, "The Voice of Calvary." See Perkins, *Let Justice Roll Down*, 92–93.

30. The Child Evangelism Fellowship was founded by Jesse Irvin Overholtzer in 1937 as a fundamentalist outreach to children. The Perkinses have been very active with this organization and services over the years.

31. Perkins, *Let Justice Roll Down*, 72.

32. Perkins, *Let Justice Roll Down*, 84.

33. Perkins, *Quiet Revolution*, 115.

34. Perkins, *Quiet Revolution*, 102.

# The Church as Family and the Politics of Food Distribution

*Lauren F. Winner*

## I.

IN 1983 JOHN M. PERKINS WAS APPOINTED TO PRESIDENT RONALD Reagan's Task Force on Food Assistance. This task force, which also included neoconservative author Midge Decter and former Massachusetts governor Edward King, was convened during an upsurge in interest in, and controversy about, hunger in the United States. Specifically, the administration's proposed cuts to food stamps had stoked the ire of hunger activists and Democrats on Capitol Hill. More generally, in part due to the 1981–1982 recession, the early 1980s saw growth in food stamp expenditures; 1983 had seen growth in food banks; and reporters were newly turning their attention to stories about hungry Americans. The White House appeared more concerned with slashing the budget than feeding the hungry. Presidential adviser Edwin Meese III dismissed stories of hunger as "anecdotal," and Reagan was coming under attack for seeming to be insensitive to the problem. The task force was to travel the country and determine whether, indeed, there was a serious hunger problem, and, if so, to suggest measures Congress might take to address it.

If Reagan thought appointing a task force to investigate hunger would placate his critics, he was wrong: the August announcement of the task force's membership only increased public furor because the task force was said to be stacked. Critics charged that too few members of the commission had any expertise in dealing with hunger, and those who did had a bias against programs like food stamps. Governor King was singled out as one who had publicly opposed food assistance programs in the past, as was pastor and activist John Perkins, the only African American member of the task force. National newspapers implied that Perkins's mind was already

16

made up, and they quoted Perkins's own words to make the case: Perkins, the *Washington Post* warned, "wrote in a 1976 book that 'the welfare system is one of the most wasteful and destructive institutions created in recent history.'"[1]

Perkins's service on this task force provides an interesting context for exploring the complexities of his political sensibilities. About Perkins's politics, one might ask: how did a man who regularly declared things like "Communism is God's chastening rod to capitalism"[2] end up a Reagan appointee? Or, from a different vantage point, one might ask how one with such a strong commitment to a radical renewal of poor black communities could have written the words cited above about "the welfare system."

Indeed, Perkins's political views in the 1970s and 1980s defy easy summary (as, perhaps, does all African American politics in the years after the civil rights movement):[3] he was a critic of the Black Power movement who worked tirelessly for black economic self-determination; a critic of the welfare state and a proponent of individual responsibility, yet also a prophet who warned that "God is going to move in judgment on our own nation" because of the many ways that big business has exploited the poor.[4] Readers of his column "Walk Your Talk," which first ran in the *Jackson Advocate* in 1979, regularly encountered gimlet-eyed analyses of the ways that racism and poverty continued to afflict African Americans—the ways that "Black people in this country are victimized by the powers that be." Readers were also frequently reminded that "real change can only come about through deep changes in individuals." For example, black-on-black crime, an issue that energized Perkins in the 1980s, may be explained in part through unemployment and other systemic problems in "the inner city." Yet "even more fundamental is the breakdown of individual spiritual life . . . [the] problem of individual selfishness and total lack of commitment to anyone but ourselves."[5] In Perkins's view, the solution to poverty and social problems did not lie solely in the realm of political economy. Perkins famously propounds a holistic gospel that aims to help people "spiritually, socially, and economically."[6] In part because social ills are at root spiritual ills, government programs "cannot bring significant change to the lives of people in the Black community."[7]

Perkins's participation on Reagan's task force—and the controversy surrounding his appointment to it—hint at the extent to which Perkins thwarts our shorthand of "left" and "right." Throughout Perkins's political analysis in the early 1980s runs a critique of the welfare state.[8] In Perkins's view, welfare programs fostered dependence and destroyed the individual's drive to succeed. The War on Poverty had created a "welfare mentality," and taught poor people that they have "a right to demand that the system take care of them. And so they lose the desire to help themselves."[9] Yet it is not enough to say that Perkins's criticisms sound like those of white conservatives; his critique sounds different if we also note that he is drinking from the same wells as, say, the African American historian and critic Manning Marable, who observed in 1979 that "the radical says, 'the welfare system as it now exists is dehumanizing and degrading to poor people.' . . . [By contrast,] the liberal uses the radical's language to achieve the conservative's aim: the preservation of the capitalist system, and the traditional ethnic-racial hierarchy within society."[10] (It is worth noting, however, that leftist activists like Marable did not share Perkins's sympathies for Reagan's food policies: "Reagan's budget cuts in food stamps," Marable would write in 1981, ". . . are . . . akin to capital punishment for the millions of ghetto class blacks."[11])

This essay does not aim to tidily systematize Perkins's political views; nor does it argue for his early-1980s criticisms of the welfare state. Rather, based principally on a reading of Perkins's occasional writings from the years leading up to his appointment on Reagan's task force, this essay begins to map one corner of Perkins's political imagination, that is, his vision of the church. I suggest that Perkins's ecclesiology—which focuses on the local church body and conceives of the church as an alternative family that both nurtures believers and announces the prophetic word of God—is one thread that helps stitch together his politics. Perkins's service on Reagan's task force—and his endorsing, in that context, what many critics deemed socially regressive policy—may be seen as inseparable from his ecclesiology.

## II.

The centrality of the church to Perkins's politics is evident from the diagram that graces the pages that divide one section from another in *A Quiet Revolution*: this diagram depicts the words "the church" enclosed in a circle. Intersecting the circle are five phrases: "the call," "justice," "economic development," "social action," and "evangelism." All of these, in Perkins's imaginary, grow from and depend upon the church; justice, economic development, indeed change will only come from the church.

But when Perkins spoke of the church as an agent—*the* agent—of change, he was not making the same point made by social scientists who focused on the church as a (generic) institution in which African Americans

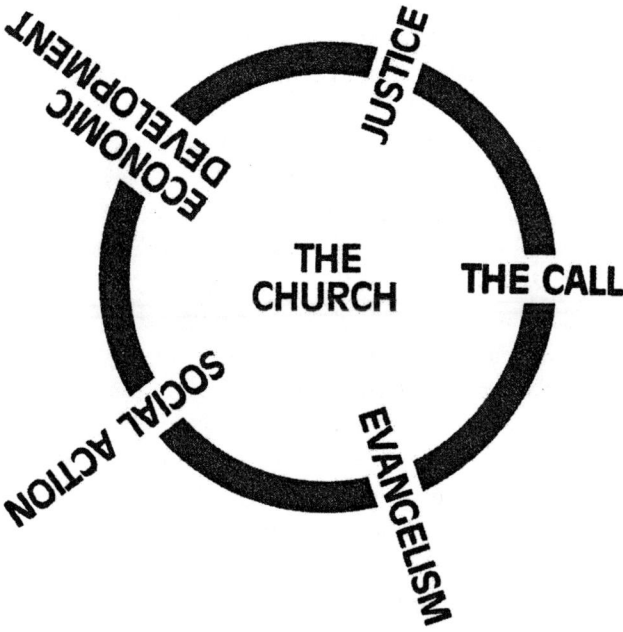

Fig. 1. From John Perkins, *A Quiet Revolution: The Christian Response to Human Need, a Strategy for Today* (Waco, Tex.: Word Books, 1976), 13.

exercised leadership, developed a communications network, raised money, and so on.[12] To the contrary, Perkins was critical of those who identified the church's transforming power exclusively or even primarily with its generic institutional strength. Indeed, Perkins wrote that people too often thought of the church as "an organization that leaders can manipulate for their own economic, political, or social gain. When leaders use the church this way, they make the church a tool of the culture, of the society, or the race."[13] The church may have been a place where black men and women developed leadership skills and where they functioned, in a racist society, with a degree of autonomy. But those institutional qualities were not the essence of the church's transforming power.

If not merely a strong institution, what was the church in Perkins's imaginary?

First, the church was the site of particular spiritual practices. In addition to Perkins's well-known "three Rs" of community development—relocation, reconciliation, and redistribution—Perkins argued that certain spiritual practices must accompany any effort to revitalize African American communities, and, indeed, America at large. These practices were nurtured in and by the church. Perhaps the most central of these practices was prayer. In a series of columns in 1981, Perkins told readers that the single most important thing individuals can do to "make a difference" is pray. Perkins teases out several scriptural models of prayer: he holds up Nehemiah's "bow[ing] low" before God; he cites James 4:3 as urging prayers that come not from "selfish motives" but rather prayers that seek the good of all of humanity.[14] But the central model is the Lord's Prayer. If people faithfully follow the model of the Lord's Prayer, they will perforce be allying their will with God's will (a will that, says Perkins, is always for humanity's flourishing). Specifically, when Jesus teaches his followers to pray "Thy kingdom come," he is "praying that He might make the community in which we live an example of God's kingdom." Confounding an oppositional spirituality in which the active and the contemplative are juxtaposed to one another, Perkins identified prayer as an integral part of political change: "People ask me, 'What can I do?' I tell them that they can pray. . . . I know someone is saying, 'You shouldn't take so much time praying, you should be working.' But I say we need to pray in order to be more effective at our work."[15]

Second, the church was the keeper of a calendar that criticized and reconfigured the calendar of secular America. Surrounding American society lived by a calendar that served the interests of a racist capitalist system. This calendar was not merely at odds with the church's calendar; it was, specifically, a parody and indeed a perversion of the church's calendar—to wit, Christmas, a central day in both calendars. Perkins wanted American Christians to "question some of the traditional ways in which we celebrate the coming of Christ."[16] "Our economic system," Perkins charged, "has taken Christmas and wrapped it up with big spending, materialism, and greed. We have been brainwashed into thinking the more a present costs, the better it is. The fancier the toys are that we get for our children the better their Christmas will be. We, as Black people are in bondage to this kind of Christmas. Black people have been convinced by white advertisers to spend a lot of money that goes back to white companies." An economic system keyed to the financial flourishing of a small elite, in other words, had perverted Christmas. The church was the keeper of the true meaning of Christmas. The real gift of Christmas was that Jesus makes it possible for people to live in a "new kind of relationship with one another." The real gift one should give at Christmas is the self-sacrificial gift of one's self, *imitatione Christi*, for the flourishing of one's downtrodden neighbor. The church should follow Jesus in going "into the community and giv[ing] ourselves to the people who need us."[17]

The church, then, carried an alternative calendar, a calendar in which sacred days did not further ensnare black Americans in economic bondage to white people, but rather a calendar whose sacred days enabled self-giving and a transformed community. Beyond the specifics of an ecclesial calendar marked by days like Christmas, the church proclaimed a historical narrative that prophetically corrected an American history of oppression. Indeed, Perkins's political vision was shaped by a keen and particular sense of history: "I believe in learning from history, and sometimes it's helpful to look back at our historical behavior," he wrote in 1976. Slavery and segregation are the historical contexts in which Perkins limns politics; he repeatedly frames social and economic problems against the backdrop of America's "two biggest domestic conflicts," arguments America had with itself—the Civil War and the civil rights movement.[18] Specifically, history provided Perkins a tool for criticizing the welfare politics he so disdained. Rather than identifying similarities between the civil rights movement and the War on Poverty, Perkins compared Jim Crow and the welfare state: both were "dehumanizing,"[19] and in the face of the degradations of welfare, "each one of us must claim the dignity that gave birth to the Civil Rights Movement and take responsibility for our own lives."[20] Shadowing Perkins's theological language is the trope of history, of memory; slavery and Jim Crow, the Civil War and the civil rights movement, form a narrative that bolsters Perkins's politics with the quasi-sacred memory of national sin and national martyrdom. Yet as central as history is to Perkins's political discourse, the church is finally the agent of change that trumps even the signal events of American history: the church is "a historical reality more viable than both the Civil War and the Civil Rights movement."[21]

Third, the church was a family. Family is a central theme in Perkins's occasional writings, and key to his ecclesiology. Perkins was concerned with the family because he saw it as the seedbed of a healthy society. Concomitantly, the disintegration of the family had led to many social ills: "what's broken in our community is the family," said Perkins in a 2006 Bible study, and problems like guns are "symptom[s] of the problem."[22] The collapse of the family is in part responsible for "the over population of our prisons" and for teenage prostitution.[23] For Perkins, the church represented—indeed, the church *was*—the true instantiation of family. The church was the family that contextualized and could redeem distorted practices of family that pervaded 1970s and 1980s America.

Perkins speaks of three kinds of families. First is the biological and nuptial family, an institution that is key to Perkins; Perkins calls this family the "individual family"[24] or "the local family."[25] This family is "the foundation of all society"; it is what "transmits value and nurture into the society."[26] This family—the individual, local, or biological family—had been under threat for over a century. Again offering a narrative grounded in American history, Perkins situates the late twentieth-century family in a long genealogy of challenges to the integrity of African American families. Slavery posed the first challenge: enslaved Africans were made to "take on the names of their masters," they could not legally marry, and "kids many times were snatched from family." In his historical narrative, Perkins compresses the striking and virtually immediate steps African Americans took to consolidate their families during Reconstruction, noting only that "when the slaves were emancipated, you can see great strides among blacks toward becoming a family." But instead of dwelling on the post–Civil War reconstitution of African American families, Perkins turns his attention to another challenge: "in the late '30s, during the time of the industrial revolution of this country many black people began to go North. The husband or wife went North with the idea of getting a job and returning for her family, but many times the family was never reunited." Decades later, the children of those men and women who moved north turned out to be self-seeking individualists with no sense of obligations to their kinfolk: "They feel no responsibility to their grandparents who are still living in misery somewhere in the South. They do not think of the sacrifices that were made from them to be where they are today."[27]

The family, in Perkins's account, thrived on stability and familiar patterns of life. Geographic mobility threatened the family because it introduced people to new, modern ways of organizing their lives. Families that survived the Great Migration soon faced another "enemy of the black family," World War II, which called men away from their families and to the front.[28] The risk was not only that men would die in service, but that those who lived often "found a new way of life elsewhere." The specific threat of "new ways[s] of life" that geographical mobility made possible included a challenge to the pronounced gender norms running throughout Perkins's vision of the family. For example, one of the reasons the Great Migration was so threatening to families was that women who moved to the North "became accustomed to a new way of life . . . and when she finally returned home, her husband was uncomfortable with her new ways and felt threatened by them." Indeed, this "threatened" man had oftentimes "established a relationship with another woman," and sent his children to live with a grandmother. The wife's absence, and her husband's discomfort with her "new ways," utterly unraveled the family.[29]

The challenges were manifold, but through it all, Perkins wrote, "the black family pulled through." But it might not pull through "the final attack on black families—the development of the welfare system." The "dehumanizing" welfare system unsettled the patriarchal structure of the ideal family: it "stepped in and took the place of the father. The way the system was set up, the family was rewarded if the husband didn't come back." Perkins was also concerned with social welfare's impact on mothers. The welfare system "began to give aid to the dependent children and mothers" (and with that turn of phrase, Perkins suggests that the problems with welfare were coded into the very name of the program, Aid to Families with Dependent Children). This cultivation of dependence undercut the long tradition of black mothers who "worked . . . with dignity" to provide for their children.[30]

The second kind of family Perkins speaks of is the fictive family. In the 1970s he wrote of "Mr. and Mrs. R. A. Buckley, a couple who joined us in our ministry and have been like parents to me and grandparents to my children." Three decades later, then himself an old man, Perkins assumed the role of being a fictive grandfather to young people in prison: "They all call me Grandpa Perkins."[31] In referring to people as though they were kin, Perkins participates in a long tradition in African American history: the stitching together of fictive familial relationships in situations where social and political circumstance, most especially slavery, threatened nuptial and biological families.[32] Indeed, Perkins recognized the challenges slavery and Jim Crow put to African American families when he marvels that "my wife and I are the first Perkins since slavery to ever stay together as a family." It is because Perkins lacked models for stable family life in his own parents and grandparents that he needed the nurture of couples like the Buckleys.[33]

Perkins sometimes calls this fictive family "the extended family," a phrase that for him pointedly does not denote only a large network of biological kin; rather, "the extended family" is that family that "can reach out and see those kids out there that need help. As black people, we need to reach out to the kids who need a home and parents." For Perkins, the "extended family" is better able to meet the needs of vulnerable people than the state: there are children who "need a home and parents," and "we need to go to the agencies who have these kids and bring them into our homes and make homes for them." In particular, "middle class black families who have jobs that are making it from $12,000 and up" have a responsibility to rescue these children from the clutches of "government programs."[34]

The extended family was one institution in which Perkins's vision of reconciliation could be worked out. He tells the story of a black woman who died, leaving a widower and three small children, one of whom was only six days old. The woman's pastor, who had just gotten married, "took the family into his family. That little black girl knows only one mother. When she is crying, no black mother can substitute for the pastor's wife, who is white." This new family would be uniquely capable of rearing a daughter who knew "reconciliation" rather than "racial preference" as a "way of life" and who would "have no problems in being reconciled in her other relationships" as an adult.[35] The extended or fictive family also effected transformation in the lives of the incarcerated people who called Perkins "Grandpa":

> When a new one comes in they can't call me Grandpa Perkins. I tell them, "If you want to call me Grandpa Perkins I've got to give you permission to call me Grandpa Perkins. Everybody who become my grandchildren have certain behavior." I say, "Now if you want to be my grandchild . . ." "Yeah, I want to be!" . . . That sets up some discipline. . . . I can say to them "You're not my grandchild acting like that." We've got to set up that environment of love. And that's what a family has an opportunity for. They're the ones who love them![36]

Beyond the borders of this extended or fictive family is Perkins's third family: the "family of God," that is, the church. This family is "a community of God . . . the body of Christ." The family is "the group of people who meet together . . . on Sunday morning."[37] In this family, which is the "greatest" family, we are given new siblings. One's relationships with the brothers and sisters one has in the new family are an even "greater tie" than the connections one has to one's natural siblings.[38] It is in this familial idiom that Perkins explains what the church is: "The church needs to be a family of [people] who have been called out of the world . . . into a new family relationship with each other." This is the theological vision that gives ballast to the "fictive kinship" Perkins described with Mr. and Mrs. Buckley.[39]

Perkins uses his own autobiography to explain that the family of God contextualizes, redefines, even trumps the local family. In childhood, Perkins says, his "human family" was "bankrupt and wrecked." After his mother died, he and his four siblings went to live with his paternal grandmother. There, he encountered cousins who were "undisciplined," "born out of wedlock," "so I was in the midst of a family that had very little fatherhood identity." He found new family in the family of the church—not only new brothers and sisters in Christ but also God the Father.[40] Yet the family of the church does not—like the welfare state—threaten or destroy "individual families." To the contrary, although conversion is described as a call to a new family, one is to continue to "care for [one's] local family." "Individual families who are part of the family of God" should model "what God intended the family to be."[41]

And here, finally, is the church that is truly a locus of transformation—not merely an instrumental institution, but rather the family of God. Beyond offering models of stable individual families, the church is "the prophetic voice of God," whose vocation is "calling for justice and righteousness."[42] This church is capable of effecting social change not, Perkins insists, simply because it provides leadership and an institutional framework for organizing black people. Rather, drawing again on familial language, Perkins says that the church is "a family whose love for each other makes God's love visible to the world."[43] The church, rather than "government programs," offers the hope of sustained and sustaining social change. Consider, for example, teenage prostitution. Girls may take to the streets in part because of "a person's basic need for economic survival," but their more primary motivation, says Perkins, is "the basic human need for affection."[44] Those "desperate emotional needs were first created by the broken family structure of our Black community," a broken family structure that, as we have seen, was on Perkins's analysis, caused by segregation, an industrializing economy that split families apart, and finally the welfare state. The solution, in Perkins's mind, lies in the extended kinship that the church ought to be practicing: teenage prostitution will end when the church reaches out to lonely, emotionally vulnerable teenage girls and gives them "the love and sense of community that they so desperately need."[45]

This notion of the family of God—the church—captures the scale of the church. The church and the church's transformation may extend to the ends of the earth, but foremost the church is a local body. Ideally, members of a church would all live in the same neighborhood.[46] "Every thing that happens to us spiritually God wants to work it out locally," Perkins wrote in 1977. Perkins grounded this vision of the local in thoroughly biblical idiom. The model for this "working out locally" was the apostle Paul, who "would never leave a city until he had formed a local fellowship," because it was in that local fellowship that Christ's body could be manifested.[47]

Because "the church . . . [is] the most potent instrument of healing and change in the world,"[48] the local was thus the scale of politics. "The local church in the Black ghettoes of America is the most logical agent for social change in the Black community."[49] Indeed, Perkins went so far as to say, when asked in 1988 what Martin Luther King Jr. would do if he were still alive, that King would have realized that "the political system was not the answer," that he would have focused on the local and would have "moved into the area of neighborhood development."[50] And scale was part of the problem with twentieth-century welfare programs that wrested control from local people and tried, with results both risible and tragic, to direct social change from Washington.

Washington's attempts to feed hungry people in Mississippi provided Perkins a vivid example of the problem:

> I remember that when Robert Kennedy came down and he said, yes, poverty here. We going to do something. And so I remember that when they started the surplus food, to send the food in. They sent the food in to Mendenhall and that's where I was living, by the ton. And the black folks fed that food, good food, they fed it to the hogs. They sent in pow[d]ered milk by the ton and black folks had never drank any powdered milk before and they fed that milk to the hogs. . . . They sent in grits, they sent in . . . grapefruit juice and people fed that grapefruit juice to the hogs, to the hogs. Cause black folks never had no grapefruit juice. . . . And so it just went on and the businessmen in the town said hey. The business people all over the country said hey, why should we have the government send this food in here. We have the best food distribution system in the world. Our supermarkets. Let's change this thing, let's now given [*sic*] them food stamps, so we can get the money. And so the poverty program. So do you know something like 50% of the money off [*sic*] all the social welfare programs are spent before it leaves Washington? Do you know the consultant[s] in Washington get the money before it leaves Washington? . . . And the money can't even come down unless it's going directly back to the big business enterprise.[51]

Local people on the ground would know how to get food into the mouths of hungry people, and how to keep money circulating in the local economy. The bureaucracy in Washington succeeds—and perhaps aims— not at getting food into the mouths of hungry people, but rather money in the pockets of big enterprise. Local communities on the ground would have far more success at distribution of food and, indeed, redistribution of wealth.[52]

## III.

This brings us back to the Task Force on Food Assistance.

Controversy surrounding the task force did not die down after the initial announcement of the makeup of the committee. Meese kept making ill-advised statements—in December he continued to insist that hunger was a myth, this time opining that people went to soup kitchens not because they were hungry but because "the food is free." The commission itself turned out to be fractious, canceling in December what was to be its final meeting "amid disagreement" among members.

In January, just days before the task force submitted its report, member George Graham made explicit the racism that was latent in Meese's charge of lazy and mendacious welfare recipients. Graham, a professor of pediatrics at Johns Hopkins, insisted that black children's "problems are not food." The height of black athletes, he said, proved that black children were well nourished and black people "take care of their little children." Ergo, "I don't think anyone in their right minds believes there is a massive hunger problem." Congressman Charles Rangel responded to Graham, saying that "Dr. Graham has used one racial stereotype to promulgate a new one." John Jacobs, president of the National Urban League, echoed Rangel, dismissing Graham's "biased and highly misinformed opinion." Benjamin Hooks, president of the National Association for the Advancement of Colored People (NAACP), topped the polemic: "Reaching back into the dark abyss of racist history in this country, Dr. Graham brought forth sentiments that many Americans thought had been buried with old Jim Crow."[53]

The final report of the Task Force on Food Assistance acknowledged that hunger was a problem in America, but insisted it was impossible to calibrate just how large a problem. It recommended numerous small changes to food assistance policy—a 100 percent guarantee of food stamps to people without an address, tax breaks to manufacturers who donated surplus foodstuffs to food pantries—but the centerpiece was a proposal to replace federal food programs with block grants to states.[54]

Though he claimed that he did not agree with every iota of the report, Perkins was comfortable signing it. Perkins clearly dissented with the Meeses of the world, who thought hunger to be anecdotal: "There is something severely wrong. There are kids out there who are not getting food, who are hungry."[55]

The proposal of block grants to states was consistent with Perkins's views about local communities and the local churches being the locus of political change. Years after the task force submitted its recommendations, Perkins continued to argue that half of the money devoted to hunger programs never left Washington: if the federal bureaucracy could be shrunk, more food could get into the hands of hungry people. "There is no doubt that the budget cuts have removed much of the resources that would be available to the poor. But that is not necessarily the most important issue. It is whether or not those resources that were getting to the poor. Perhaps they weren't. I suspect that's the reason Reagan cut it." In the context of the task force, Perkins spelled out a political view that was consistent with, and indeed may have partially emerged from, his ecclesiology, an ecclesiology that points to the local, neighborhood church as the only source for true change: the federal government was an inefficient behemoth, and local institutions—presumably not least the local church—could more effectively address pressing problems like widespread hunger. "Local people could come up with more innovative and creative programs to provide food assistance to their own people."[56]

These arguments were unpersuasive to many. The report was not popular among hunger activists, who charged that the task force had degenerated into a "farce."[57] Nor did the report come in for much praise in the black press, which was irked that the task force had spent $350,000 of "taxpayer dollars" to offer such retrograde conclusions, and they charged that many of the task force members skipped more than one of the hearings. "The Task Force and its report are a sham"[58] opined the *Baltimore Afro-American*. Norman Hill, president of the A. Phillip Randolph Institute, lambasted an administration that had "gutted food stamps and school lunch programs," and that, through the task force, "seeks to explain away the hunger that exists"; Hill connected Reagan's food policies with his "dismal record" of enforcing civil rights.[59] Frank Lomax III, president of the Columbus Urban League, writing in the *Call and Post*, declared, "We denounce the final findings of the President's Task Force on Food Assistance, as being clearly wrong and not based upon reality, as well as being unfeeling and not responsive to . . . human suffering."[60] Robert L. Gordon, president of Kappa Alpha Psi, called the task force "a national disgrace."[61] Yet despite the many criticisms African American leaders made of the presidential task force, before the year was out the Pasadena, California, NAACP had honored Perkins with the Ruby McKnight Williams award—and his service on the task force was one of Perkins's many accomplishments noted with pride when the award was announced.[62]

## NOTES

1. Spencer Rich, "Adversaries on List for Hunger Unit," *Washington Post*, April 25, 1983; Bill Peterson, "Critics See Reagan Food Panel Bias against Welfare," *Washington Post*, April 26, 1983; "Task Force Probes Hunger," *Black Enterprise*, November 1983, 22.

2. John M. Perkins, "Nahum," 7, in the records of Voice of Calvary Ministries, 1969–1986, in the archives of Wheaton College, Wheaton, Ill. (hereafter cited as VOC/Wheaton).

3. On the complexities of African American politics after the civil rights movement, and especially on African American support for Reagan, see David L. Chappell, "The Lost Decade of Civil Rights," *Historically Speaking* (April 2009): 37–41.

4. Perkins, "Nahum," 8.

5. John Perkins, "Walk Your Talk" column (hereafter cited as WYT), March 27–April 2, 1980; WYT, May 22–28, 1980. All "Walk Your Talk" columns may be found in VOC/Wheaton, Box Tk, folder tk. Unless otherwise noted, I am citing the version of the "Walk Your Talk" column that ran in the *Jackson Advocate*.

6. WYT, *California Advocate*, June 19, 1981.

7. WYT, June 26–July 2, 1980.

8. For a discussion of Perkins's views on welfare in the context of his larger theological and political vision, see Charles Marsh and John Perkins, *Welcoming Justice: God's Movement toward Beloved Community* (Downers Grove, Ill.: InterVarsity Press, 2009), 30–32. For one interpretation of African American criticisms of welfare, see Jennifer L. Hochschild, *Facing Up to the American Dream: Race, Class, and the Soul of the Nation* (Princeton, N.J.: Princeton University Press, 1996), 166.

9. WYT, December 27–January 2, 1980.

10. Manning Marable, "Liberalism's Short-Term Solution Holds No Cure for Ills of Blacks," *Afro-American*, July 21, 1979, 5.

11. "The Question of Genocide," *Afro-American*, December 12, 1981, 5.

12. See, for example, Aldon D. Morris, *The Origins of the Civil Rights Movement* (New York: Free Press, 1984).

13. WYT, June 26–July 2, 1980.

14. WYT, September 10–16, 1981.

15. WYT, September 10–16, 1981; WYT, September 24–October 1, 1981.

16. *Voice of Calvary Ministries Quarterly Fellowship Letter*, December 1976, 3, VOC/Wheaton, Box 31, folder 18.

17. WYT, "The Real Meaning of Christmas." See also John Perkins, "Christmas: A History and Story of Reconciliation," *Reconciler* (December 1977): 1, 4. All *Reconciler* columns are found in VOC/Wheaton, Box 25, folder 10.

18. "Behavior and the Bicentennial," part I, draft, 2, VOC/Wheaton, Box 13, folder 4.

19. For Perkins's description of segregation as "dehumanizing," see WYT, December 27–January 2, 1980; WYT July 10–16, 1980; "Interview with John Perkins: Proposition 13," *Reconciler* (October 1978): 4; Gospel Light Staff Meeting, April 6, 1977, 2, VOC/Wheaton, Box 113, folder 8.

20. WYT, December 27–January 2, 1980.

21. "Behavior and the Bicentennial," part II, draft, 2.

22. John Perkins, "Thursday Morning Bible Study," Community Christian Development Association (CCDA), 2006, http://www.urbansermons.org/f/audio/drjohn-perkins -thursday-morning-bible-study-ccda-2006-audio.

23. "A Message That Changes Lives," *Reconciler* (November 1977): 1.

24. "Can the Family Survive?" *Reconciler* (January 1979): 1, 4.

25. "The Family of God," 2, VOC/Wheaton, Box 13, folder 8.

26. Perkins, "Thursday Morning Bible Study," 2006.

27. "Can the Family Survive?" 1; "The Gospel: Giving Youth Vision," *Reconciler* (February 1978): 4.

28. "Can the Family Survive?" 1.

29. "Can the Family Survive?" 1.

30. "Can the Family Survive?" 1.

31. John Perkins, "Saturday Morning Bible Study," CCDA, 2006, http://www.urban sermons.org/f/audio/dr-john-perkins-saturday-morning-bible-study-ccda-2006-audio.

32. On the importance of the fictive family in African American history, see Emily Clark, *Masterless Mistresses: The New Orleans Ursulines and the Development of a New World Society, 1727–1834* (Chapel Hill: University of North Carolina Press, 2007), 178, 194.

33. "Behavior and the Bicentennial," part II, draft, 6.

34. "Can the Family Survive?" 1, 4.

35. "Becoming as Little Children," *Reconciler* (June 1978): 1, 4.

36. Perkins, "Saturday Morning Bible Study."

37. "Family of God," 1.

38. "Family of God," 5.

39. "Can the Family Survive?"; "Family of God," 2–3.

40. On the importance of acknowledging "God as our Father," see WYT, September 10–16, 1981.

41. "Can the Family Survive?"

42. WYT, June 26–July 2, 1980.

43. WYT, July 3–July 9, 1980.

44. WYT, July 17–23, 1980.

45. WYT, July 17–23, 1980.

46. WYT, July 3–July 9, 1980.

47. Gospel Light, 5–6.

48. "Behavior and the Bicentennial," part II, draft, 2, VOC/Wheaton, Box 13, folder 4.

49. WYT, July 17–23, 1980.

50. "What Would He Do Today?" *Christianity Today*, April 8, 1988, 42.

51. Perkins, "Nahum," 5.

52. Perkins's position on welfare suggests not only the complexities of African American politics after the civil rights movement; arguably, his politics suggests that "left" and "right" as we typically conceive them are unhelpful or even irrelevant on the questions of welfare policy and the poor. At the dawn of the Reagan administration, Perkins raised questions about the state's capacity to alleviate poverty—questions that, three decades after Perkins's service on Regan's task force, very much still animate American political discourse. The challenge that half of the money funneled through Great Society programs never got to the

poor, if true, and the challenge that the War on Poverty centrally enriched a cabal of social workers and economists, are, of course, serious ones. See Allen J, Matusow, *The Unraveling of America: A History of Liberalism in the 1960s*, 2nd ed. (Athens: University of Georgia Press, 2009), especially chapter 8.

53. Simon Anekwe, "Rangel: Graham Is Insensitive," *New York Amsterdam News*, January 7, 1984.

54. Spencer Rich, "Presidential Task Force Findings; 42 Groups Join in Hunger Report Criticism," *Washington Post*, January 11, 1984; Ronald F. King, *Budgeting Entitlements: The Politics of Food Stamps* (Washington, D.C.: Georgetown University Press, 2000), 131–134; W. Timothy Coombs, "The Failure of the Task Force on Food Assistance: A Case Study of the Role of Legitimacy in Issue Management," *Journal of Public Relations Research* 4:2 (1992): 109–115; "Hunger Commission: No Surprises," *Washington Post*, January 9, 1984.

55. Robert Pear, "Hunger Panel Cancels Final Meeting," *New York Times*, December 13, 1983.

56. "An Interview with John Perkins," VOC/Wheaton, Box 36, folder 15.

56. Pear, "Cancels."

58. "Hunger Is Very Real in a Land of Plenty," *Afro-American*, February 4, 1984.

59. Norman Hill, "Social Justice, Civil Rights, President Reagan," *Los Angeles Sentinel*, February 9, 1984.

60. Frank Lomax III, "A Cold, Indifferent Side of Hunger," *Call and Post*, February 23, 1984.

61. "Hunger Report Assailed," *Philadelphia Tribune*, July 31, 1984.

62. "NAACP Honors Perkins," *Los Angeles Sentinel*, May 22, 1986.

# Brotherhood and Its Limits

*Ted Ownby*

IN 1994 JOHN PERKINS AND FORMER KLANSMAN THOMAS TARRANTS published *He's My Brother: Former Racial Foes Offer Strategy for Reconciliation.* The book consists of alternating narratives and religious reflections of the two men as they describe how their journeys to overcome their own forms of hatred and to embrace similar understandings of racial reconciliation became essential to their definitions of Christian life. The idea that racism violates essential Christian principles has become so prevalent that it may seem, at least in many circles of Christian thought, an easy point to make. Even the urge within the Christian Left to criticize conservative or comfortably apolitical forms of Christianity can seem canned or somewhat obvious—perhaps something closer to an ordinary introduction to an ordinary sermon than a point of inspiration or theological depth. How, then, can one approach a book with an African American man and a white man on the cover of a book with an apparently bland title like *He's My Brother*?

This chapter approaches Perkins through the concept of brotherhood, the concept announced in the title of the Perkins-Tarrants volume. In using the language of brotherhood as a Christian response to issues of race, Perkins and his coauthor were drawing on some words with a long history, multiple meanings, and plenty of controversy. The concept of brotherhood, often defined as the brotherhood of man under the fatherhood of God, was crucial to the early, optimistic phases of the civil rights movement, then faced criticism from both the Right and the Left, and now strikes most people as either naive or simply irrelevant. Compared to many other topics, Perkins has never had a great deal to say about brotherhood. However, on the occasions when he has written about it and especially when he uses the term "brother" in the title of a book coauthored with a former Klansman, it seems particularly significant.

The concept of brotherhood is revealing for reasons beyond the title of *He's My Brother.* In that volume, as in others, John Perkins tells the story of the 1946 murder of his brother Clyde as the crucial moment in his youth.

That was when, at age sixteen, he learned the degree of terror African Americans could face if they chose to fight the rules of Jim Crow society. In fact, one could easily imagine that the title refers both to the bond between Perkins and Tarrants and the memories of bonds between Clyde and John. When Perkins first mentions brotherhood in *He's My Brother*, he is pointing out something lacking in white Christians. At the end of the passionate chapter on the murder of Clyde, Perkins makes the point that he grew up in a state with a great number of Christian churches and an extraordinary degree of racism.

Well before he coauthored *He's My Brother*, Perkins had already made clear how the death of his brother had shaped his perspective on the world. In the first chapter (entitled "Clyde") of his 1976 memoir, *Let Justice Roll Down*, Perkins began his story with painfully familiar themes in Mississippi life: a sweaty summer, picking cotton, poor whites and poorer blacks, white resentment about African Americans in the military, racist language and violence by the police, and the impossibility of demanding justice. The teenaged John Perkins ran to see Clyde after a local deputy marshal had shot him. He arrived in time to beg his brother, "Brother, don't die."[1] His responses to the murder set up major issues for the rest of his life. First were anger and the possibility of revenge: "we *had* to get even."[2] He wrote that he would have shot the deputy if he had a weapon. Second was frustration that no one was held accountable and that he, like many others, might lapse into resignation and complacency. Third, he decided to leave Mississippi for California as a direct response to the murder. "Mississippi was behind me. Forever, I told myself."[3]

By introducing division and hatred, the desire for revenge, and the appeal of flight, the chapter sets up what comes later in the book. Since racist hatred killed John Perkins's own brother, he started his adult life a long way from thinking of all people as brothers and sisters. And of course the people who killed Clyde would never have thought of the Perkins family as brothers and sisters in Christ. The chapter immediately following the discussion of the murder of Clyde Perkins is Thomas Tarrants's chapter, "How I Learned to Hate." The book, fortunately, never equates Tarrants's violent racism with Perkins's anger—Tarrants had a lot farther to go toward brotherhood, or reconciliation, or love than Perkins—but it sets up an interesting parallel in which both chose to do serious work to overcome hatred and eventually to embrace each other as brothers.

By all accounts, John Perkins is not a conventional figure who exemplifies larger trends. His life and ideas cannot be examples of generalizations about the black church or racial reconciliation or Christian activism. Perhaps studying how he has used the concept of brotherhood helps dramatize some of the difficulties of racial definition and interracial work in the wake of the civil rights movement. Perkins believes in pursuing friendship and brotherhood, struggling for justice, and overcoming barriers that keep people from knowing and caring about each other. Above all, he believes in Christian work. Brotherhood, for him, is a project, and like many projects, it requires persistent effort.

Without understanding the roles brotherhood played in the history of thinking about race in the twentieth-century American South, it is not possible to see why it was such an important step for Perkins and Tarrants to claim each other as brothers. In the early decades of the twentieth century, Christian brotherhood was, as language, above all for white Christians who wanted to express something positive toward black Christians. Brotherhood meant goodwill and the absence of violence and overt hatred. It had the serious limits of not necessarily calling for equality, legal rights, or desegregation, but it had its place for religious believers wanting to work toward a kinder world. Until late in the civil rights movement, most people in the South who discussed brotherhood as part of a Christian understanding of race relations did so with an optimism that the world was moving in the right direction, away from separation and hatred and toward unity and shared kinship. Many, but not all, of those who used the concept believed brotherhood to be a basic reality—a true state of human being that God had created and sinful mankind had left behind through selfishness and division.

When Perkins came to the concept of brotherhood, however, it had been going out of style for some time, attacked by some African Americans as naive or irrelevant to their concerns, condemned by some conservatives as bad politics and bad theology, and abandoned by many white liberals as a failed experiment. Thus when Perkins began writing about his work in the 1970s—and when he used it as a book title in the 1990s—the concept was not an obvious or easy term to embrace.

A shortcut to the history of the concept involves studying a few groups and individuals who made considerable use of the concept of brotherhood in the years before John Perkins began his work. In the South, those were groups that dealt with issues of race relations by emphasizing face-to-face contact and discussion, kindness, and respect (not necessarily equality), all in Christian settings and with Christian language. The Commission on Interracial Cooperation (CIC) was the first group consisting primarily of white southerners to call on notions of Christian brotherhood. Largely urban, the CIC began in Atlanta in 1919 as an effort to allay post–World War I violence between whites and blacks. The CIC tried to bring leaders together first in times of potential trouble to get to know each other and to discuss ways to avoid conflict. CIC educational director Robert B. Eleazer, a Methodist minister and writer as well as a CIC worker, offered some of the more hopeful meanings of brotherhood. In the 1930s he authored a range of educational publications designed to help teachers, especially white teachers, do a better job discussing African American history in their classes. In one CIC pamphlet called *What the Bible Tells Me About Race Relations*, Eleazer began with the story of God's creation of all people to make a point about the definition of family. "As children of one Heavenly Father, I must think of all men as brothers. No, not in terms of sentiment and gush; but in understanding, in sympathy, in goodwill and helpfulness."[4] He made clear that he wrote about southern racial issues as an insider. Like many southern writers, he used a family metaphor to make that point. "I am interested in the South's problem of race relation not as an outside critic, but as a member of the family, frankly discussing here in the family circle our family responsibilities."[5]

In the 1940s Eleazer increased his civil rights activism with a barrage of discussions of brotherhood. In a wartime sermon, "Christianity in an Unchristian World," he argued that brotherhood was "a fundamental fact of life" and sin was "anything which destroys brotherhood—as caste, prejudice, intolerance, extreme nationalism, war, religious narrowness."[6] He broadened the point even more in a 1947 essay, "Reason, Religion, and Race." Arguing that both good religion and good science made clear that all people were in fact related, he rejected the possible suggestion that brotherhood was "just a pretty sentiment." Instead, the concept of brotherhood, which necessitated the recognition of human interdependence, was responsible for all improvement in the world. "This fact of mutual dependence— of practical brotherhood—means also mutual obligation and gratitude on the widest scale." Eleazer stressed a worldwide system of relationships, and wrote that unless humans recognized their interdependence, based on an understanding of the truth of shared kinship, global relations would rely simply on force.

By the late 1940s and early 1950s the language of brotherhood as the opposite of racial division was becoming a common if minority opinion among Christian preachers white and black. Eleazer was writing articles for the CIC when it merged into the Southern Regional Council (SRC), and in

1946 the SRC republished and publicized a 1941 sermon by Atlanta Presbyterian leader J. McDowell Richards, "Brothers in Black." Richards structured his sermon around God's question to Cain, "Where is . . . thy brother?," answering that it should be obvious that whites and blacks were brothers. Science proved a single human origin, Christianity upheld a common religious kinship, and racial division stood in the way of God's plan.[7] Harold L. Trigg, associate executive director of the SRC, wrote an article in early 1946 asking the question, "Brothers or Bombs?" Trigg discussed poverty and hatred in the world, arguing that Americans needed to begin the process of "interracial brotherhood" at home as part of a goal of "world brotherhood" led by Christians.[8] When Paul D. Williams retired as president of the SRC in 1952, he reminded members that "our purpose derives from that deceptively simple but mighty truth which is the essence of the Judeo-Christian tradition—the inescapable, indestructible truth that all men are brothers."[9]

Prior to the civil rights era, African American leaders had reason to be wary of the concept of brotherhood. Many feared it meant good intentions but empty promises. James Weldon Johnson's 1934 volume *Negro Americans, What Now?* addressed the issue of brotherhood directly to warn readers against pursuing it as an end in itself. A powerful and prolific author and NAACP organizer, Johnson stressed that African Americans had to work for equal rights within the American legal, political, and economic systems and urged black churches to redirect their energies away from "hypnotic religion" so they might confront "the fundamental current questions of life," which only "applied Christianity" could address.[10] Johnson made a short list of techniques for making progress: education, politics, unions, black-owned business, and the development of black leadership. Last on his list was a call for better relations with white Americans. But Johnson made that call with the proviso that knowing and working with whites was a technique rather than a goal. African Americans needed to work with whites because that would create greater opportunities, not because integration created a necessarily better world. "We should establish and cultivate friendly interracial relations whenever we can do so without loss of self-respect. I do not put this on the grounds of brotherly love or any of the other humanitarian shibboleths; I put it squarely on the grounds of necessity and common sense."[11] Johnson did not want to overstate the importance of groups that got together to discuss improving race relations, such as the CIC, and he said he feared that many well-intentioned whites tended more toward patronizing than brotherly attitudes toward blacks. Using hyperbole associated with the language of progressive Christianity, he especially warned African

Americans to be wary of the white individual who makes some small step and acts as if "he has just solved the race problem and brought in the millennium."[12]

Robert Russa Moton, the successor to Booker T. Washington as president of Tuskegee Institute and thus an important spokesperson for African American progress, tended to be more optimistic and less combative than Johnson, but he also had reservations about brotherhood as a goal. He dedicated his 1932 volume *What the Negro Thinks* to "those noble and beautiful spirits of my own and other races who have with the greatest courage and utmost unselfishness given their very lives for the cultivation of a brotherhood among all men which is the finest flower of the Christian spirit."[13] Moton only mentioned that finest flower one other time, and then he directed it toward whites. Discussing segregation, he said the typical African American "sees quite clearly just where the white man's professions of Christianity and his practice of the code in his relations with his darker brother in Christ do not harmonize." Thus when he mentioned brotherhood, it was something white Americans needed to realize and live, but it was not a concept that was very important in what Moton called "the advancing Negro."[14] Both Moton and Johnson identified brotherhood as a language some white Christians—maybe a small minority—were using to discuss progress in race relations.

World War II, with its extraordinary fears and possibilities and confrontation with extraordinary evil, inspired much more aggressive and hopeful uses of the concept of brotherhood. The war invigorated African Americans' demands on the federal government, as it proved their contributions to the national war effort at the same time Nazi genocide was dramatizing the evils of racism. For African American leaders, brotherhood emerged as a concept relevant to both Christianity and representative government. One sign that the civil rights movement was beginning to use the language of brotherhood in discussing specific issues was a 1944 collection of essays, *What the Negro Wants*, edited by Rayford W. Logan. The concept appeared several times in the collection, sometimes in broadly rhetorical ways and sometimes as something the authors were urging whites to understand and live. Gordon B. Hancock, dean of theology at Virginia Union University, restated that it was whites in America who needed to live up to notions of Christian brotherhood. Hancock wrote optimistically, "there is a growing feeling among whites favoring full citizenship for the Negro both as a fulfillment of race integrity idealism and as a fulfillment of the higher ideal of human brotherhood proclaimed in the Gospel of Jesus Christ." He called for more "moral daring" from such white Americans.[15] In a speech in Richmond in 1943, Hancock emphasized that brotherhood was the responsibility of whites. "The South must save the Negro or itself be lost. . . . Men must be brotherized or they will be brutalized."[16] Sterling A. Brown's concluding essay in *What the Negro Wants* made brief mention of the growing respect between some African Americans and whites, and saw in the efforts of white editors, union organizers, antilynching organizers, and writer-activists like Lillian Smith and Arthur Raper the goal of "treating Negroes in the spirit of brotherhood."[17] However, much like Hancock and James Weldon Johnson, Brown worried that brotherhood was less common than paternalism even among the white men and women who were happy to offer blacks advice but not willing to treat them as equals or kin.

On a few occasions, authors in *What the Negro Wants* mentioned brotherhood in broader ways that were more about African Americans' place in a broad understanding of world brotherhood. Mary McLeod Bethune, longtime educational and reform leader, closed her piece, "Certain Inalienable Rights," with a question. "In order for us to have peace and justice and democracy for all, may I urge that we follow the example of the great humanitarian—Jesus Christ—in exemplifying in our lives both by word and action the fatherhood of God and the brotherhood of man?"[18] In the postwar years Bethune increased her rhetorical uses of brotherhood. For years she had mentioned it as one of many positive virtues, but in the 1940s and 1950s she rarely wrote or spoke publicly without praising brotherhood as a living reality on the march. In 1946 she penned a short and personal essay about her own spiritual life. Consistently optimistic about the power of God's love working in human history, she joined brotherhood to international interconnectedness and the workings of a loving God. "I am in a state of spiritual readiness at all times. I am ready to read the signs of the times and interpret them for my people, for the world. I am ready to act in faith and love and wisdom and justice for peace. I am ready to keep an open mind—to follow the guides toward upward trends and forward progress which will make our world THE ONE GREAT WORLD—A world where all men are brothers."[19] Coming to the end of her long life, the reformer found in brotherhood a favorite way to conclude talks and papers. Bethune ended a 1955 *Chicago Defender* essay on the *Brown v. Board of Education* decision by connecting world brotherhood to equal opportunity for education. "All enlightened Christian people who have a sense of human values, who believe in world brotherhood and who have heard the conscience of America speak through the Supreme Court will work with zeal for the full implementation of the

Court's decision."[20] And in her ambitious 1955 essay "My Last Will and Testament," Bethune left to her many friends and students the gifts of hope, confidence, education, faith, dignity, the goal of harmony, respect for the use of power, and, above all, love. She concluded that love "connotes brotherhood, and, to me, brotherhood of man is the noblest concept in all human relations."[21]

Only in the mid-1950s through the early 1960s—and then only briefly—were black and white activists united in using the language of brotherhood. Many of the most active protest groups and leaders in many of the most visible protests made brotherhood a central part of their vision or at least their rhetoric. For example, workers in the Congress of Racial Equality (CORE) used the language of brotherhood as their primary concept both in how they organized their work and how they understood their goals. Executive Director George Houser described CORE efforts to desegregate Washington, D.C., swimming pools and bus stations as "Project: Brotherhood." In 1952 CORE urged everyone who heard its message to join its Pledge Brotherhood Campaign during Brotherhood Month—February. Organizers urged that people truly committed to the practice of desegregation "could turn the world upside down. For them, brotherhood is not an idea, or a meeting—it is a way of life." CORE was especially proud, among the 50,000 people who signed the Brotherhood Pledge, of a woman who refused to go to her church until it admitted African Americans, because she had overturned segregation "with the reality of brotherhood!"[22]

Most of the major moments and organizations of the civil rights movement used the language of brotherhood. A song written and first sung at Dexter Avenue Baptist Church during the Montgomery, Alabama, bus boycott in 1956, included the lines:

We know love is the watchword
For peace and liberty.
Black and white, all are brothers
To live in harmony.[23]

Beginning four years later with a similar goal of direct action, the Student Nonviolent Coordinating Committee (SNCC) made considerable use of the concept, especially in its early years. At work in Albany, Georgia, in 1961, SNCC activists distributed a handbill spelling out religious ideals of brotherhood: "We believe in the Fatherhood of God and the brotherhood of man. We believe that God made of one blood all nations for to dwell on the face of the earth. . . . If we are of one blood, children of one common Father, brothers in the household of God, then we must be of equal worth in His family, entitled to equal opportunity in the society of men." The Albany handbill stressed that SNCC workers were both optimistic and realistic, knowing there would be problems ahead but believing that the future had to be better. Ultimately, they hoped, "As prejudice feeds on prejudice, so brotherhood will feed on brotherhood."[24]

In the 1950s and early 1960s Martin Luther King Jr. became the leading voice for a vision of brotherhood that meant racial integration and, ultimately, more than integration. Often King placed brotherhood in a list of positives, suggesting that while embracing it was part of doing God's work and bringing on a better world, it was not the only goal worth pursuing. He concluded a 1956 sermon, "Jesus says in substance, I will not be content until justice, goodwill, brotherhood, love, yes, the kingdom of God are established upon the earth."[25] King used the concept in countless sermons and speeches, especially but not exclusively at large events attended by both whites and African Americans. In one of the earliest sermons he developed in divinity school, King held out the hope of a brotherhood that could do away with racism and unite all people. Sermonizing on "three dimensions of a complete life," King discussed the length of life as the achievements of the individual, but saw the breadth of life as connections to other people. Raising the possibility of "a beautiful symphony of brotherhood"—a phrase he used throughout his life as a minister—King stressed the interdependence of all people. "We are inevitably our brother's keeper because of the interrelated structure of all reality." Too many of "our white brothers," he said, were only concerned with material things, prestige, and power, but they would become better humans if they stretched their interests to share interests with all people, including black people. "The recognition of the oneness of humanity and the need of an active brotherly concern for the welfare of others is the breadth of man's life."[26]

The need for white men and women to recognize shared kinship with all people characterized some of King's most famous statements. In the "I Have a Dream" speech in 1963, King dreamed "that one day on the red hills of Georgia, the sons of former slaves and the sons of former slave owners will be able to sit down together at the table of brotherhood." Later in the speech, King used brotherhood and sisterhood to address school desegregation. "I have a dream that one day down in Alabama, with its vicious racists, with its governor having his lips dripping with the words of 'interposition' and 'nullification,' one day right there in Alabama little black boys and black girls will be able to join hands with little white boys and white girls as sisters and brothers."

To the optimistic notion of brotherhood as the recognition of an underlying truth, and the equally optimistic idea that human beings were increasingly understanding how to live out that truth, King added an essential point. Brotherhood meant recognizing people with problems and trying to help them. King frequently stressed that human beings should see neighbors as brothers and sisters with shared interests. In the sermon "On Being a Good Neighbor," he criticized all the categories of religion or race or nationality that separated people from each other. Lecturing on the Good Samaritan, King concluded, "The good neighbor looks beyond the external accidents and discerns those inner qualities that make all men human and, therefore, brothers." King stressed that at their best, real neighbors—real brothers—risk reputation and life for fellow humans because they realize their relation. "I must not ignore the wounded man on life's Jericho Road, because he is a part of me and I am a part of him."[27]

The other meaning of brotherhood, beyond shared humanity, the goal of desegregation, and a challenge to the racism of white southerners, involved personal transformation available through forgiveness. Here King addressed the goal of brotherhood to African Americans, who, he believed, could never experience true kinship with fellow human beings until they forgave their enemies, in essence making brothers and sisters of their former enemies. King thus offered something many activists had never offered: methods of reform that could make individual reformers better human beings. It is important to see that King meant numerous things by brotherhood, in part because so many people in his time identified brotherhood as meaning nothing other than racial desegregation. For King, it meant goodwill and the hope of working together for integration, the absence of division and the possibility of shared identity and interests of all people, the imperative for all people to help the weak and troubled, and, finally, the need to forgive enemies.

Numerous white southern Christians believed they were marching straight toward a world of brotherhood by supporting implementation of the *Brown v. Board of Education* decision. The groups that really filled the concept of brotherhood with meaning were liberal Christians, black and white. It is not sufficient to say the language of Christian brotherhood was common in the early and mid-1950s; it was central and crucial in the discussions many black and white church groups had about desegregation. In the 1950s and 1960s a startling number of mainstream evangelical groups came to support the goal of breaking down segregation laws. Given how few supported it or even gave the issue much thought a generation earlier, and given the power of the opposition, it is, as David Chappell emphasizes, amazing how many white southerners supported the desegregation of schools in the mid-1950s.[28] Their reasons were numerous: they obeyed the law, they believed education benefited all people, they believed in the principles of the American government, they did not want to follow the logic of some alternatives.[29] The essentially Christian reason to oppose segregation was rooted in notions of the fatherhood of God and the brotherhood of mankind.

When leaders of one church group after another explained their support for the *Brown* decision with an emphatic Christian directness that shocked supporters of segregation, they consistently used the language of brotherhood. In fact, hardly any of the official statements of various denominations did *not* rely on the idea, and religious speakers and writers mentioned few themes as often as brotherhood in the civil rights years. The religious language of brotherhood so common among white Christians who supported some form of desegregation suggested that all white Christians really knew they should be treating blacks as brothers and sisters, if only they would realize what their religion teaches. As T. B. Maston, a professor at Southwestern Baptist Seminary, wrote, "All of us who are in the family of God, regardless of class or color, are brothers and sisters in Christ and should treat each other as such."[30] By the 1960s the language of Christian brotherhood had moved far beyond the seminaries and a few liberals into the mainstream of churches' thinking. After racial violence in Columbia, Tennessee, Charles Trentham, minister of the First Baptist Church in Knoxville, offered a sermon called "One Father—One Blood." Trentham quoted Benjamin Mays's charge that "if we accept the verdict of science and the Christian religion, we must admit that either all men are brothers or no men are brothers."[31] When a group of Methodist ministers in Mississippi decided to stand united against racial segregation, their "Born of Conviction" statement relied on an old Methodist principle, "We believe that God is Father of all people and races, that Jesus Christ is His Son, that all men are brothers, and that man is of infinite worth as a child of God."[32]

James McBride Dabbs offered a memorable distinction in discussing Christian brotherhood. A ministerial association in Little Rock, Arkansas, asked the Presbyterian Dabbs to talk about race relations on what they called Brotherhood Sunday in 1960. Dabbs was happy to speak, but he began by saying he did not want to speak of "race relations" because the concept suggested people should only categorize each other as "white" or "colored." In a quick deconstruction of the idea of race, he continued, "Let us leave, therefore, Christian race relations with its contradictory implications, and discuss brotherhood."[33] Shared experience as humans, in this case as Christians, meant shattering notions of racial difference. The basic Christian message, for Dabbs, was that all humans are "brothers for whom Christ died."[34] As brothers, we can and must be concerned with each other, not just in issues of religion, but in all matters of importance. As Dabbs stressed, "Spirit in this world is inseparable from matter; and to be concerned about the spiritual welfare of men is to be concerned about their hunger, their pain, their frustrations—all the shock and weariness of human life in this world." Why? Because "if my brother hungers, would I not give him bread?"[35] Dabbs concluded with a combination of day-to-day pragmatic activism under a stirring and unique definition of Jesus. "As the old phrase has it, we should improve every occasion. To improve any occasion is to discover and to create within it more of the spirit of brotherly love which we have learned from Christ, our elder brother in God."[36]

Seeing Jesus as an older brother, Dabbs was perhaps the clearest example of a white southerner who embraced the concept of brotherhood as a way to use evangelical traditions in southern culture to change southern culture. Born in 1896, the Presbyterian writer and farmer from western South Carolina wrote countless essays for secular and religious magazines, spoke to large and small groups, and often became directly involved in groups such as the SRC. He offered inspiration to the many white southerners who worried that addressing and trying to improve race relations meant turning their backs on the South. No, Dabbs counseled, getting involved in improving race relations was in fact the truest endorsement of the best traditions of southern life, especially religious life.

Dabbs, more than many reformers, knew that most evangelicals believed that nothing was worth much if it did not involve the saving of souls. He began with the central question of what salvation had to do with improving human relations and remained careful never to get too close to the older social gospel, with its leader Walter Rauschenbusch's concept of social salvation. Society, Dabbs believed, would never be saved, and it was a failure of Christian thinking to assume that people would solve all social problems. He was especially important as a thinker because he said gaining salvation and recognizing brotherhood were part of the same process. He did not call for people to be saved first and then go on to pursue brotherhood or that good Christians should know that applying their faith to social problems is an admirable next step after one becomes a Christian. Instead, he said that recognizing the reality of brotherhood was part of the *process* of becoming a saved Christian person. For a person to recognize that Jesus died for all people, not just for him or her, was to recognize that all people face the same situation—that we are all cut off from God and needing connection to both God and all of those other people. In a sermon called "Brothers in Love's Eclipse," Dabbs explained, "We Christians say that for us every man is the brother for whom Christ died; that our brotherhood consists in the fact that he died to save us all." Dabbs stressed that Jesus's love for all people that led to his sacrifice was the example for all people—that we must sacrifice for each other. All people feel despair about their own lives and the purpose of life itself; the Christian life entailed recognizing that we share experiences and needs and possibilities with other people who feel cosmic despair and need something grand to fix it. "We are saved because love lives and dies and is born again in us. This is the key to human brotherhood; in all men love lives and dies and may be born again. All men are brothers in love's eclipse. And we are saved by this realization of brotherhood."[37]

In a revealing essay entitled "The Cotton Curtain," Dabbs argued that overcoming separation of many kinds is essential to Christian living. The lines whites drew that separated them from African Americans, he said, were sinful because of Jesus's life and death, which united all people in a great cosmic drama. Dabbs wrote that society was justified in separating from itself criminals and people with contagious diseases, "But beyond this we go at our peril, and every step in separation must be justified. In the Christian view, Christ lived and died to close these separations: between man and God, between man and man." Dabbs wrote of many things that united or could and should unite people in the South; the sense of trouble and defeat was one of them. "It may be hard for Southern whites and Southern Negroes to admit that they are brothers; the cotton curtain has dimmed our vision so long."[38]

If civil rights activists emphasized family issues in their opposition to segregation, their opponents stressed family as well. But their meanings were different. While civil rights leaders called on the notion of brotherhood, figures in the movement for massive resistance held up the ideal of parental authority as the key to a decent and safe society that passed truths from one generation to the next. If civil rights leaders stressed New Testament notions that all of God's children were part of a big, interconnected brotherhood, their opponents consistently cited as their central authorities the patriarchs of the Old Testament. In the civil rights movement,

brotherhood implied the absence of hierarchy, while in the countermove-
ment of Massive Resistance, ideas about family were based on a hierarchy
within a permanent relationship.

It may seem surprising that anyone would oppose an apparently in-
nocuous concept like brotherhood. But the leaders of massive resistance
frequently condemned the ways opponents of segregation used the concept.
Mississippi governor Ross Barnett, for example, claimed that the "average
white American" did not want racial integration, "in spite of all the propaganda the race-mixers can produce, in spite of all the phony 'brotherhood'
being talked."[39] When Barnett's attempt to prevent the desegregation of the
University of Mississippi ended in violence and disgrace, the *Jackson Daily
News* sneered, "Watch the peace-lovers come to the fore, grab a nigger-
neck and start bellowing brotherly love."[40] The publications of the *Citizens'
Council* repeatedly ridiculed the concept in editorials and cartoons. Editor
William J. Simmons sneered at the few southern journalists who claimed
that while the region was economically backward and racially oppressive,
"with overdoses of brotherhoodism, the South would begin to see the light
and join the twentieth Century by becoming another Brazil." One cartoon
portrayed a tank named "Christian Brotherhood" running over a southern
white man named "States' Rights."[41] In the first issue of that journal Simmons claimed that all white southerners opposed the *Brown* decision, with
the important exceptions of people who thought keeping the schools open
was more important than preserving segregation and clergymen upholding
ideas of Christian brotherhood.[42]

"Why," a white preacher in the South told *Look* magazine in 1964, "it's
gotten so you can't preach justice and brotherhood without someone thinking you mean *nigras*."[43] Supporters of segregation were troubled to the point
of exhaustion that brotherhood had come only to mean opposition to segregation. Fairly frequently, Massive Resistance speakers addressed the topic
directly, rejecting the ways civil rights figures used the term. In a volume
that mixed opposition to desegregation with attempts at humor, North Carolina author W. E. Debnam's *Then My Old Kentucky Home, Good Night!* fell
back on the traditions of southern evangelicalism that claimed Christianity
was really all about salvation. Debnam worried that "this perverted Fatherhood of God and Brotherhood of Men business can wipe out two entire
Races" if people continue to misinterpret the doctrine. He argued that those
doctrines were in fact central elements of Christianity and indeed "the final
hope and refuge of Mankind. . . . But the Fatherhood-Brotherhood doctrine

as taught by Jesus was of the Spirit, pure and undefiled." Brotherhood, Debnam concluded, meant that all humans stood in equal need of conversion,
but it did not fit the political platform or passing worldly concerns of any
group. He sneered, "As taught by the Cult of the Latter Day Abolitionists, it's
(the Fatherhood-Brotherhood doctrine) of the Flesh and reeks of corruption."[44] A Memphis lawyer writing for the Tennessee Federation for Consti-
tutional Government offered a similar theological dismissal of the concept.
"Let's first dispose of the often made suggestion that 'brotherhood' calls for
racial integration. My friends, that term at this time has a new meaning
entirely disassociated with its former meaning—it now simply means the
social integration of the white and Negro races in all aspects of our personal, social and business lives."[45]

In many ways, massive resistance was successful in opposing notions
of brotherhood. By putting up such a violent front against the civil rights
movement, Massive Resistors dramatized the weakness of easy ideas that
all people were God's children who, as family members, shared essential interests in each other's welfare. Massive resistance dramatized separateness,
in effect denying that whites were related to African Americans through
blood, religion, or metaphor. Through hateful words and violent actions,
Massive Resistors told African Americans they were not their brothers, and
many African Americans listened.

In the mid-1960s brotherhood also became less useful and less popular
among civil rights activists in the South. Calling for kinship and forgiveness
of people who were shooting or jailing them grew tiresome, frustrating, and
ultimately maddening. Massive resistance had made clear that numerous
white southerners with power did not embrace African Americans as members of a big family. Other activists simply found the concept of brotherhood too limited and moved on to issues where it was not very helpful.

By the early 1960s some CORE workers, notably James Farmer, started
to doubt that pursuing or implementing brotherhood could achieve their
goals. Writing in 1965, Farmer looked back at the 1940s and 1950s as "our
days of youthful idealism when we loved to tell a story about a boy who told
his mother about a new friend at school." When the mother asked if the
new friend was "white or colored," the boy told her he would have to check.
"We laughed. Oh, how we laughed. Brothers and Sisters, is this not indeed
the way it will be some day."[46] For Farmer, that scene had come to seem
quaint and naive as he faced violence and prison, and he grew uncomfortable with the notion that integration always seemed to be on whites' terms
and increasingly did not see desegregation as his main objective.

New notions of brotherhood were emerging that did not unite blacks and whites. Farmer was moved by a man who stood up at a CORE convention in San Francisco in 1964 and proclaimed, "Brother Farmer, we've got to dig being black." Brothers became those who shared the same background and the same problems. People were related less by universal membership in the human race under the same God than by shared struggles. All people of African descent were brothers, because they had shared the experience of being enslaved or colonized or both. Increasingly in the early 1960s, "We sensed the presence of black men all over the world who were engaged in efforts parallel to our own, calling us brother and asking us to call them brother. In the movement we found an identity." Farmer was stunned on his first trip to Africa. "Like most American Negroes I know nothing of my grandparents. . . . Yet all over Africa black men made me feel as if they were my family." And Farmer encouraged African Americans to celebrate and teach these connections. In the conclusion of his book, he addressed the cultural and educational dimensions of CORE's new direction. "CORE intends to teach Negro history; and to study the world with an eye to the history our brothers are making."[47]

As many historians have detailed, SNCC made some of the most dramatic changes on issues related to racial segregation. Fairly quickly in SNCC, concerns about brotherhood as an idealistic image of an integrated society faded as activists in the group shifted their interests beyond the goal of desegregation to a range of specific strategies and objectives in which brotherhood was not particularly relevant. Many activists simply stopped referring to brotherhood, and others pointedly rejected the ways the concept seemed to hide problems and make whites feel good. In this way, the activism of the mid-1960s recalled the worries James Weldon Johnson and others had about the message of brotherhood decades earlier. When SNCC leaders decided to remove all white members from the organization in 1966, they mentioned the limits of brotherhood. Whites, they said, "cannot relate to the Black experience, cannot relate to the word 'black.'" Whites could not understand the depths of blacks' anger and could not understand blacks' food, language, religion, history, or aspirations. Instead, whites tended only to see the goal of desegregation as an end point that did away with past problems and allowed new generations to start over without the problems of the past. Communication was crucial, and SNCC leaders argued that blacks could not express themselves freely around even the hardest working and best-intentioned white people. "One white person can come into a meeting of Black people and change the complexion of that meeting, whereas one

Black person would not change the complexion of that meeting unless he was an obvious Uncle Tom. People would immediately start talking about 'brotherhood,' 'love,' etc.; race would not be discussed."[48]

Numerous African American writers in the mid-1960s were making the same points. In *Black Man's Burden*, Georgia-born novelist John Oliver Killens rejected as hypocritical the white liberals throughout America who wanted to imagine the end of human difference. Addressing white Americans, he wrote, "You'd like to wish us out of existence so that the whole world would not see us, because our very life in this country, as black people, gives the lie before the world to your protestations of freedom and human brotherhood." Like James Farmer, Killens confronted a deeper meaning of family on a trip to Africa. "Everywhere I went people called me brother." The term was important because Africans used it with a sense of sharing experiences with their "American brother." On the contrary, Killens condemned Americans who used the metaphor of keeping things within the family when they warned blacks against taking their criticisms of American race relations to a world audience. "If there is one thing we black folk should know by now it's that the American people are not one big happy family. We never have been. We are not even one big unhappy family."[49] In *The Negro Mood and Other Essays*, published in 1964, Mississippi native Lerone Bennett captured the growing African American frustration with white liberals who, he said, loved to talk about their own guilt but rarely took part in the hard work necessary for social change. The language of brotherhood seemed crucial in defining a liberal and also in showing a liberal's limitations. "The fundamental trait of the white liberal is his desire to differentiate himself psychologically from white Americans on the issue of race. He wants to think and he wants others to think he is a man of brotherhood. The white liberal talks brotherhood; he writes about it, prays for it, and honors it." But, Bennett emphasized, he did not actually work for "revolt and rebellion."[50] Julius Lester, a native of St. Louis who went to Fisk University on the way to becoming a SNCC worker, condemned how sentimental understandings and descriptions of family stood in the way of addressing real problems. In his 1968 book *Look Out Whitey! Black Power's Gon' Get Your Mama!* Lester, much like James Farmer, wrote with amusement about the idealism of the early movement. The Freedom Riders of 1961 and the Freedom Summer volunteers of 1964, he said, "talked of creating the 'Beloved Society' in which all men were brothers and, oh, yes, Peace! It was wonderful."[51]

Stokely Carmichael explicitly rejected notions of political action that, like those common earlier in the civil rights movement, seemed to be based on love and high moral principle. Notions of politics based on "a moral, friendly or sentimental basis, or on appeals to conscience" represented "a myth because we believe that political relations are based on self-interest: benefits to be gained and losses to be avoided."[52] Carmichael and his compatriots did not reject brotherhood; instead, they made the concept specific and, they hoped, more useful. Brotherhood, defined as desegregation, forgiveness of oppressors, and unity with all people under God, seemed irrelevant. Instead, "brother" and "sister" identified those Americans who were united by the shared experience of facing slavery, racial violence, and racial segregation in America. For some, brotherhood was also coming to mean sharing background, interests, and kinship with Africans, both those colonized and those who were newly independent. Carmichael urged an all-black communal economy that would both reject the economic power of white-run American capitalism and build on the potential for brotherhood within the black community. Spelling out the programmatic meanings of Black Power, Carmichael and coauthor Charles V. Hamilton encouraged "an attitude of brotherly, communal responsibility among all black people for one another."[53] In his memorable 1966 essay "Power and Racism," Carmichael held up the ideal of a black society "in which the spirit of community and humanistic love prevail.... The love we seek to encourage is within the black community, the only American community where men call each other 'brother' when they meet."[54] The terms "brother" and "sister" as meaning black man and woman were not new in this period, but the popularity of the usage dramatically increased to the point that it began to appear in dictionaries in the 1970s.[55]

Many SNCC leaders urged a sense of brotherhood and sisterhood not with white Americans and Europeans who oppressed blacks on two continents, but with all people who faced imperialism and economic exploitation. In 1967 SNCC's new chairman, H. Rap Brown, sent out letters to "Dear Brothers and Sisters in Black Communities throughout the United States." He wanted to unite black Americans around the need to support "our brothers and sisters in South Africa" in an armed struggle against apartheid. Brown urged boycotts of all companies and governments that invested in South Africa and asked for contributions to the African National Congress and a general self-education in order to "support our blood brothers."[56] SNCC condemned the war in Vietnam and asked why black Americans should go off to fight people who were "victims of the same oppression that our brothers in Vietnam suffer."[57] SNCC worker Cleveland Sellers used the concept repeatedly and poetically in a long rejection of the Vietnam draft in 1967: "How do we stop the exploitation of our brothers' territories and goods by a wealthy, hungry nation such as this?" Sellers answered, "I am committed to give support to my brothers in Vietnam as they fight to keep America from taking their tungsten, tin, and rubber. I shall be prepared to support my brothers in Iran when they move to overthrow their puppet regime which gives that country's rich oil deposits to the U.S." He continued that he was "prepared to back my brothers in the Congo when they tell the U.S. 'Hell, no,' this copper belongs to me. I shall stand ready when my brothers in South Africa move to overthrow that apartheid regime. . . . I shall not serve in this Army or any others that seek by force to use the resources of my black brothers here at the expense of my brothers in Asia, Africa, and Latin America."[58]

By the late 1960s brotherhood was having a difficult time. It seemed too white, too optimistic, certainly too much about desegregation and not enough about justice and power. To some activists, it may have seemed too male—although it is hard to find anyone making that point in a direct way.[59] The activists with new uses of the concept were defining all black people as brothers and sisters who had faced the same experiences and developed a sense of the kinship of the oppressed and struggling. A recurring theme is that brotherhood had a great deal to do with the hopes and expectations white southern Christians had about racial integration. Many white Christians either believed the civil rights movement had succeeded and no longer needed to be addressed, or they worried that the directions it was taking had no room for a vision of brotherhood that united all whites and blacks.

This historical background of the various meanings of brotherhood helps clarify the ways Perkins used the concept, why he used the concept in a book cowritten with a former Klansman, and also why he used the concept relatively infrequently and only on a few topics. Perkins understood the concerns of the civil rights activists who rejected the concept because he had felt troubled by it himself. What Perkins ultimately described as the experience of Christian brotherhood was something he discovered long after he had been working for justice. He was apprehensive to embrace the concept of brotherhood, fearing it for many of the reasons African American leaders had been wary of it in the past.

Perkins shared with James Weldon Johnson, James Foreman, and many others the fear that the concept of brotherhood could be too sugary to have much lasting value. For example, his 1976 volume *Let Justice Roll Down* includes an early statement agreeing with the worries so many African Americans have had that brotherhood, poorly defined, carried implications that could become far too optimistic. In a quick and revealing passage on the first page of the preface, Perkins wrote, "Ours is not a story of bitterness—it is a story of love and the triumphs of the God of love. But it is a story carved out of the realities of violence and poverty, ending not in some sugarcoated sense of brotherly love but the deep conviction that only the power of Christ's crucifixion on the cross and the glory of His resurrection can heal the deep racial wounds in both black and white people in America."[60] The language of "some sugarcoated sense of brotherly love" sounds a great deal like the many people—from James Weldon Johnson in the 1930s to James Farmer in the 1960s—who claimed that shared experience and goodwill, defined as brotherhood between whites and blacks, was not their primary goal.

An intriguing feature of Perkins's use of the concept of brotherhood is that in some of his books, he does not mention the concept early, instead waiting until fairly late in the volume before describing it as a goal that is difficult to approach. In both *A Quiet Revolution* and *With Justice for All*, brotherhood appears only slowly. In the former book, published in 1976, brotherhood first appears at the end of an important section, "The Failure of the Evangelical Church." In that chapter Perkins criticizes white churches in the South for talking but not acting, or for taking only passing notice of the problems facing African Americans. Using language of past African American leaders who addressed the concept of brotherhood particularly to white liberals, he took note of the small numbers of evangelicals who "broke away from the popular propaganda against the civil rights movement. . . . I praise God for those few people who as Christians, many of them white, have stayed with us and are even now stepping out in courage to influence in love their brothers and sisters."[61] Perkins continued in that chapter in a way that dramatizes a crucial point about how he understands and uses the concept of brotherhood. He recalled that "in the late 1960s I was more damaged than I am now." Anger and bitterness were part of what had "damaged" him, and Perkins wrote that for years he had only been concerned with "the deep needs of black people." However, brotherhood became part of his story when he came to believe he needed to deal with whites as well as African Americans. "It would be several years before God would give me a burden for the deep needs among people in the white community, needs for reconciliation and love. It would be several years before I realized that it would not be possible to deal with one and not the other, and that the models of reconciliation and brotherhood that would need to be built among whites would be the basis for real community development in the black neighborhood."[62]

Perkins's slow movement toward using the concept of brotherhood is also evident in *With Justice for All*, a book on community development Perkins first published in 1982. He first refers to brotherhood in a challenge to white Christians. "As we embark on our mission, we must invite our white brothers and sisters to join us—to join us as partners in a way that reconciles us to each other even as we labor together." That statement was a welcome to people who should, if they were truly brothers and sisters, be working together but a cautionary note that separation belies any claims to brotherhood. It seems more pointed when Perkins wrote that he and his African American colleagues needed to continue their work even if no whites joined them. In that case, "we must start without them."[63]

Later in *With Justice for All*, Perkins offered his first serious discussion of the meaning of brotherhood as a positive virtue and a Christian responsibility. Using numerous examples from projects Perkins and his associates had developed in Mississippi and California, the volume argued for a three-step process of relocation, reconciliation, and redistribution. Continuing the tendency to use brotherhood to discuss racial definitions and interracial work, Perkins only discussed it in the chapters on reconciliation. Relocation meant a range of things, beginning with decisions to move into poor areas where people need help so the people moving in could get to know better the people they are helping. Redistribution has been crucial to his vision of a Christian society, and also had multiple meanings, extending from talent and energy to finances. Brotherhood did not appear in the start and end of the book; it is only significant in the middle chapters, where it is a central, crucial part of reconciliation.

For several years Perkins had little interest in working with white people. As many activists were saying in the mid and late 1960s, he believed for some time that power and justice were the goals of the civil rights movement. As he described the early years of his ministry, "My whole drive for those first 10 years was to lift blacks from their oppression. I heard the voices calling for black self-determination and black liberation, and I accepted that. What I really wanted in the sixties was for the white man to leave us alone, to let us be. Because of the hostility, I had very little contact with the white Mississippi community."[64] By the 1970s, however, that seemed a combination of bad strategy and bad theology. Reconciliation was the strategic and theological solution: "As a Christian, my responsibility was to seek to be reconciled. Then out of that reconciliation, justice would flow."[65] As a crucial component of reconciliation, brotherhood, for Perkins, meant a personal kinship with people working for reconciliation and justice. Perkins emphasized scriptural support for brotherhood, referring to John's command that someone cannot truly love God and hate his brother, and Jesus's statement in the Sermon on the Mount that people should not seek reconciliation with God while they were angry with their brothers.

In *He's My Brother* Perkins adds a particularly personal approach to his discussion of brotherhood as part of reconciliation. He offers more discussion of his own Christian conversion experience in part as a way to introduce issues related to brotherhood. Growing up outside any church, Perkins recalled that he thought of Christianity as the "white man's religion" and was working for power and justice for African Americans well before he had his own conversion experience.[66] Unlike many southern evangelicals who grew up assuming that religious life was about church life and individual conversion experiences, Perkins knew from the beginning of his life as a Christian that working for justice was part of his religious commitment. When he returned from California to Mississippi in 1960, he knew he wanted to work in churches and with poor people. As Charles Marsh writes, "Perkins understood that the first order of business in any serious attempt to build community with the poor was to get involved in a local church."[67]

The way Perkins used the concept of brotherhood emerged especially clearly from his confrontation with hatred—especially his hatred of people who hated and mistreated him and other African Americans. In 1970 he was arrested and beaten in jail in response to an economic boycott in Mendenhall, Mississippi. Lying in a hospital bed suffering from injuries, he said he experienced a form of hatred almost as powerful as the hatred of those who had beaten him. He wrote that he knew at that moment "why so many leaders of the civil rights movement were so vehemently anti-white," and he wondered if cooperation between whites and African Americans might simply be impossible.[68] Experiencing what he called something close to a second conversion experience, Perkins first recalled a few helpful white individuals, and, far more important, he imagined Jesus on the cross, forgiving his tormenters. "The Holy Spirit would not let that image leave me. He seemed to be whispering to me again and again, 'John, you've got to love them.'"[69] Taking the emphasis on forgiveness so prominent in the work of Martin Luther King Jr., Perkins describes the practice of forgiving as a broader practice of understanding the love God has for humanity. Probably more specific to Perkins, though, is his emphasis on love as a process—recognizing shared interests, working together, not as an end product but in the shared goal of addressing poverty and injustice.[70]

Perkins and former Klansman Thomas Tarrants both discuss overcoming hatred, and both use the concept of brotherhood to describe that process. As a descriptive term, "friend" might by itself have been too generic and nontheological, so Perkins wrote of Tarrants, "The better I got to know him, the more I loved him as a brother, and the more impressed and amazed I was by what God had done in his life. Once we would have been the worst of enemies. Now we are the best of friends, brothers in Christ, working hand-in-hand for the sake of the Gospel." Perkins describes this kind of brotherhood between people whose personal histories seemed to make them enemies for life as a contemporary miracle, similar to biblical stories of healing.[71]

Later in *He's My Brother* Perkins made one of his clearest links between Christian conversion, racial reconciliation, and efforts to work for justice for poor people.[72] Very much like James McBride Dabbs, Perkins argued that the need to be reconciled to God puts human beings in a very social position of sharing the same problem. Beginning with lost sinners separated from God, Perkins describes the need to be reconciled, and then immediately continues to the need to overcome social barriers. God "expects us to tell people how they can be reconciled to God through the cross, and He also expects us to reconcile people to people across whatever barriers might divide us—including barriers of race, ethnicity and class."[73] The difference between the language Perkins and Dabbs used to describe brotherhood is that while Dabbs discussed people's need to recognize the preexisting truth of brotherhood, Perkins sees brotherhood as more of an active approach, closer to making brotherhood than to recognizing it. In a section entitled "Because the Theological Foundation of Our Faith Is Reconciliation," Perkins discusses brotherhood more than he has anywhere else in his written work. He quotes James's command to help "if a brother or sister is naked and destitute of daily food," and he makes clear that action is the only way to show that high ideals that people discuss are genuine and meaningful. "That call to reach out a loving hand of assistance to the poorer brother or sister crosses culture, racial and international barriers. If the gospel we preach is genuine, it is the power to reconcile alienated men and women to a holy God and to one another across all these barriers. It is the only means and hope for international brotherhood and peace, and the only means and hope for brotherhood and peace between different races and ethnic groups here at home."[74] Here Perkins comes very close to one of Martin Luther King's key meanings of brotherhood. It was not simply about coming together; it was about coming together, across all possible lines that separate them, to help people who need it.

To draw conclusions about the ways John Perkins has chosen to use the concept of brotherhood in his books, one can start with what brotherhood is not. First, brotherhood is not an underlying reality human beings only need to discover or realize. He does not refer to science and the Bible working together to undermine the idea of race and other reasons for human separation and hatred. The apparently easy plea of so many people on the idea of race—if only people understood the truth, they would reject the concept—is not an important part of his work. He would not have agreed with Robert Eleazer or Mary McLeod Bethune that brotherhood is real, while human creations that separate people are fakes and lies. Second, Perkins does not discuss phases of history moving from selfishness and separation toward a greater day of brotherly love. At least in his books, Perkins does not seem to have much use for stages of history, and while he certainly can see progress, he does not use the grand language of many earlier activists who saw brotherhood as a new stage of history. Finally, he would disagree with Stokely Carmichael's description of brotherhood in *Black Power*. All human beings can be brothers or sisters—there is no way to claim that only black people should call each other "brother" or "sister."

Perkins has continued traditions associated with several of the intellectual leaders who have discussed brotherhood. He continues Martin Luther King Jr.'s call for brotherhood that involves helping people in trouble to solve their problems and King's emphasis on forgiveness as part of Christian life. He also continues the emphasis James McBride Dabbs placed on brotherhood as an essential part of Christian salvation. Sometimes Perkins has agreed with people like James Weldon Johnson, who feared that brotherhood was a kind of light and sugarcoated covering of deeper, harder issues, and he continues to emphasize that getting whites and African Americans together to know and respect each other is a just a step toward broader goals of fighting poverty and powerlessness. But his most inspired discussions overcome these worries to portray brotherhood as a crucial part of reconciliation and Christian salvation. Perhaps the most succinct summary Perkins has made of his theology of brotherhood came in a short paragraph in *With Justice for All*: "To be reconciled to my brother I must first be reconciled to God; to remain reconciled to God I must be reconciled to my brother. I cannot have one without the other."[75]

It seems fair to conclude that Perkins has not said (or tried to say) anything about brotherhood that is distinctive. The concept has not dominated his thinking, and analyzing it does not unlock a mysterious secret about his theology and how he applies it. Perhaps his use of a concept that many have rejected as obsolete or irrelevant to real issues shows the courage of an unconventional activist. It seems that the most important way Perkins uses the concept is to say there is little about brotherhood that is easy. If it is not a human or spiritual reality waiting for human beings to find or a next and better stage of history, what is it? Brotherhood in *With Justice for All* is necessary before moving on to the work of the third R, redistribution. And in *He's My Brother*, brotherhood is part of learning that reconciliation is "an ongoing process."[76] Above all, brotherhood is a goal, a job, an imperative to keep doing hard work, and a commitment to the inseparability of social action and Christian life.

## NOTES

1. John Perkins, *Let Justice Roll Down* (Ventura, Calif.: Regal Books, 1976), 21.

2. Perkins, *Let Justice Roll Down*, 20.

3. Perkins, *Let Justice Roll Down*, 24. On the importance of the murder of Clyde Perkins in the life of John Perkins, see Charles Marsh, *The Beloved Community: How Faith Shapes Social Justice, from the Civil Rights Movement to Today* (New York: Basic Books, 2005), 156–157; Stephen E. Berk, *A Time to Heal: John Perkins, Community Development, and Racial Reconciliation* (Grand Rapids, Mich.: Baker Books, 1997); Peter Goodwin Heltzel, *Jesus & Justice: Evangelicals, Race & American Politics* (New Haven, Conn.: Yale University Press, 2009).

4. Robert B. Eleazer, "What the Bible Tells Me About Race Relations," 2, in Howard Kester Papers, Reel 13 (Glen Rock, N.J.: Microfilming Corporation of America, 1973). On Eleazer's work for using schools to oppose racism, see Robert B. Eleazer, "My First Eighty Years," unpublished manuscript, 65–68, in Eleazer Papers, Vanderbilt University Library, Nashville, Tenn.; Robert B. Eleazer, "The Quest for Understanding: Education in the Art of Getting Along Together," in *Education and Racial Adjustment: Report of the Peabody Conference on Dual Education in the South* (Atlanta: Executive Committee of the Conference, 1931), 17–23; Robert B. Eleazer, *School Books and Racial Antagonism: A Study of Omissions and Inclusions That Make for Misunderstanding*, pamphlet published by the Conference on Education and Race Relations, Atlanta, 1935, Eleazer Papers, Vanderbilt; *College Courses in Race Relations: An Effort to Meet the Challenge of the Southern Situation*, pamphlet published by the Conference on Education and Race Relations, Atlanta, 1939, Eleazer Papers, Vanderbilt.

5. Robert B. Eleazer, "A Southerner Talks to the South," MSS File, 1, Eleazer Papers, Vanderbilt.

6. Robert B. Eleazer, "Christianity in an Unchristian World," MSS File, Eleazer Papers, Vanderbilt.

7. J. McDowell Richards, *Brothers in Black* (1941; repr., Atlanta: Southern Regional Council, 1946).

8. Harold L. Trigg, "Brothers or Bombs?" *New South* (February 1946): 3.

9. Paul D. Williams, "Wings of Eagles," *New South* (January 1952): 2.

10. James Weldon Johnson, *Negro Americans, What Now?* (1934; repr., New York: Viking Press, 1938), 22.

11. Johnson, *Negro Americans*, 81.

12. Johnson, *Negro Americans*, 84.

13. Robert Russa Moton, *What the Negro Thinks* (Garden City, N.Y.: Doubleday, Doran, 1932), vii.

14. Moton, *What the Negro Thinks*, 66.

15. Gordon B. Hancock, "Race Relations in the United States: A Summary," in *What the Negro Wants*, ed. Rayford W. Logan (Chapel Hill: University of North Carolina Press, 1944), 227.

16. Quoted in John Egerton, *Speak Now Against the Day: The Generation before the Civil Rights Movement in the South* (New York: Alfred A. Knopf, 1994), 309.

17. Sterling A. Brown, "Count Us In," in Logan, *What the Negro Wants*, 314.

18. Mary McLeod Bethune, "Certain Inalienable Rights," in Logan, *What the Negro Wants*, 258.

19. Mary McLeod Bethune, "Spiritual Autobiography," in *Mary McLeod Bethune: Building a Better World, Essays and Selected Documents*, ed. Audrey Thomas McCluskey and Elaine M. Smith (Bloomington: Indiana University Press, 1999), 54.

20. Mary McLeod Bethune, "U.S. Will Make 'the Grade' in Integrating All Its Schools," in McCluskey and Smith, *Mary McLeod Bethune*, 274.

21. Mary McLeod Bethune, "My Last Will and Testament," in McCluskey and Smith, *Mary McLeod Bethune*, 59, 61.

22. Fellowship of Reconciliation and Congress of Racial Equality, "Pledge Brotherhood," 1952, flyer, State Historical Society of Wisconsin, microfilm.

23. Bayard Rustin, "Montgomery Diary," in *Time on Two Crosses: Collected Writings of Bayard Rustin*, ed. Devon W. Carbado and Donald Weise (San Francisco: Cleis Press, 2003), 59.

24. Handbill of the Albany Nonviolent Movement, November 9, 1961, in Stephen Lawson, Charles Payne, and James T. Patterson, eds., *Debating the Civil Rights Movement, 1945–1968* (New York: Rowman & Littlefield, 2006), 141–142.

25. *The Papers of Martin Luther King, Jr.*, Vol. 3, *Birth of a New Age, December 1955–December 1956*, ed. Clayborne Carson (Berkeley: University of California Press, 1977), 208, 323, 328.

26. Martin Luther King Jr., *Strength to Love* (New York: Pocket Books, 1964), 88–90.

27. Martin Luther King Jr., *Stride Toward Freedom* (New York: Perennial/Harper & Row, 1964), 23, 29.

28. David Chappell, *A Stone of Hope: Prophetic Religion and the Death of Jim Crow* (Chapel Hill: University of North Carolina Press, 2004).

29. See Mark Newman, *Getting Right with God: Southern Baptists and Desegregation, 1945–1995* (Tuscaloosa: University of Alabama Press, 2001).

30. T. B. Maston, *The Christian and Race Relations* (Memphis, Tenn.: Southern Baptist Convention, Brotherhood Commission, Seminar Pilot Series for Men, n.d.), 4.

31. Charles Trentham, "One Father—One Blood," in *Baptists See Black*, ed. Wayne Dehoney (Waco, Tex.: Word Books, 1969), 21.

32. *Mississippi Methodist Advocate*, January 2, 1963, 2, www.mississippi-umc.org/console/files/oFiles_Library_XZXLCZ/Born_of_Conviction_4QQJSQYW.pdf.

33. James McBride Dabbs, "The Tragic Fellowship of Southerners," Address at interchurch meeting, Greater Little Rock Ministerial Association, on Brotherhood Sunday, 1960, 3, in Southern Regional Council File, OCSMMSS, Box 22, Special Collections, University of Mississippi, Oxford.

34. James McBride Dabbs, "Southern Churchmen: Fellowship to Committee," *Katallagete* 1 (1965): 10.

35. Dabbs, "Tragic Fellowship," 4.

36. Dabbs, "Tragic Fellowship," 12.

37. James McBride Dabbs, "Brothers in Love's Eclipse," Folder 13, Box 4, Dabbs Papers, Southern Historical Collection (SHC), University of North Carolina, Chapel Hill.

38. James McBride Dabbs, "The Cotton Curtain," Box 8, Folder 220, Dabbs Papers, SHC.

39. Ross R. Barnett, "Strength Through Unity!" Address to Citizens' Council Rally, New Orleans, March 7, 1960, 4, Citizens' Council Collection, Folder 14, Special Collections, University of Mississippi.

40. *Jackson Daily News*, quoted in Paul Hendrickson, *Sons of Mississippi: A Story of Race and Its Legacy* (New York: Alfred A. Knopf, 2003), 126.

41. Both the editorial and the cartoon appeared in the *Citizens' Council*, October 1957, 1.

42. *Citizens' Council*, October 1955, 1.

43. "Mississippi: The Attack on Bigotry," *Look*, September 8, 1964, 28.

44. W. E. Debnam, *Then My Old Kentucky Home, Good Night!* (Raleigh, N.C.: W. E. Debnam, 1955), 70.

45. Marvin Brooks Norfleet, *Forced Racial Integration! In Its Religious, Social and Political Aspects—Principally Applied to School Integration of the White and Negro Races*, pamphlet published by the Tennessee Federation for Constitution, West Tennessee District, 1960, 4, Donald Davidson Papers, Vanderbilt University Libraries, Special Collections, Box 44, Folder 1.

46. James Farmer, *Freedom—When?* (New York: Random House, 1965), 86.

47. Farmer, *Freedom—When?* 87, 134, 196.

48. Student Nonviolent Coordinating Committee Position Paper, "The Basis of Black Power," 1966, Race and History website, www.raceandhistory.com/historicalviews/2004/The_Basis_of_Black_Power.html.

49. John Oliver Killens, *Black Man's Burden* (New York: Trident Press, 1965), 19, 160, 168.

50. Lerone Bennett, *The Negro Mood and Other Essays* (Chicago: Johnson Publishing, 1964), 78, 77.

51. Julius Lester, *Look Out Whitey! Black Power's Gon' Get Your Mama!* (New York: Dial Press, 1968), 6, 4.

52. Stokely Carmichael and Charles V. Hamilton, *Black Power: The Politics of Liberation in America* (New York: Vintage Books, 1967), 75.

53. Carmichael and Hamilton, *Black Power*, vii.

54. Stokely Carmichael, "Power and Racism," in *The Black Power Revolt: A Collection of Essays*, ed. Floyd B. Barbour (Beacon, Mass.: Extending Horizons Books, 1968), 70.

55. On the term "brother" as a synonym for African American male, see Herb Boyd and Robert L. Allen, eds., *Brotherman: The Odyssey of Black Men in America* (New York: One World, 1995); Jonathan Rieder, *The Word of the Lord Is Upon Me: The Righteous Performance of Martin Luther King, Jr.* (Cambridge, Mass.: Belknap Press of Harvard University Press, 2008), 32–49.

56. H. Rap Brown to "Dear Brothers and Sisters in Black Communities throughout the United States," August 28, 1967, SNCC Papers, Reel 11, The King Center, Atlanta.

57. SNCC Policy Statement, Atlanta, 1967, *Freedom Information Service Mississippi Newsletter*, June 2, 1967, 2.

58. Cleveland Sellers, in *Freedom Information Service Mississippi Newsletter*, October 13, 1967, 2.

59. On the complications of applying all-male definitions of activism within the civil rights movement, see Steve Estes, *I Am a Man! Race, Manhood, and the Civil Rights Movement* (Chapel Hill: University of North Carolina Press, 2005).

60. Perkins, *Let Justice Roll Down*, 11.

61. John Perkins, *A Quiet Revolution: Meeting Human Needs Today: A Biblical Challenge to Christians*, rev. ed. (Pasadena, Calif.: Urban Family Publications with Network Unlimited International, 1976), 99.

62. Perkins, *Quiet Revolution*, 102.

63. Perkins, *Let Justice Roll Down*, 40.

64. John M. Perkins, *With Justice for All*, foreword by Chuck Colson (Ventura, Calif.: Regal Books, 1982), 110–111.

65. Perkins, *With Justice for All*, 112.

66. John M. Perkins and Thomas A. Tarrants III, with David Wimbish, *He's My Brother: Former Racial Foes Offer Strategy for Reconciliation* (Grand Rapids, Mich.: Chosen Books, 1994), 56.

67. Marsh, *Beloved Community*, 165.

68. Perkins and Tarrants, *He's My Brother*, 131.

69. Perkins and Tarrants, *He's My Brother*, 133.

70. On the influence of King on Perkins, see Marsh, *Beloved Community*; Heltzel, *Jesus & Justice*.

71. Perkins and Tarrants, *He's My Brother*, 145, 144.

72. See Marsh, *Beloved Community*, 182.

73. Perkins and Tarrants, *He's My Brother*, 176.

74. Perkins and Tarrants, *He's My Brother*, 177.

75. Perkins, *With Justice for All*, 126.

76. Perkins, *With Justice for All*, 158–208; Perkins and Tarrants, *He's My Brother*, 228. On reconciliation as an ongoing process, see Berk, *Time to Heal*, 375.

# A Quiet Revolution and the Culture Wars

*Peter Slade*

THE STORY OF THE CIVIL RIGHTS MOVEMENT DRAMATIZES THE MORAL failure and cultural captivity of the white evangelical church in the United States of America. Evangelicals' active resistance to integration in the 1960s stemmed from their rejection of the social gospel movement and separation from modernist and progressive Protestants earlier that century. The civil rights movement was only one act in a theological drama that continues to play out in the sanctuaries, seminaries, and city streets of twenty-first-century America. John Perkins is a key character in this unfolding drama. As an African American prophet to contemporary white evangelicals, Perkins confronts them with their complicity in rejecting the prophets while at the same time inviting them to expand their theology to include what he calls the holistic gospel. More than forty years after Martin Luther King Jr.'s death, Perkins's unique life story enables a new generation of evangelicals to relocate themselves as participants in the continuing civil rights movement without rejecting their evangelical heritage. In the latest act of this theological drama, we find a theology of the social gospel alive and well in the most surprising of places—as a grassroots movement within the mainstream of American evangelicalism.

## THE SOCIAL GOSPEL

The story of John and Vera Mae Perkins's return to Mississippi in 1960 and the foundation of Voice of Calvary Ministries in Mendenhall is a familiar one. It is told by John Perkins and retold as the founding narrative of the Christian Community Development Association (CCDA).[1] Also well known is Perkins's strategy for Christian community development condensed into his three Rs of relocation, reconciliation, and redistribution.[2] Perhaps less well known is the theological distance Perkins traveled from his fundamentalist/evangelical roots to preaching his holistic gospel of the kingdom of God that "see[s] people not just as souls, but as whole people."[3] His original reason for returning to Mississippi was to bring biblical literacy to the black churches in his home state, whose preachers and congregations, in his opinion, had plenty of zeal and emotion but lacked "enlightenment."[4] Driven by this vision, Perkins first established a Bible institute and engaged in evangelism at every opportunity. Three years after returning to Mississippi, motivated by a desire to help their neighbors as well as their own children, Vera Mae started running a day care center from their home. "[It] was," Perkins remembers, "the first real social action we got into."[5] The day care flourished, and from 1966 to 1968 it became part of the federally funded Head Start program.[6] By the mid-1970s Voice of Calvary, now located in both Jackson and Mendenhall, was operating thrift stores, health clinics, a housing cooperative, as well as classes in Bible and theology.

The notion that the gospel of Jesus Christ is good news not just to an individual's soul but also to his or her whole person and community is not a new idea to American Christianity; it found its most pronounced expression in the social gospel movement of the early 1900s. The fact that Perkins had to rediscover this dimension of the gospel for himself is an embarrassing testimony to the self-imposed theological segregation of American evangelicals in the middle of the twentieth century, a tendency that continues to this day. In the 1960s evangelicals desired to remain holy and separate from the corrupting influence of liberal Christianity with its social gospel, ecumenical, and universalist tendencies.

The influential writings of the great prophets of the social gospel movement—Washington Gladden, Walter Rauschenbusch, Richard Ely, Shailer Mathews, et al.—were shaped by a number of factors that came together in the churches and seminaries of America's Gilded Age. By the time Rauschenbusch published his landmark work *Christianity and the Social Crisis* in 1907, this form of socially progressive Protestantism was a complex ideological laminate with its own distinctive properties. This laminate was formed in part by, and in part in response to, the rapid expansion and industrialization of America's cities. These cities filled to overflowing with migrants and immigrants, and the churches struggled to find ways to respond to the vice and poverty of this new urban landscape. In a huge burst of energy following the Civil War, encouraged by the success of the abolitionist cause, Protestant churches created a plethora of societies, organizations, and leagues to bring the civilizing gospel light to the cities. In 1869 the *New York Times* reported a meeting of just such an organization: at this particular meeting of the American Christian Commission, the speakers called on "Christians of all denominations [to] set aside their doctrinal differences" better to engage in "Christianizing the masses."[7] Facing these new challenges, churches sought new ways to understand both the masses and what it meant to Christianize them. By the beginning of the twentieth century, the social gospel had brought together the new science of sociology, the findings of modern biblical criticism, and the progressive politics of the era.[8] "For the first time in history," Rauschenbusch reflected, "the spirit of Christianity has had a chance to form a working partnership with real social and psychological science. . . . The social gospel is the old message of salvation, but enlarged and intensified."[9]

The prophets of the social gospel insisted that their message was rooted in an evangelical belief in the salvific work of Christ and not a reduction of the gospel to a simplistic optimism in the progress of Anglo-Saxon Protestant civilization. "It takes regenerate souls to make a regenerated society," Shailer Mathews explained. "The gospel is the message of salvation assured to individuals and society who accept Jesus as their Lord."[10] Rauschenbusch wanted to expand the challenge of the gospel and "bring men under repentance for their collective sins." With this came the hope not only of personal salvation but also the "regeneration of the social order."[11] The condensed account of twentieth-century theology taught in seminaries today is that postwar liberal disillusionment and the rise of the Christian realism led by theologian Reinhold Niebuhr dashed this optimism.[12] It is important to note that Niebuhr's problem with the social gospel was not that it wanted to expand the mission of the church to redeeming the social order, rather that it did not have a right understanding of society itself. He argued in his landmark *Moral Man and Immoral Society: A Study in Ethics and Politics* that no matter how much regeneration an individual moral Christian might experience, when these individuals get together they form immoral—not regenerated—societies.[13]

While it is true that the optimism of men like Rauschenbusch and their talk of "the salvation of nations" seemed absurd and irresponsible in the face of global depression and the rise of totalitarian regimes in the interwar years, such a dismissal of the social gospel movement downplays the remarkable successes it had in shaping churchgoers' social concern and the impact this popular concern had on American society.[14] The theology was neatly summarized by the Congregational minister from Topeka, Kansas, Charles M. Sheldon in his popular novel *In His Steps* with the question, "What would Jesus do?"[15] The practical outworking of this theology was a movement that built "institutional" churches in the inner city offering a range of social services including language and literacy classes, job training, bathhouses, as well as movements to reform slum housing, organize labor, close saloons, prosecute lynching, improve prisons, build hospitals, and ensure world peace through a league of nations.[16]

The social gospel movement experienced its most serious challenge not from Niebuhr's Christian realism but from a group of people who came to call themselves fundamentalists. Rauschenbusch anticipated what historians came to call "the Great Reversal"—the division between social concern and evangelism—when he recognized the tendency for churches to divide between those who persisted in an exclusively "individualistic theology" and those who adopted a socially progressive theology.[17] He called this a "dumb-bell system of thought, with the social gospel at one end and individual salvation at the other."[18] This polarization that Rauschenbusch decried entered a new and divisive phase when the fundamentalist-modernist war ripped through the Protestant denominations in the 1920s. At the start of 1924, *Christian Century* ran an editorial with the self-explanatory title "Fundamentalism and Modernism: Two Religions."[19] The modernists came to be associated with the mainstream churches that were members of the Federal Council of Churches, founded in 1908. These churches withdrew from emphasizing personal evangelism and foreign mission tending to leave these areas to the evangelical, Pentecostal, and fundamentalist churches.[20] By the 1940s a group of conservative Protestants came together with a desire to reject liberal theology while at the same time distancing themselves from the mud-slinging and ant-intellectualism of the fundamentalists. This movement, championed by Billy Graham, founded the National Association of Evangelicals in 1942, established Fuller Theological Seminary in 1947, and started publishing its own journal, *Christianity Today*, in 1954 to challenge the liberal *Christian Century*.[21]


## THE CIVIL RIGHTS MOVEMENT

Liberal and evangelical Protestants had clearly established themselves in separate camps by 1954, when, with the Supreme Court's decision in the case of *Brown v. Board of Education*, the theological drama of the modern civil rights movement began.[22] Revealed in this drama is the fundamental weakness of evangelical theology, which dogmatically rejected what Rauschenbusch described as the gospel of salvation "enlarged and intensified" to include the redemption of social institutions and what Perkins came

to call the "holistic gospel." In the 1950s in the South—where most evangelicals could be found—an ecclesial marriage of convenience was taking place
between social conservatives concerned with preserving the "southern way
of life" and theological conservatives defending the inerrancy of Scripture:
since the modernist-fundamentalist battles of the 1920s, northern fundamentalist preachers needing churches had been welcomed in southern pulpits.[23] Following the Supreme Court's ruling in *Brown* in 1954, the struggle
over desegregation provided the heat and pressure that bonded these elements into a strong laminate. Adding strength and durability to this bond
was the patriotism fashioned in opposition to Communism and the threat
of civil unrest.

This bonding (or bondage) can clearly be seen if one reads through issues of *Christianity Today* from the 1950s and 1960s. Through this period
the editors of *Christianity Today*—the most widely read evangelical publication[24]—classified themselves as "earnest moderates" and "evangelical moderates" on the issue of race.[25] They carefully tried to position themselves
*for* desegregation and in support of the Supreme Court's ruling in *Brown*
in 1954, and the passage of the Civil Rights Act in 1964, while at the same
time being *against* "forced integration."[26] In 1958 L. Nelson Bell, the executive editor of *Christianity Today* and Billy Graham's father-in-law, captured
this balancing act in a widely adopted statement, "The Race Issue and a
Christian Principle."[27] Evangelical Christians should remove "all barriers
to spiritual fellowship in Christ, without at the same time attempting to
force un-natural social relationships." The "un-natural social relationships"
of particular concern to evangelicals were those of interracial marriage and
integrated churches that affected family and congregational life.[28]

Evangelical's relationship with the civil rights movement comes into
clear focus in *Christianity Today*'s treatment of Martin Luther King Jr. In
the journal's review of King's book *Stride toward Freedom*, the author—a
professor of theology at Southern Baptist Theological Seminary, Louisville,
Kentucky—warned that "the philosophy underlying racial integration is
racial socialism" and that King's goal is "a state imposed classless society."[29]
"Dr. King properly recognizes communism as a Christian heresy," the re-
viewer explained, "but fails to realize that a part of its heretical character
is implicit in his integrationist ideology."[30] While eschewing the Citizens'
Council's insistence that King was a Communist, these evangelical moderates believed he was a socialist and an unwitting heretic—a fine distinction!

It was clear to the readers of *Christianity Today* in the 1950s and 1960s
where the root of King's confusion lay: liberal theology that failed to take

into account the doctrine of original sin and human depravity. Such liberal "philosophers of religion" might argue differently, "but the believing Church" knew that the real solution to "racial antipathy" lay in the "indispensability of regeneration."[31] These evangelical moderates frequently bemoaned the absence of evangelical leadership in the civil rights movement to correct this liberal theology; however, they could not blame evangelical leaders for choosing to avoid association with a movement that did not insist on conversion: they wrote, "One can well understand . . . a lack of enthusiasm for integration without regeneration."[32]

Evangelicals were at least correct in recognizing the influence of the social gospel in Martin Luther King Jr.'s mission; King's beloved community owed its vision to the earlier social gospel movement.[33] In 1960 he described his encounter with Walter Rauschenbusch's writings in the "early fifties" as leaving an "indelible imprint on my thinking."[34] What was imprinted on King was the conviction that "the gospel at its best deals with the whole man, not only his soul but his body, not only his spiritual well-being, but his material well-being as well."[35]

By the late 1960s these socially conservative evangelical moderates watched the television news with horror as images of African Americans engaging in nonviolent protests gave way to scenes of rioting in the urban ghettos. Following King's assassination in April 1968, L. Nelson Bell wrote in his column in *Christianity Today* blaming King's legacy of nonviolent direct action for the unrest. "Civil disobedience is not the 'harmless gesture of protest' it was once said to be"; rather, "calculated civil disobedience, seemingly so innocent, has brought in an era of lawlessness and bloodshed that can plunge our nation into unbelievable chaos." Taking stock, evangelical readers of *Christianity Today* were able to disapprove of racial discrimination and speak in favor of civil rights, while at the same time denouncing the movement's principles as heresy, its leaders as Communist stooges, its methods as destructive of America, and its aims as a threat to the private institutions of family and church.


## THE CULTURE WARS

The discrediting of King's message and the movement's methods and goals in the minds of evangelicals had profound repercussions for John Perkins as he attempted to build his ministry in Mendenhall. In the 1960s and 1970s Perkins received much of his financial support from his contacts in churches in California. He often had to field hard questions about his proximity to and sympathies with the civil rights movement. In the heightened atmosphere of the 1960s it was inevitable that Perkins's ministry—working for economic development and political enfranchisement with African Americans in Mississippi—would be guilty by association. Such associations made it easy for evangelicals to dismiss Perkins's message of love and justice.

Perkins frequently tells a painful story to illustrate the white churches' failure to seek racial reconciliation and justice because of their fearful rejection of the civil rights movement. It is the story of his friendship with Robert Odenwald, the minister of Mendenhall's First Baptist Church during his early years in Mendenhall. The result of this interracial friendship—as Perkins tells it—was that Odenwald was moved to "try to express something of God's love for *all* people in a couple of sermons."[36] As the leadership of the National Association of Evangelicals sought to remain "moderate" on the question of the civil rights movement so as not to alienate their southern base, brave men such as Odenwald faced their congregations alone.[37] Tragically, the opposition from within his own congregation led to Odenwald's suicide.[38]

Most of Perkins's ministry of Christian community development has taken place after the end of the period that most associate with the civil rights movement; however, he has had to negotiate and challenge Christians in the context of an ongoing ideological conflict that did not simply stop with the passing of the Civil Rights Act in 1964 or the death of King in 1968. Historians Maurice Isserman and Michael Kazin contend that "for better than three decades, the United States has been in the midst of an ongoing 'culture war,' fought over issues of political philosophy, race relations, gender roles, and personal morality left unresolved since the end of the 1960s."[39] Sociologist James Davison Hunter applied the term "culture war" to what he defined as the "competing moral visions" of two sides in an increasingly polarized America, with the "progressive" on one side and the "orthodox" on the other.[40] Southern historian Andrew M. Manis develops Hunter's thesis and contends that these two sides are competing civil religions. On one side is "a homogenous civil religion of exclusion," and on the other "a pluralistic civil religion."[41] This pluralistic civil religion gained its energy in the civil rights movement and found clear articulation in King's preaching and speeches. According to Manis, the movement was "a revitalization of a black civil religion, which . . . highlighted the idea of pluralism to argue that desegregation fulfilled the American purpose. As a microcosm of the world's diversity, America was called by God to be an exemplar nation, revealing how the rest of the world might live together as a family of nations."[42]

America's churches have played influential roles in this culture war and have had their dramatic narratives shaped by these competing civil religions. For liberal Protestants, the high point of this pluralistic impulse came in 1965 when King called for clergy to come to Selma, Alabama, to take part in a "Ministers March to Montgomery."[43] In the decades that followed, mainline Protestants became increasingly absorbed in the politics first of gender and then of sexuality, all of which took place in the context of their dwindling numbers. Evangelicals took their stand on the other side of the culture war by embracing the "homogenous civil religion of exclusion." By the time Ronald Reagan became president in 1980, evangelicals were in lockstep with the Republican Party.[44] Evangelical churches freed from defending segregation poured their energies into defending their social institutions—families, schools, and churches—from incursions by liberal notions of pluralism. Historian Paul Harvey provocatively suggests that "for religious conservatives generally, patriarchy has supplanted race as the defining first principle of God-ordained inequality."[45] Meanwhile, as liberals and conservative Christians manned the parapets in this culture war, America's cities experienced catastrophic urban decline.

## THE HOLISTIC GOSPEL

It is at this point that Perkins's contribution to this unfolding drama becomes apparent. In 1989 he brought together the leaders of evangelical Protestant communities that were "expressing the love of Christ in America's poor communities" to form the CCDA.[46] Many of these men and women were known to Perkins personally through the networks he had built over the preceding twenty years. Committed to Perkins's holistic gospel and guided by his three Rs, the CCDA held its first annual conference that same year in Chicago. The organization grew in scope and influence; twenty years later over 2,500 people attended the 2009 CCDA conference in Cincinnati. Every morning the main hall was full to hear Perkins lead a Bible study. This association of evangelical grassroots community organizations bringing their evangelical social gospel to bare in the poorest neighborhoods of America's cities—"the abandoned places of the empire"[47]—is the unrecognized story: this is a quiet revolution in the midst of the culture wars.

How has this happened? How has an African American preacher from Mississippi with ties to the civil rights movement had so much influence over white evangelicals? How has the social gospel that was anathema for American evangelicals come to find perhaps its most vibrant home within modern American evangelicalism?

To be sure, the holistic gospel of Perkins and the CCDA does not perfectly correspond to the social gospel of Rauschenbusch, Gladden, and Mathews—the CCDA's emphasis on racial reconciliation and developing indigenous leadership distinguishes it from the paternalistic impulses and white middle-class values of their Victorian forbears. Nonetheless, the theological DNA of the CCDA is from the same gene pool as the social gospel movement: the CCDA is a direct descendent, not distant cousin, of the social gospel. Both embrace the idea that the gospel radically challenges social sin as well as personal sin and that Christians born again to a living hope and inspired by a vision of the kingdom of God should work for that kingdom to come on earth as it is in heaven. In addition to this theological inheritance, there is an interesting symmetry between the institutional churches and city missions of the social gospel and the church plants and community projects of the CCDA. In the nineteenth century the social gospel was a response to the problems caused by modern industrial capitalism and the growth of the cities; over a century later, the CCDA is pioneering a response from evangelical churches to the problems of postindustrial consumerism with its outsourcing of jobs and abandoning of urban centers.

In 2004, I interviewed John Perkins in Jackson, Mississippi, in a back room of one of the buildings that make up the John M. Perkins Foundation for Reconciliation & Development. My opening gambit was to ask, "Why do white churches like you so much?" The extended conversation that flowed from this question provides some insights into how and why Perkins has worked with white evangelicals for so long and with such effect.

The first and most significant reason Perkins gave for his influence on white evangelicals is that he identifies himself as an evangelical: these are his people. No matter how badly they treated him and his friends because of his race or his message, from the beginning he understood the evangelical church as his constituency. "It's difficult to change society apart from violence unless you have a deep sense of ownership of that society," Perkins explained. "As a nation Mandela changed [South] Africa because he claimed it as his very own. [In the same way] I claimed Christianity and I claimed evangelical Christianity."[48] It is a striking image: the evangelical church is a country and Perkins is a freedom fighter, not going into exile, but working from within to free the land and its citizens of its oppressive white apartheid government. And why not go into exile? As Perkins has explained, "I was called to preach the good news of Jesus Christ to white people."[49]

For the last forty years white evangelical churches, conferences, and colleges have invited Perkins to speak precisely *because* he is a black evangelical. Because he is an evangelical, a native of the country, he does not set off their liberal heretic alarms that are set on a hair trigger. He speaks their language when it comes to the Bible and shares their concerns about African American churches that he considers to rely on emotionalism and the personality of the preacher and lack knowledge of the Bible and the evangelical gospel.

Because he is black, Perkins understands that he serves a peculiar function for white evangelicals. "Racism is so bad in America and so engulfed in the church in America . . . they need a person like me every once in a while to even justify their existence as a church."[50] He believes that at some fundamental level white evangelicals understand that a racist church is not the church of Jesus Christ: that a racist church is not preaching the gospel. Perkins's continued presence in the white evangelical churches allows them to postpone passing this judgment on themselves; he pulls them back from the edge of this theological abyss, which threatens to discredit them. "I think I serve sometimes as a means of releasing some of their guilt without hearing somebody who is going to tell them that they are totally absolutely lost."[51]

While Perkins recognizes this dynamic of white guilt and self-justification that gains him access to white evangelical congregations, he is not there to serve their purposes. He is there to confront evangelicals with the radical call of his evangelical social gospel to relocate themselves to America's economically impoverished communities, be reconciled with their neighbors, and redistribute their talents and resources to empower the poor and excluded. Even if his evangelical credentials have given Perkins access to white pulpits for the better part of forty years, his insistence on seeing systemic and societal sin as well as the sin of the individual has been a difficult message for conservative white Protestants to assimilate. The sociologists Christian Smith and Michael Emerson argue that white evangelicals listen to this message through their filter of free will individualism and hear a deracinated gospel of personal salvation that does not see systemic forces of oppression, racialization, and injustice.[52]

Over the years Perkins has found enough churches that will give him a hearing to enable him to play his most subversive role: a pied piper. Starting in the late 1960s, congregations across the country have trusted this African American Bible preacher with their children. Countless idealistic young white evangelicals—including some of the contributors to this volume— traveled to Mendenhall and Jackson and the Harambee house in Pasadena, California, for retreats, service projects, spring breaks, semesters off, and years out. In 1964 Perkins watched as the Council of Federated Organizations (COFO) brought white middle-class students to Mississippi to work alongside local civil rights leaders in freedom schools and voter registration campaigns—some even stayed in his house. Even as the Student Nonviolent Coordinating Committee (SNCC) abandoned working with whites, Perkins saw this as a strategy he could use in Mendenhall. Voice of Calvary attracted its first white volunteers in 1966 to work with the Head Start program.[53] It is this insistence on the "relocation" of middle-class whites to work in grassroots community development projects that is the most tangible link between the CCDA and SNCC. Perkins said in 1976, "It is a part of the civil rights movement that we have held on to."[54] Just as the organizers of Mississippi Freedom Summer in 1964 hoped that the involvement of white northern volunteers would focus attention and support on their work in the state, Perkins gains financial support from and influence within the volunteer's white evangelical networks.[55] Over the years, as thousands of these young white people have been challenged by Perkins's three Rs of Christian community development, they have participated in transforming the shape of the evangelical church in America.

Back to the metaphor of a laminate: the fusing together of theological conservatives who rejected biblical criticism and the social gospel with social conservatives resisting integration proved to be a remarkably enduring and rigid new material. Racism was the glue that originally locked evangelicals into this particular form. Even though by the 1970s the political climate had changed and previously outspoken evangelical segregationists had changed their tune on race, reactionary social conservatism and evangelical theology remained firmly stuck together.[56]

Having established this metaphor, I want to suggest that Perkins's growing network of influence and persistent message of racial reconciliation— even if the full implication of what he was saying passed many white evangelicals by—acted as a solvent on this laminate. This ungluing of the rigid white evangelical laminate with the solvent of racial reconciliation loosened the bonding between the layers of social conservatism and biblical literalism, allowing Perkins to infiltrate the evangelical church with the holistic (social) gospel. By the time he started the CCDA in 1989, Perkins was part of a movement bringing new elements together to form a new laminate: a social gospel freed from the extraneous trappings of white paternalism and liberal theology that connected strongly with a reading of Jesus's message of the kingdom and the social pronouncements of the Hebrew prophets as the inspired Word of God.

## THE JOSHUA GENERATION

Even if I were a sociologist, it is still beyond the scope of my research to quantify the extent to which American evangelicals have embraced this new evangelicalism. Anecdotal evidence points to a significant shift having taken place. The apostles of this evangelical social gospel who have been preaching this message in the post–civil rights era wilderness for decades report a change. Professor of sociology and evangelical preacher Tony Campolo wrote in an essay on the centenary of the publication of Rauschenbusch's *Christianity and the Social Crisis*, "It is hard for most current Evangelicals to understand how our predecessors could have missed the more than two thousand biblical admonitions to seek justice and well-being for those whom Jesus called 'the least of these.'"[57] As Perkins entered his eightieth decade he found young people responding to his evangelical social gospel with what appeared to him to be a remarkable degree of interest. "We've seen a huge shift in evangelical churches," he wrote in 2009, "the division between personal faith and social action has been bridged by a new generation . . . justice [is] becoming a discipleship issue for evangelicals."[58]

Perkins sees biblical significance in the fact that this is happening forty years after the civil rights movement. Just as God worked on the chosen people in the wilderness for forty years, Perkins writes, "I believe that's what God has been doing for these past forty years. He has been tilling the soil, scattering the seed and preparing the church for a new thing."[59]

The national press took interest in this "new generation"—particularly the ones who were evangelicals—as they organized across campuses in the 2008 presidential elections in support of Barack Obama. Obama, throughout his campaign, embodied the American civil religion of pluralism that had been revitalized during the civil rights movement and crystallized in King's "I Have a Dream" speech. In 2007 Obama spoke at the anniversary of the march from Selma to Montgomery and talked of a Joshua generation. "I stand on the shoulders of giants. I thank the Moses generation; but we've got to remember, now, that Joshua still had a job to do. As great as Moses was, despite all that he did, leading a people out of bondage, he didn't cross over the river to see the Promised Land."[60] Though not coined by Obama, this phrase—"Joshua generation"—spun out into the press's reporting of the election race. The results of the 2008 presidential election showed that America's civil religion of pluralism was for a time in the ascendancy over the civil religion of homogenous exclusion. There were also signs of a growing movement within evangelicalism that was breaking from the Republican Party. *Newsweek* reported that "young Christians liked Obama much better than Kerry: a third of white evangelicals ages 18 to 29 voted Democratic this time, compared with 16 percent in 2004." This gain for the Democrats was offset by "their grandparents [who] liked Obama less: a quarter voted for him, compared with a third for Kerry."[61]

It is far too soon to predict how this Joshua generation of white evangelicals will embrace the holistic gospel of Perkins and the CCDA: if they will free themselves from the ties that bind them to the theological strictures of their grandparents or if they will cling to the familiar gospel of a personal salvation that is unable or unwilling to preach good news to the poor. This will be the true test of Perkins's legacy. There are reasons to believe that such a fundamental shift in American evangelicalism could take place.[62] Evangelical members of this Joshua generation are two generations removed from the civil rights movement, and an increasing number of them did not grow up in the South.[63] They are not living in a postracial America, but they are worshipping and pioneering new ministries in churches whose pastors and seminary professors came of age in post–civil rights movement America.

Finally, whether you call them the Joshua generation or "Hipster Christians,"[64] Perkins is of particular significance to them *because* of his connection with the civil rights movement. To these evangelicals, Perkins is not simply a modern-day prophet calling for evangelicals to embrace a gospel of relocation, redistribution, and reconciliation; Perkins's story enables them to trace their lineage back to the Moses generation of the civil rights movement. Perkins enables evangelicals to have a sense of place in the new Joshua generation's narrative *as* evangelicals: they do not have to renounce their evangelical heritage to have a legitimate place in this story.

A particularly visible group of standard-bearers of the social gospel for this new generation are the participants in what has been dubbed the new monastic movement—small Christian communities in inner-city neighborhoods.[65] The unofficial spokesman for this movement is Shane Claiborne, a white dreadlocked member of the Simple Way community in Philadelphia. Claiborne, a highly sought-after speaker on the evangelical youth circuit and best-selling author, considers Perkins a mentor and an inspiration and serves on the board of the CCDA.⁶⁶ In 2009 Claiborne and Perkins coauthored the book *Follow Me to Freedom: Leading and Following as an Ordinary Radical*, which is a transcript of their extended conversation on grassroots Christian activism. In reading Claiborne's words, there is a startling correspondence in his thinking between King and Perkins. "Dr. King and John [Perkins] looked into the eyes of those who were threatening their lives and beating their friends and said 'We still love you.'"⁶⁷ In another section on Christian leadership, Claiborne states: "Moses and Dr. Martin Luther King Jr. were leading people to a Promised Land, to that Beloved Community. Really, with CCDA and his whole life, that is what John Perkins has done."⁶⁸

For Claiborne and the new generation of pioneers and social prophets in the CCDA, Perkins is their Martin Luther King Jr., he is their (almost) martyr, he is their hero of the civil rights movement. In Perkins, a new generation of Christian activists connects with the civil rights movement. They do so not with the discomfort of preceding generations of evangelicals for whom King's salvation was in doubt but with pride that, to quote Claiborne's historically dubious claim, "in the 1960s . . . John Perkins was a radical evangelical who advocated for civil rights."⁶⁹

This marks a sea change in white evangelicals' relationship to the civil rights movement in general and Martin Luther King Jr. in particular. Responding to the new attitudes and interests of Joshua generation evangelicals, Perkins has changed the way he talks about the civil rights movement. "These days," Perkins observed in 2009, "I'm often asked about the Civil Rights movement."⁷⁰ In the 1960s and 1970s, as Perkins spoke to evangelicals—black and white—across America, such questions were cause for concern and caution. In his 1976 book *Let Justice Roll Down*, he bemoaned how being associated with the movement called his theology into question. "I would try to defuse some of the standard objections. I could usually see them coming. For instance, if a questioner asked, 'What do you think of Martin Luther King?' I knew where the question was leading."⁷¹ Others would be more direct: 'Do you think Dr. Martin Luther King is a Christian?' or 'Do you think Dr. King is a communist?'"⁷²

In the 1970s Perkins was careful in public and in print to distance his religious beliefs from those of the civil rights activists (which implicitly included King). These activists "were committed to the cause. And to the struggle," Perkins wrote; unfortunately, those who led the movement had "either a bankrupt theology or no theology at all."⁷³ Thirty years later Perkins is happy to associate his evangelical social gospel of Christian community development with Martin Luther King, even crediting King as its inspiration. "For black evangelicals in the sixties," Perkins said in an interview in 2008, "King was our prophet of justice."[74] Perkins told Claiborne, "It was King's message of having a dream of freedom that inspired my family and me in 1963."[75] One needs to treat Perkins's statements with care; this change in his account tells us much more about the shift in the attitudes of his white evangelical audience than it does about Perkins's own relationship to King and the liberal Protestants—black and white—who were among the leaders in the civil rights movement.

For the theologian (and coeditor of this volume) Charles Marsh, Perkins is not a substitute for King; rather, Perkins rescues King's Christian vision that was abandoned by many of the leading activists of the movement. By embracing Perkins's prophetic witness, evangelicals can come, late in the day, as laborers in the movement's "unfinished business."[76] This, as Peter Heltzel (another coeditor) notes in his book *Jesus and Justice: Evangelicals, Race, and American Politics*, "marks the beginning of a new genealogy of American evangelicalism."[77]

In all the excitement it is important to remember that Perkins himself took time to come around to having "the old message of salvation . . . enlarged and intensified" to include elements of the social gospel that inspired King.[78] Because its advocates lay outside the evangelical fold, Perkins had considered King's a "bankrupt theology."[79] This should come as no surprise because a spirit of theological hubris and triumphalism rather than humility and collaboration has distinguished mainstream American evangelicalism throughout its history. This hubris and triumphalism have led to the evangelical church's vulnerability to enslavement by the homogenous civil religion of exclusion.

This new generation of evangelicals' identification with and claim on the civil rights movement through Perkins, combined with Marsh's and Heltzel's new genealogy of American evangelicalism, offers exciting insights and direction for the church in America. However, it seems clear to me that this movement is in peril of falling captive to the arrogance that permeates the evangelical church: it is in danger of its followers claiming the moral victory of others as their own. In doing so the inspiring stories of faith and the civil rights movement—of King in Birmingham, Alabama, and Perkins in Brandon, Mississippi—become an uncritical endorsement of evangelical theology and a way of dismissing nonevangelical Christians.

This is why setting the story of the civil rights movement, Perkins, and the CCDA in the wider narrative of the social gospel in America is so important. In the 1920s and 1930s the bitter theological divisions between modernists and fundamentalists separated the social demands of the gospel of Jesus Christ from what Rauschenbusch called "the old message of salvation."[80] By the time of the civil rights movement, evangelicals (who considered themselves the righteous guardians of this old message of salvation) were in opposition to King and the other prophets crying out for justice. The new generation of evangelicals who find inspiration from these stories of the movement must reckon with their own tradition's moral and theological failure and its complicity with the social evils of racism and oppression. Doing so should cause serious reconsideration of a constricted evangelical theology limited to personal salvation and dismissive of all other branches of Christianity. For evangelicals to claim the moral capital of the civil rights movement without facing these hard facts leaves them guilty of the same crime as the Pharisees whom Jesus condemned, saying, "Woe to you! For you build the tombs of the prophets whom your ancestors killed" (Luke 11:47).

Considering Perkins's life and work in the context of this larger story points to his real achievement and legacy. His persistence over forty years as an African American apostle of the holistic gospel to white evangelicals helped loosen the bonds between a reactionary social conservatism and an evangelical biblical hermeneutic. Perkins, and the movement of which he is a part, has created the space for an evangelical social gospel that is repairing the rupture between "the old message of salvation" and the social gospel.

## NOTES

1. "History of CCDA," http://www.ccda.org/history.

2. Charles Marsh, *The Beloved Community: How Faith Shapes Social Justice, from the Civil Rights Movement to Today* (New York: Basic Books, 2005), 174–175.

3. John Perkins, *A Quiet Revolution: Meeting Human Needs Today: A Biblical Challenge to Christians*, rev. ed. (Pasadena, Calif.: Urban Family Publications with Network Unlimited International, 1976), 62.

4. John Perkins, *Let Justice Roll Down* (Ventura, Calif.: Regal Books, 1976), 80.

5. Perkins, *Quiet Revolution*, 69.

6. Perkins, *Quiet Revolution*, 71.

7. "The American Christian Commission," *New York Times*, May 28, 1869.

8. George M. Marsden, *Understanding Fundamentalism and Evangelicalism* (Grand Rapids, Mich.: Eerdmans, 1991), 29.

9. Walter Rauschenbusch, *A Theology for the Social Gospel* (New York: Macmillan, 1917), 5.

10. Shailer Mathews, *The Social Gospel* (Philadelphia: Griffith & Rowland Press, 1910), 11.

11. Rauschenbusch, *Theology for the Social Gospel*, 7.

12. Justo L. González, *The Story of Christianity*, Vol. 2, *The Reformation to the Present Day*, rev. and updated 2nd ed. (New York: HarperCollins), 377.

13. Reinhold Niebuhr, *Moral Man and Immoral Society: A Study in Ethics and Politics* (New York: C. Scribner's Sons, 1932).

14. Rauschenbusch, *Theology for the Social Gospel*, 6.

15. Charles M. Seddon, *In His Steps, What Would Jesus Do?* (Chicago: Advance Publishing, 1898).

16. George M. Marsden draws a distinction between the social gospel movement of the twentieth century and the evangelical social concern movements of the nineteenth century. He does this to explain the fundamentalists' reaction to the social gospel. It is a mistake, however, to push this distinction too far and to fail to see the chronological and practical continuity between the two. George M. Marsden, *Fundamentalism and American Culture: The Shaping of Twentieth Century Evangelicalism, 1870–1925* (New York: Oxford University Press, 1980), 91.

17. David O. Moberg, *The Great Reversal: Evangelism versus Social Concern* (Philadelphia: J. B. Lippincott, 1972); Marsden, *Fundamentalism and American Culture*, 85.

18. Rauschenbusch, *Theology for the Social Gospel*, 9. Sociologist James Davison Hunter, in his book *Culture Wars*, recognized that the roots of the contemporary political struggle in America stretched back to this struggle over the social gospel. James Davison Hunter, *Culture Wars: The Struggle to Define America* (New York: Basic Books, 1991), 78.

19. "Fundamentalism and Modernism: Two Religions." *Christian Century* 41 (January 3, 1924).

20. Martin E. Marty, *Modern American Religion: The Noise of Conflict, 1919–1941*, 3 vols. (Chicago: University of Chicago Press, 1986), 2:217.

21. D. G. Hart, *Deconstructing Evangelicalism: Conservative Protestantism in the Age of Billy Graham* (Grand Rapids, Mich.: Baker Academic, 2004), 23–26, 111; Marsden, *Understanding Fundamentalism and Evangelicalism*, 62–82; Martin E. Marty, *Modern American Religion: Under God, Indivisible, 1941–1960*, 3 vols. (Chicago: University of Chicago Press, 1996), 3:434–448.

22. I am playing with the notion of theological drama following the suggestion of Charles Marsh. Charles Marsh, "The Civil Rights Movement as Theological Drama: Interpretation and Application," *Modern Theology* 18 (April 2002): 231–250.

23. Peter Slade, *Open Friendship in a Closed Society: Mission Mississippi and a Theology of Friendship* (New York: Oxford University Press, 2009), 103–107.

24. Curtis J. Evans, "White Evangelical Protestant Responses to the Civil Rights Movement," *Harvard Theological Review* 102 (2009): 269.

25. "Race Tensions and Social Change," *Christianity Today* 3 (January 19, 1959): 21, 22.

26. "Civil Rights and Christian Concern," *Christianity Today* 8 (May 8, 1964): 28–29.

27. "Desegregation and Regeneration," *Christianity Today* 2 (September 29, 1958): 21.

28. "What of Racial Intermarriage?" *Christianity Today* 8 (October 11, 1963): 26–28.

29. E. Earle Ellis, "Segregation and Dr. King," *Christianity Today* 3 (January 19, 1959): 35–36.

30. Ellis, "Segregation and Dr. King," 35.

31. "Desegregation and Regeneration," 20; Evans, "White Evangelical Protestant Responses to the Civil Rights Movement," 266.

32. "The Washington March and the Negro Cause," *Christianity Today* 7 (September 13, 1963): 28; "Desegregation and Regeneration," 20.

33. Ralph Luker, *The Social Gospel in Black and White: American Racial Reform, 1885–1912* (Chapel Hill: University of North Carolina Press, 1991), 323.

34. Martin Luther King Jr., "Pilgrimage to Nonviolence," *Christian Century* 77 (April 13, 1960): 439–441, reprinted in Martin Luther King Jr. and James Melvin Washington, *A Testament of Hope: The Essential Writings of Martin Luther King, Jr.* (San Francisco: Harper & Row, 1986), 37.

35. King and Washington, *Testament of Hope*, 37–38. Over the succeeding decade (and without the benefit of King's graduate education), Perkins reached similar conclusions and started to preach his holistic gospel, which brings the gospel of salvation to the whole person.

36. Perkins, *Let Justice Roll Down*, 99.

37. Paul Harvey, *Freedom's Coming: Religious Culture and the Shaping of the South from the Civil War through the Civil Rights Era* (Chapel Hill: University of North Carolina Press, 2005), 244.

38. Perkins, *Let Justice Roll Down*, 100; Clayton Sullivan, *Called to Preach, Condemned to Survive: The Education of Clayton Sullivan* (Macon, Ga.: Mercer University Press, 1985), 165.

39. Maurice Isserman and Michael Kazin, *America Divided: The Civil War of the 1960s* (New York: Oxford University Press, 2000), 4.

40. Hunter, *Culture Wars*, 107–108.

41. Andrew Michael Manis, *Southern Civil Religions in Conflict: Civil Rights and the Culture Wars* (Macon, Ga.: Mercer University Press, 2002), 183.

42. Andrew Michael Manis, "The Civil Religions of the South," in *Religion and Public Life in the South: In the Evangelical Mode*, ed. Charles Reagan Wilson and Mark Silk (Walnut Creek, Calif.: AltaMira Press, 2005), 167.

43. James F. Findlay, *Church People in the Struggle: The National Council of Churches and the Black Freedom Movement, 1950–1970* (New York: Oxford University Press, 1993), 64; Michael B. Friedland, *Lift Up Your Voice Like a Trumpet: White Clergy and the Civil Rights and Antiwar Movements, 1954–1973* (Chapel Hill: University of North Carolina Press, 1998), 122.

44. For a detailed analysis, see Joseph H. Crespino, *In Search of Another Country: Mississippi and the Conservative Counterrevolution* (Princeton, N.J.: Princeton University Press, 2007); Manis, *Southern Civil Religions in Conflict*; Darren Dochuk, "Evangelicalism Becomes Southern, Politics Becomes Evangelical," in *Religion and American Politics from the Colonial Period to the Present*, ed. Mark A. Noll and Luke E. Harlow (New York: Oxford University Press, 2007).

45. Paul Harvey, "At Ease in Zion, Uneasy in Babylon: White Evangelicals," in *Religion and Public Life in the South: In the Evangelical Mode*, ed. Charles Reagan Wilson and Mark Silk (Walnut Creek, Calif.: AltaMira Press, 2005), 75.

46. "History of CCDA," http://www.ccda.org/history.

47. Shane Claiborne, *The Irresistible Revolution: Living as an Ordinary Radical* (Grand Rapids, Mich.: Zondervan, 2006), 166.

48. John Perkins, interview by the author, October 12, 2004, Jackson, Miss.

49. Charles Marsh and John Perkins, *Welcoming Justice: God's Movement toward Beloved Community* (Downers Grove, Ill.: InterVarsity Press, 2009), 37.

50. Perkins, interview.

51. Perkins, interview.

52. Michael O. Emerson and Christian Smith, *Divided by Faith: Evangelical Religion and the Problem of Race in America* (New York: Oxford University Press, 2000), 52, 67.

53. Perkins, *Let Justice Roll Down*, 132.

54. Perkins, *Quiet Revolution*, 72.

55. A recent example of this is a student volunteer from Seattle Pacific University (SPU) who insisted that the president of the college go with a group of students to Jackson. SPU now houses the John Perkins Center.

56. Harvey, *Freedom's Coming*, 246.

57. Walter Rauschenbusch, Anthony Campolo, and Paul B. Raushenbush, *Christianity and the Social Crisis in the 21st Century: The Classic That Woke Up the Church*, 1st ed. (New York: HarperOne, 2007), 77.

58. Marsh and Perkins, *Welcoming Justice*, 48.

59. Marsh and Perkins, *Welcoming Justice*, 50.

60. "Selma Voting Rights March Commemoration" March 4, 2007, Obama News & Speeches, http://www.barackobama.com/2007/03/04/selma_voting_rights_march_comm.php.

61. Tony Dokoupil and Lisa Miller, "Faith Beyond His Fathers," *Newsweek*, January 26, 2009.

62. It is important to realize that it is far more than their evangelical heritage working against this new generation becoming socially engaged. Christian Smith's recent study of young adults in the United States argues that "almost all emerging adults today are either apathetic, uninformed, distrustful, disempowered, or, at most only marginally interested when it comes to politics and public life." Christian Smith, Kari Christofferson, and Patricia Snell Herzog, *Lost in Translation: The Dark Side of Emerging Adulthood* (New York: Oxford University Press, 2011), 225.

63. Robert Wuthnow, *After the Baby Boomers: How Twenty- and Thirty-Somethings Are Shaping the Future of American Religion* (Princeton, N.J.: Princeton University Press, 2007), 80.

64. Brett McCracken, "Hipster Faith," *Christianity Today* (September 2010), www.christiantitytoday.com/ct/2010/September/9.24html.

65. Jonathan Wilson-Hargrove, *New Monasticism: What It Has to Say to Today's Church* (Grand Rapids, Mich.: Brazos Press, 2008).

66. Tom Sine, *The New Conspirators: Creating the Future One Mustard Seed at a Time* (Downers Grove, Ill.: InterVarsity Press, 2008), 32.

67. John Perkins and Shane Claiborne, *Follow Me to Freedom: Leading and Following as an Ordinary Radical* (Ventura, Calif.: Regal Books, 2009), 141.

68. Perkins and Claiborne, *Follow Me to Freedom*, 107.

69. Peter Heltzel, *Jesus and Justice: Evangelicals, Race, and American Politics* (New Haven, Conn.: Yale University Press, 2009), 177.

70. Marsh and Perkins, *Welcoming Justice*, 119.

71. Perkins, *Let Justice Roll Down*, 109–110.

72. Perkins, *Quiet Revolution*, 99.

73. Perkins, *Let Justice Roll Down*, 103.

74. John Perkins, interview with Peter Heltzel, September 14, 2008, in Heltzel, *Jesus and Justice*, 165.

75. Perkins and Claiborne, *Follow Me to Freedom*, 225.

76. Marsh and Perkins, *Welcoming Justice*, 34.

77. Heltzel, *Jesus and Justice*, 161.

78. Rauschenbusch, *Theology for the Social Gospel*, 5.

79. Perkins, *Let Justice Roll Down*, 103.

80. Rauschenbusch, *Theology for the Social Gospel*, 5.

Part II

# REDISTRIBUTION

*Challenging the Church*

✝

# A Prophetic Vision in an Age of Profit

*Paul Louis Metzger* @ Multnomah School of the Bible, Portland, OR. Probably Dr. Metzger's son.

"We have substituted a gospel of church growth for a gospel of reconciliation."
—JOHN M. PERKINS, *With Justice for All*

## A VOICE CRYING OUT IN A CONSUMER WASTELAND

THE GOSPEL MESSAGE CENTERED IN JESUS INVOLVES SUSTAINED CONSIDERation of the economics of the kingdom. The apostle Paul writes, "For you know the grace of our Lord Jesus Christ, that though he was rich, yet for your sakes he became poor, so that you through his poverty might become rich" (2 Cor. 8:9). Paul is speaking of a spiritual-physical reality, which has a bearing on our whole being and the whole Christian community. Yet we often spiritualize texts like this one and rarely think of their implications for how we redistribute our wealth, talents, resources, and gifts as Jesus's followers. John M. Perkins has served the church as a prophetic voice, crying out in a consumer wasteland for many years. He has challenged us to think strategically about how we can respond to God's love poured out in Jesus through the Spirit by working with Jesus among the poor. This chapter reflects upon Perkins's redemptive, prophetic message of the economics of God's kingdom in an age of consumer profit, and how that message must become mainstream in the twenty-first century evangelical church. This essay begins by recounting my initial exposure to Perkins's thought, and how God transformed my thinking during an address Perkins gave at Reed College in 2001.

## OPIATE OF THE MASSES, NEW WINE OF THE KINGDOM

My first significant exposure to Perkins and his work took place in 2001. I had invited him to serve as our keynote speaker for a conference I was hosting on kingdom justice for the Institute for the Theology of Culture: New Wine, New Wineskins, which I direct at Multnomah Biblical Seminary in Portland, Oregon. During the week, he also had an opportunity to speak at Reed College in Portland. In addition to having a reputation for academic excellence, Reed College was known at the time as a very secular and irreligious school. Still, Perkins determined to share a good part of his testimony with the Reed students gathered there in the auditorium. Perkins told them of how white people's religion in the Deep South was often an opiate for the black masses, of his near fatal beating in a Mississippi jail cell at the hands of white police officers, and of how God led him through that trauma to give his life to working for redemptive change for all people oppressed by poverty and racism.[2] At the close of his talk, and without any prompting, the Reed students stood up in unison to give a two-minute standing ovation for a life so well lived. While they may not have agreed with Perkins's Christian convictions, their critical assessment of the Christian religion could not account for this transformed life. Nor could I—an evangelical seminary professor. Perkins's words and the Reed students' response left me reeling, as I drank from new wineskins his new wine message of the kingdom. Perkins powerfully conveyed to the Reed students—and to me—that the Christian religion is not the opiate of the masses that the American church so often makes it, but the life-giving and society-changing new wine of Jesus's kingdom community.

While the Reed students present there that evening went away deeply moved by Perkins's gospel message, some in my evangelical circles struggle with Perkins's call, mistakenly seeing him as divisive rather than as prophetic and redemptive. I find this so ironic—and troubling—given that Perkins's message and ministry are all about bringing people together. And yet given our individualistic and market-driven culture, I should not be too surprised. Redemption in this culture often involves exchanging goods and services (even religious ones) to expand one's individual stock and spiritual portfolio, not interpersonal, indissoluble communion that overcomes barriers of class and race. Other evangelicals mistakenly view Perkins's prophetic message as an appendix to the gospel rather than as core to gospel witness.

It is very difficult for the evangelical movement to hear God's word proclaimed by Perkins aright. The movement has given too much attention to prophetic talk of the near or distant future, separating the future from the present and overshadowing the main thrust of the prophets—calling people back to God's word to build a community that lives in light of the eschatological kingdom reality that has dawned in Christ in the Spirit. Furthermore, the evangelical movement has often devalued the holistic nature of the gospel in favor of an otherworldly and individualistic spirituality, and so has failed to see how caring for the poor has always been a critical component of the prophetic call of Old Testament and New Testament prophetic work centered in Jesus the Messiah and enlivened and empowered by the Spirit. No doubt as a result of these and other reasons, we are ill-prepared to challenge those who intentionally or unintentionally replace "prophet" with "profit" and concern for the gospel of just relations and reconciliation with a gospel of church growth and consumerism.[3]

Attention will be given to these various issues, and theological-cultural recommendations will be made pertaining to Perkins's life and work for their bearing on the church and theology. Such analysis will assist us in breaking new ground in the hope that the church can grow as the prophetic kingdom movement the triune God envisions and enlivens it to be rather than as a consumer, profit-oriented monument that symbolizes the market-driven culture at large. In what follows I discuss Perkins's revolutionary principles of relocation, reconciliation, and redistribution, setting forth these principles' profound theological and cultural significance in the context of Jesus's ministry in and through the Spirit recorded in Luke 4.[4]

## THE STOCK MARKET AND THE SYNAGOGUE

Evangelicals prize personal relationship with Jesus—but which Jesus? Stock Market Jesus, who helps us acquire greater wealth and affluence for ourselves, or Jubilee Justice Jesus of the synagogue in Luke 4, who would have us leverage our resources and influence to benefit the least of these? The Jesus of Luke 4 presents us with a very different model of Jesus than that which we often find in American cultural consumer Christianity, which Will Ferrell parodies as Ricky Bobby in *Talladega Nights* in his dinner prayer to the eight-pound six-ounce baby Jesus to help him gain more money, success, and fame. The Jesus we find in Luke 4 does not come to be served or to be prosperous, but to serve and to identify with the poor, bringing justice to them. He does not come to make us prosperous and self-serving, but to lead us to serve others, especially the least, the last, and the lost.

In Luke 4 we find Jesus in the synagogue of God-forsaken Nazareth in Galilee of the Gentiles. Nothing good comes from Nazareth (see John 1:46). Nazareth is by no means a center of power or of wealth, like Jerusalem,

Washington, D.C., or New York City, and Jesus is not viewed as coming from the best stock that this town has to offer (Luke 4:22). Apart from initially wowing the crowds with his charisma and miracles (Luke 4:14–15, 22), his message to his own people to move beyond their tribalism built on an exclusionary form of religious tradition rather than the grace of God leads to his rejection (Luke 4:23–30).

While God raises up noble and noteworthy types to bring the good news to centers of power like Paul in the New Testament or Daniel in the Old Testament, this is not his normal means. And yet, as a movement, evangelicals have sought to engage and even take back centers of power, and have not done so through concrete community development among the masses, especially the poor.

Perkins's life and thought forms reflect the gospel drama. Working in "God-forsaken" Mendenhall and West Jackson, Mississippi, and hailing from bootlegging stock, Perkins is not by flesh viewed as a model evangelical witness. Certainly Perkins's life story has the makings of a great movie, and his accomplishments and accolades over the years put him in the company of the greats, but still his background, his relational commitments to the dispossessed, and his heart passions place him in humbler circumstances and cultural contexts. Beyond Perkins's celebrity status in some circles, his life and message of relocation, reconciliation, and redistribution are truly iconic and gospel-centric—bearing witness to God's Son's incarnate life and message, as reflected in such passages as Luke 4.


## RELOCATION

Jesus opens and searches the scroll of the prophet Isaiah to read the text that will mark the launch of his public ministry. Quoting from Isaiah 61, the prophet Jesus indicates that the Spirit of the Lord is on him, signifying that the messianic age—the eschatological future—has dawned in Jesus's person and ministry. With this in mind, rightful prophetic consideration of eschatology involves giving attention to Jesus's incarnation, for the eschatological future dawns in him. To put it differently, to think eschatologically includes thinking incarnationally. Moreover, to think incarnationally involves thinking compassionately. The fact that the Spirit is upon Jesus to preach good news to the poor involves the notion that eschatology rightly conceived includes consideration of Jesus's incarnation, and with it his concern for jubilee justice for the poor and outsider in the here and now.[5] Bound up with Jesus's "relocation" from heaven to earth in his incarnation is his vital concern for jubilee justice for the poor and foreigner.

In contrast to those supposedly prophetic figures who would claim that Jesus has come to make us prosperous, that the Spirit lives in us solely for the purpose of giving us ecstatic experiences, and that eschatology is about escaping this world, Christology, pneumatology, and eschatology as framed in Luke 4 involve engaging this world sacrificially and compassionately—especially the poor.[6] In contrast to the upward mobility model of much prosperity gospel "prophetic" preaching, which claims that God wants us to be prosperous, that he wants us to bless others *so that* we might be blessed (a self-serving rather than others-centered orientation), and that he wants us to leave poorer surroundings behind, the prophet Jesus empowered by the Spirit of the future is all about downward mobility and solidarity. In this context, it is worthy noting what Perkins says of the prosperity gospel movement:        *typo?*

> The prosperity movement is heavily accepted among the poor but has done very little in terms of real community development at the grass-roots level. It takes people's attention away from the real problem, and if those people succeed it encourages them to remove themselves from the very people they ought to be identifying with and working among.[7]

Over against this individualistic and escapist viewpoint, Perkins prophetically challenges the church to identify with the poor and oppressed in Jesus through the Spirit, for the kingdom of God has come in Jesus's person. What we find here is the communal being and comissional action of God, as the Father sends his Son in the Spirit into the world. The triune God invites us to participate in this reality of relocation, and with it reconciliation and redistribution.[8]

## RECONCILIATION AND REDISTRIBUTION

The Spirit of the Lord is on Jesus to preach good news to the poor. The Spirit is not on Jesus for a privatized, self-centered, or ecstatic spiritual experience. The Spirit is upon him to care compassionately for the poor. Those of us who are poor in spirit will care for the poor given how much the poor mean to Jesus and given the Spirit's work in our own hearts. As an evangelical in the best sense of the term, Perkins understands that both aspects—the "poor" of Luke 6:20 and the "poor in spirit" of Matthew 5:3—are important, and that both are biblical.[9]

Perkins's two Rs of reconciliation and redistribution reflect the Scripture's dual emphasis on the poor in spirit and the poor. Regarding reconciliation, Perkins claims that we are to be reconciled to God—to be "born from above," as John puts it in John 3:16, and with it to be reconciled to one another based on God's forgiveness of each of us. Matthew puts it in different terms. We are to be "poor in spirit" (Matt. 5:3): "Blessed are the poor in spirit, for theirs is the kingdom of heaven." Jesus's disciples are "poor in spirit;" John R. W. Stott interprets this trait to signify "spiritual bankruptcy."[10] Jesus's followers understand their great spiritual need or state of spiritual bankruptcy before God, and as a result are meek, merciful, and makers of peace (see Matt. 5:3, 5, 7, 9).

There is more, though—namely, the concern for redistribution. Not only are Jesus's disciples to be spiritually bankrupt but also they are to concern themselves with those who are bankrupt in other ways. God is concerned for the poor in spirit *and* for the poor. Regarding the latter, Jesus says, "Blessed are you who are poor, for yours is the kingdom of God" (Luke 6:20). Concern for the poor involves redistribution. Perkins's discussion of voluntary redistribution in a variety of ways (including resources, talents, experiences, and so forth) resonates with this text and Jesus's message in Luke's gospel as a whole, including Luke 4.

We live now in light of what has been and will be, not disconnected from Jesus's past or from his future; for we live with and in Jesus, who is our ascended and reigning and returning prophet, high priest, and king (see Heb. 1:1–3, Col. 3:1–4) in and through the Spirit (see Acts 1:8) in the eschatological age (see Luke 4:17–21). As a result, we have confidence and hope that his kingdom will come and that his will is going to be done on earth as it is in heaven. As a prophetic spokesperson for Jesus and his kingdom in the power of the Spirit, Perkins exhorts the church to reenvision and reenact the story of salvation involving the communal economics of relocation, reconciliation, and redistribution of the eschatological kingdom.

## REIMAGING THE GOSPEL OF THE KINGDOM

God's kingdom centered in Jubilee Justice Jesus, empowered by the Spirit, and disclosed in Christian Scripture calls into question the counterfeit gospel narrative of consumer capitalism conveyed by Stock Market Jesus, who elevates the individual consumer as king. However, given our culture's fixation with free market capitalism, it is very difficult for the church not to confuse the two. We are tempted to base human value on the amount of goods we can acquire in an age dominated by the fear of scarcity rather than on the wealth of relationships wherein we share life together secured by God's abundant love that overcomes barriers of race and class.[11] We need to reimage the gospel of the kingdom through prophetic witness, reenvisioning and reenacting the good news of relocation, reconciliation, and redistribution in word and deed.

Such prophetic witness entails being centered on Jubilee Justice Jesus revealed in the synagogue in Nazareth, and not Stock Market Jesus, who sells out to the highest bidder and bails out to cut his losses when the going gets tough. We should take note of Jesus and the crowds who react to him and his message in Luke 4, and make sure that we follow Jesus prophetically and not for profit. True prophetic voices and practical theologians like John Perkins do not sell out to the highest bidder or change their tune if their popularity wanes (and I have known of situations where Perkins's popularity has waned—even among his supporters). Rather than cater to market preferences or focus on fame and success, they take their cue from Luke 4's Jesus in the synagogue and faithfully bear witness in the power of the Spirit to Jesus's eschatological kingdom no matter the cost. I now close by reflecting on prophetic witness bound up with faithfulness over against fame.

## JESUS AND THE PROPHETIC CHARISMA, NOT THE CHARISMATIC HIGH PRIEST OF PROFIT

As God's great prophet, Jesus bears the "charisma" or gift of prophecy. This charisma must not be confused with "charismatic" as defined by contemporary culture. The Jesus revealed in the synagogue as God's great prophet embodies the charisma of the Spirit, unlike Stock Market Jesus, who embodies the spirit of the age as the charismatic celebrity high priest of profit. We tend to think of a charismatic as appealing and entertaining, and that charismatic figures are winsome, popular, and famous. While Jesus's audience in the synagogue is initially impressed with his words and message (Luke 4:22a), their view of him quickly changes when he challenges their niche preferences. Given our popular rendering of charismatic, we might wonder how the Spirit could be on Jesus; if the Spirit were on him, his ministry would be much more effective and popular—especially among his own people. We fail to note that a true prophet is without honor in his hometown (Luke 4:24).

The movement of the Spirit involves not only a sense that God is with Jesus but also that Jesus will be rejected by his own kind of people. While Jesus contextualizes his message to his audience, he does not cater his message to them and their preferences. The hometown crowd initially stumbles over the fact that Jesus is Joseph's son (Luke 4:22b), and then rises up against him when he challenges their false sense of superiority over Gentiles (see Luke 4:23–30). Prophetic witness that reflects the charisma or prophetic gift of the Spirit involves rejection, and draws its strength from the affirmation of God's word and divine favor, not popularity or fame.

The lack of attention to prophetic *witness* in our circles may make those drawn to Perkins and his work susceptible to viewing him as a celebrity rather than as a saint in our celebrity culture. Those who are attracted to Perkins's message must guard against simply being enamored with his unique charisma, passion, humor, and charm; otherwise they are in danger of turning his novel prophetic, biblical vision into a novelty and commodifying him, failing to delve beneath the surface and reflect upon the structural theological and institutional changes that are needed to bring his message home to the church today.

While Perkins may appear to some of us as a charismatic celebrity, he does not fit that label if we associate self-absorption with the image of a charismatic celebrity. As a living icon in the best Christian sense of that term, Perkins serves as an effective lens or window to Jubilee Justice Jesus. I find that he points us in Jesus's direction, and in the direction of those most in need.

This point was brought home to me one evening back in 2007 in Portland. I was driving Perkins and his daughter Elizabeth to a benefit dinner where he was to serve as the keynote speaker for an inner-city ministry aimed at community development work that brought jobs and housing to ex-offenders and youth without purpose and hope. As we drove along Martin Luther King Jr. Blvd., I asked him what it was like for him now in Mississippi—decades after his beating. Perkins matter-of-factly said, "I'm kind of a hero now in Mississippi. It seems that every time the state newspapers write something about reconciliation, they quote me." "It's as if I created the word," he said with a laugh. There was a pause in the conversation. And then as he was looking out the window of the car, he went on to say something that will always stay with me, "But when I think about how many homes my fame has built for the poor in Mississippi, I realize that my fame hasn't built any homes for the poor. So I don't put no stock in my fame." There were no television or newspaper reporters in the car—just Perkins, his daughter Elizabeth, and me. I almost lost control of the wheel, for I rarely come across such a value system.

Perkins's practical theology of relocation, reconciliation, and redistribution accompanied by his life of prophetic witness envisions the eschatological kingdom reality centered in Jesus and empowered by the Spirit. Will we take up Perkins's prophetic mantle and reimage Jesus's kingdom vision through the Spirit in an age of consumer profit?[12]

## NOTES

1. John M. Perkins, *With Justice for All*, foreword by Chuck Colson (Ventura, Calif.: Regal Books, 1982). See the context for this statement on 107–108.

2. Much of what he shared that night is narrated in John M. Perkins, *Let Justice Roll Down* (Ventura, Calif.: Regal Books, 1976).

3. Michael Andres writes that above and beyond the prosperity gospel thinking among many sectors of the American evangelical population, there "is a sort of tacit acquiescence to consumerism through *silence*." Among other things, he draws attention to the Focus on the Family website, and notes the lack of consideration given there to consumerism, materialism, and the plight of the poor. See Michael Andres, "Will Evangelicals Teach Them Economic Obedience or Consumer Theology?" *Cultural Encounters: A Journal for the Theology of Culture* 4, no. 2 (Summer 2008): 14–15. See also the insightful discussion on the ongoing problems with racism and theology's role in it in "Theologians and White Supremacy: An Interview with James H. Cone," *America: The National Catholic Weekly*, November 20, 2006, http://www.americamagazine.org/content/article.cfm?article_id=5103.

4. For an example of the exposition of Perkins's community development paradigm, see his book *With Justice for All*. Perkins's theological methodology itself reflects Jesus's and his disciples' own model of the union of theology and praxis: both are rooted in incarnate presence and missional encounter. Any prophetic theology worthy of the name "Christian" will be rooted in the triune God's missional presence in the world and will involve dialectical engagement between text and context—going to the Bible for theological and practical solutions for the pressing needs at hand. For an example of this framework, see John M. Perkins, *A Quiet Revolution: The Christian Response to Human Need, a Strategy for Today* (Waco, Tex.: Word Books, 1976).

5. "The year of the Lord's favor" refers to the Jubilee in the Old Testament, the fiftieth year where debts were erased and property was to be returned to those who had lost their possessions, and where impoverished Jewish people who had sold themselves to their fellow Jews were to be released. See Leviticus 25.

6. In a telephone interview with John Perkins on October 5, 2009, he maintained that while the Spirit's work is not exclusively bound up with caring for the poor, the Spirit's work does entail vital concern for addressing the poor's plight.

7. John M. Perkins, *Beyond Charity: The Call to Christian Community Development* (Grand Rapids, Mich.: Baker Books, 1993), 71.

8. Here I am synthesizing Perkins's model of the three Rs with George Hunsberger's discussion of the triune God's communal being and co-missional action in the world. See George R. Hunsberger, "Missional Vocation: Called and Sent to Represent the Reign of God," in *Missional Church: A Vision for the Sending of the Church in North America*, ed. Darrell L. Guder (Grand Rapids, Mich.: Eerdmans, 1998), 82.

9. See Gordon D. Fee and Douglas Stuart's discussion of this subject in *How to Read the Bible for All Its Worth*, 2nd ed. (Grand Rapids, Mich.: Zondervan, 1993), 125. *see p88*

10. John R. W. Stott, *The Message of the Sermon on the Mount*, The Bible Speaks Today (Downers Grove, Ill.: InterVarsity Press, 1978), 39.

11. Gordon Bigelow has argued that the market serves as the reigning narrative of contemporary culture, even shaping the evangelical church. See Gordon Bigelow, "Let There Be Markets: The Evangelical Roots of Economics," *Harper's* 310, no. 1860 (May 2005), 33.

12. I have reflected theologically on Perkins's paradigm in chapter 6 of *Consuming Jesus: Beyond Race and Class Divisions in a Consumer Church* (Grand Rapids, Mich.: Eerdmans, 2007), for which Perkins wrote the afterword, and in chapter 15 of *Exploring Ecclesiology: An Evangelical and Ecumenical Introduction* (Grand Rapids, Mich.: Brazos, 2009), which I coauthored with Brad Harper.

# Between Two Gardens

*An Organic Salvation for Community Development
from the Biblical Narrative*

## Michael Andres

BETWEEN TWO GARDENS LIES A PLANTATION; IT IS A CURSED GARDEN, A
sharecropper's field. Between Eden and the new earth, there is the cursed
land of thorns, thistles, and cotton, marked by the pain, toil, and sweat of
the oppressed. This is the ground from which John Perkins sprouted. He
is son of a sharecropper scraping out a living from borrowed land, infant
of a dying mother bequeathing her final drops of milk, sibling to a murdered brother seeping his last drops of blood. This is the earth out of which
both his person and theology were formed.[1] He himself bears the bodily
wounds of a Brandon jail beating and the internal scars of racism. In Perkins we have an embodied grace, a lived theology, grown in communities
of brokenness, suffering, and despair. He is a theologian with dirt under his
fingernails. This is a clue to arguably his most enduring theological contribution: Perkins has passionately insisted on a transcendent faith and divine
presence that will not be uprooted from the vicissitudes of earth and the
cracked skin of poverty, an organic salvation that refuses to dislodge the
grace of justification from the call to justice.

On the eve of the social convulsions of the sixties, various Christian
theological permutations awaited the ultimate test of their version of the
gospel and the garden. In 1959, John Osteen founded Lakewood Church
in Houston, eventually to become the largest church in America, enticing
its customers with a steady diet of prosperity gospel. In 1959, Paul Tillich
published his *Theology of Culture*, offering a method of correlation seeking
the revelatory power of a culture that shifts according to the sands of time.[2]
Here and elsewhere we find the incipient Pelagianism of a therapeutic soteriology that looks towards the promise of an optimism-induced material at-
tainment or looks inward towards the reunion of the existentially estranged

self. Here the garden looks suspiciously like a suburb, a gated community, and becomes a mere instrument to discover the human potential or self-actualization of the gardener.

In 1959, the Cuban Revolution furrowed the ground preparing the way, along with the Second Vatican Council, for the germination of liberation theology.[3] Here we have an over-realized eschatology of this-worldly political salvation. In this case, the garden is disputed territory that must be freed from those who rule it, not a place of regeneration and forgiveness for those who dwell in it.

In 1959, one can detect a creeping cultural Docetism in many evangelicals' story of future salvation for individual souls detached from present human suffering. As one dispensationalist evangelical stated frankly,

> The premillennial view holds no prospect of a golden age before the Second Advent, and presents no commands to improve society as a whole. The apostles are notably silent on any program of political, social, moral, or physical improvement of the unsaved world. Paul made no effort to correct social abuses or to influence the political government for good. The program of the early church was one of evangelism and Bible teaching. It was a matter of saving souls out of the world rather than saving the world.[4]

In such a vision, there is no garden, only clouds.

In 1959, John Perkins felt called by God to return from thriving California to the grinding poverty of Mississippi to preach the gospel of reconciliation and restoration.[5] While liberal theologies offered a story of sociopolitical liberation hopelessly tied to human cultural flux, and many evangelicals offered the promise of pie-in-the-sky-when-you-die, Perkins offered another story.[6] Perkins not only extended, but also embodied, a compelling model for viewing the organic nature of the "both/and" gospel. All too often salvation has become a variant of the "either/or" gospel, one that forces us to choose between *either* saving souls *or* doing justice, one that insists that the gospel is *either* about being made right with God *or* a call to live out God's love, or one that promises *either* going to heaven in the future *or* redemption in this world now. We are at times given a deceptive dichotomy between a liberal social agenda and an evangelical spiritual quick fix. To be sure, some things are meant to be either/or: Scripture speaks of children of light or children of darkness, obedience or disobedience, serving God or mammon. But John Perkins, in his life and theology, has shown that the gospel is not a binary choice. For Perkins, the garden is a holistic sacred space of communion and cultivation.

In this chapter, I show some biblical and theological contributions of Perkins's *organic soteriology*, including its creational, Christological, and eschatological dimensions. From bitter experience, and through the black prophetic evangelical tradition, Perkins teaches (or reminds) us of a soteriology that redeems whole persons from social and personal sin, both in this earthly life and the next. It is organic because it is soteriologically earthy and holistic, and captures the material metaphor of the garden. The garden image is apt for Perkins, since he himself employs it, and not only grew up working in cotton fields but also enjoys gardening.[7]

For Perkins the garden supremely means *communion*. His soteriology emphasizes the concept and imagery of communion, or relationship, in the alienation-reconciliation biblical motif. He often speaks of the centrality of "fellowship" and "relationship."[8] The Christian community development movement, inspired by Perkins, is a loosely knit group of broadly evangelical churches and ministries, with the common vision to holistically restore communities with Christians fully engaged in the process of transformation. They espouse the three Rs of relocation, reconciliation, and redistribution.[9] Recently Perkins has explained, "The idea of the three Rs is the gospel in a nutshell—the Good News and incarnation of God." He continues, "What is the purpose of the gospel? Man is alienated from God and because of this, we are alienated from each other. The whole redemption message is to reconcile people to God, so we made reconciliation the centerpiece."[10] This fellowship is both divine and human, and involves personal communion and public community, thus reconciliation for the estranged is between both God and fellow human beings, at both an individual and communal level.

The garden also means *cultivation*. The garden needs tilling and development, for both communities as well as individuals. "Only God can send the rain," says Perkins, "but we can till the ground by committing to a place."[11] This cultivation is creational and incarnational, one which affirms the goodness of the body, and food, and work, and shelter. Perkins preaches an enfleshed soteriology of personal presence that involves whole persons, including whole bodies. This is why, for Perkins, God's plan of rescue consistently involves justification and justice, both spiritual and material, including redemption of social, economic and political human spheres.

Evangelicals are people of the Book and Perkins is a man ripped right from the pages of the Bible. He is a Moses who stands up for the mistreatment of his people, an Amos who prophetically denounces injustice among a tribe not his own, an Ezra called to return to his homeland, and a Paul made to be an evangelist to those not of his race. This deep connection to Scripture is further evidenced by his famous early morning Bible studies and his prodigious recitation of biblical passages in both his speaking and writing. To illuminate Perkins's theological legacy and to show its truth, his organic soteriological vision can be framed in terms of the overall arc of the biblical narrative. Thus the story of organic salvation according to Perkins is fruitfully conveyed as a narrative retelling of God's Word and work, through his redemptive agents, between two gardens.

Traditionally, this has been spelled out in a biblical theology of Creation-Fall-Redemption-Consummation, but perhaps better in terms of Creation-Cursed Creation-New Creation-Restored Creation. This follows if we consider the "in the beginning" creational language of Genesis 1:1–John 1:1–Revelation 21:1, linking the biblical movement of God's salvific plan. The Johannine biblical framework is one directly provided in Scripture and has the benefit of clearly showing that salvation is both creational and communal, connecting God the Creator to God the Reconciler. For Perkins, salvation, the gospel, and the garden, from Genesis to Revelation, are about reconciled relationships and restored communities in a new creation. He connects the Garden of Eden with the Garden of Gethsemane, and finally to the restored Garden of the New Earth.

## CREATION AND COMMUNITY—GENESIS 1–2

"In the beginning God created . . ." (Gen. 1:1). God speaks the world into existence. Everything is made out of nothing. First silence, stillness, nothing is there: then the divine creative word is uttered, the curtain is opened, and the chorus of comets and quasars, the seas and the volcanoes, the oaks and the toads, come forth. He makes a wonderfully diverse biotic *community*. God is a community—Father, Son, and Holy Spirit—and we too are by nature communal, built to live together in harmony. *Eden is a community garden.*

God calls creation "good" (Gen. 1:31). It is the first "good news." God affirms material creation. Elohim cares about our physical well-being, as well as our spiritual state. He is the God of soil and skin, as well as souls. Indeed God actually covenants with all creation through Noah (Gen. 9:12), promising through a resplendent spectrum of colors to re-create and never again destroy. The creation is characterized by shalom and justice, well-being and harmony; things are the way they are supposed to be. There is no scarcity—instead, only abundance for everyone. They can feast from any tree, which is good for eating. Resources are shared, and no one is excluded. With no lack, no conflict, no pain, *Eden is a peaceful garden.*

In this garden there is perfect *communion* between male and female, humans and other creatures, God and all his creation. God walks in the cool of the garden; he relocates from heaven to walk with his people and creation. But there is a unique communion between God and humanity. A *relationship* has begun, which can be seen by noting God's unique communication to the first pair ("do not eat . . ."), by their unique creation by the breath of life breathed into their nostrils, that they alone are made in the *imago Dei*, and by the use of the name Yahweh (God's covenant name) in the second creation account (one focused upon human creation). The garden models this communion between human and divine. *Eden is a lover's garden.*

God the Creator weaves human creatures in his own image; they too are designed for creative work. This is a garden, not a wilderness.[12] God is the first gardener, working to cultivate and make it blossom. To "cultivate" means "tillage; improvement; increase of fertility; the bestowing of labor and care upon a plant, so as to *develop* and improve its qualities; the devoting of special attention or study to the *development* of, or to progress in; the *developing*, fostering, or improving by education and training."[13] God *develops* his creational community. One could make the case that God is continually cultivating his creation, what John Calvin called a *creatio continuata*, throughout redemptive history, taking it from embryo to adulthood, until maturity in the final *eschaton*.[14] God may be the first gardener, but *humanity* is called to cultivate the earth and "to work the ground" (Gen. 2:5). Fruitful labor is part of God's plan, not welfare. Human beings were given the opportunity to engage in productive work. So God is interested in cultivating a *community*: first with all creation, then with a family (Adam and Eve, then Noah), eventually with a clan (Abraham) and finally with a nation (Israel). *Eden is a cultivated garden.*

## CURSED CREATION AND DISUNITY—GENESIS 3–11

The communion and shalom of the original creation was shattered by human sin (Gen. 3–11). The first pair "took and ate," grabbed and consumed, the fruity commodity. The first humans broke covenant, rejected God's rightful and just rule; they attempted to usurp his authority and take what was not theirs for themselves. The results of this broken communion were catastrophic: shame, guilt, fear, alienation, and ultimately judgment. There is now brokenness and alienation between human beings (male and female), between humans and other creatures, and between humans and God. Human reproduction becomes painful and less fruitful, work is burdensome and less productive, and resources become scarcer as God expels them from the plentiful garden.

So God's design for *development* is abated. Adam's sin was not a Fall, but a Wall; it was not so much a tragic suicidal jump from personal glory, but a separation from gracious fellowship in community. From the garden humans are banished to a wilderness. From the cool of the garden to the burning flames of angels, human beings are kept out of perfect fellowship and abundant life. God's creation is now called "cursed" (Gen 3:14, 17). God does not give up on material creation, but now it "groans" for its redemption (Rom. 8:22).

Community then curves in on itself, disintegrates, and brother destroys brother.[15] Cain, who is supposed to develop and cultivate the soil (Gen. 4:3–4), instead stains it with blood (4:10). In a perverse question, "Am I my brother's keeper?" Cain renounces his family and community responsibility to care and protect and keep one another. In a sad reversal, the ground now curses Cain (Gen. 4:11). In Genesis 1, God creates the world; in Genesis 6, God uncreates it through the chaotic waters of the flood. Eventually, in Genesis 11, we see the division of peoples based on language, nationality, and race as they are scattered at the tower of Babel. God also separates them geographically—a reverse-relocation around the globe. The *community* becomes a *disunity*: first with all creation, then with a family (Cain and Abel, Lamech), eventually with a clan (Adam's descendants in Gen. 5), and finally with all nations (Babel). Humanity no longer images the divine community—Father, Son, and Holy Spirit—as it should. But there is a promise of the ultimate defeat of evil (Gen. 3:15) and the hope of reconciliation.


## NEW CREATION AND NEW COMMUNITY—GENESIS TO MALACHI

God's work now involves community restoration and the creation of a new people. Thus, God has an organic, community plan of salvation. His people are to steward resources, possessions, money, talents, and power. He begins by calling one man to create a new people of God. God gives Abraham wealth and power, social and political influence, and he uses it directly for God's purposes to build the family and community of God's chosen people (Gen. 12:2–3; 13:2).

God's concern for shalom and justice in community is demonstrated in Moses's *sermon* from *Mount* Sinai. God cares about forgiveness of guilt, both individual and communal. Yahweh seeks communion with his people, by covenants with Abraham and Israel, and models reconciliation, forgiveness, and justification through the Passover, Day of Atonement, and sacrificial system as a means to meeting God in the tabernacle.

But God also shows that he cares for and seeks to holistically redeem the community in its social, political, and economic brokenness. Israel is liberated by God from the racism and oppression of Egypt, in order to freely worship. The Torah speaks of unjust social conditions that keep persons in poverty (Exod. 22:21–27), such as social systems weighted in favor of the powerful (Lev. 19:15) and high-interest loans (Exod. 22:25–27). In response, the Torah not only calls God's people to give direct relief to meet material and social needs, but also to intentionally develop persons and communities toward self-sufficiency.[16] For example, when a slave's debt was erased and he was released, God directed his former master to send him out with grain, tools, and resources for a new, self-sufficient economic life (Deut. 15:13–14). At times even social reform was necessary to change social conditions and structures that aggravate or cause dependency. For example, Israelites were to oppose legal systems weighted in favor of the wealthy and powerful (Lev. 19:15; Deut. 24:17) and any system of lending capital that gouges the person of modest means (Exod. 22:25–27; Lev. 19:35–37; 25:37). Development and reform are seen in the "garden" of the nation Israel. For example, Sabbath, sabbatical year, and Jubilee are all designed to afford rest, limit material accumulation, free Hebrew indentured servants, and cancel debts (Exod. 23:10–12; Deut. 15). God's plan continues later through the prophets, the emissaries for the Torah, who boldly denounced the economic and social injustice of their society.[17] They explained that the exile was in part due to their failure to cultivate the land (Jer. 12:4; Hos. 4:1–3).

Yet both communion and cultivation remain broken by human moral failure and corrupt social structures. Creation continues to wear "man's smudge and share man's smell."[18] The result is oppression, injustice, and poverty, as well as real guilt, just penalty, and final judgment. Human sin and its consequences are manifold, requiring holistic rescue. The garden is fallow, needing regeneration by the Gardener.

## NEW CREATION AND RECONCILED COMMUNITY— JOHN 1 AND LUKE 4–7

### *Incarnation and Relocation*

"In the beginning was the Word . . ." (Jn. 1:1). In the first century came the beginning of the new creation, a new garden. In this seedling of the new *eschaton* God reveals a radical development in his holistic plan of development through re-creation and reconciliation. Jesus Christ is the good news. He is its messenger and content.

The triune creator and cultivator of the universe responds to this manifold personal and communal sin, as the loving Father *sends* the Son and Spirit, showing God's missional aim.[19] God interjected himself into our messy world. He came right down into the muck in the person of a vulnerable babe in the squalor of a borrowed stable. The Word became flesh and dwelt among us, as Immanuel, to be our God and us his people. This is the incarnation, the first advent. Jesus himself does not present a model of upward mobility, but rather downward mobility, unlike the prosperity gospel. Jesus does not simply give handouts, or minister at arm's length. In love, he relocates and lives amongst the broken, powerless, and marginalized. He builds community by becoming one of them and belonging to the community. As the Christian Community Development Association (CCDA) has explained, "He didn't commute back and forth to heaven . . . Relocation transforms 'you, them, and theirs' to 'we, us, and ours.'"[20] Presence precedes communion.

### *Reconciliation and the "Both/And" Gospel*

Now relocated, Jesus gives the first words and explanation of his earthly ministry in Luke 4:18–19, an event in Jesus's hometown synagogue that occurs after his baptism and temptation.

> The Spirit of the Lord is on me,
> because he has anointed me
> to preach good news to the poor.
> He has sent me to proclaim freedom for the prisoners
> and recovery of sight for the blind,
> to release the oppressed,
> to proclaim the year of the Lord's favor.

The Nazareth Manifesto, intentionally placed in a position of prominence in Luke's Gospel, is meant to typify Jesus's ministry and message; it is "programmatic" in the Third Gospel.[21] As such Luke 4 reveals a gospel that is *both* a spiritual *and* material salvation, and *both* about forgiveness *and* a call to a way of life.

### Spiritual and Material, Individual and Communal

From Luke 4 we see that the gospel is *spiritual*. Jesus acts in the power of the Holy Spirit (4:14) and casts out evil spirits (4:31ff.). God gives us the gift of life through his Son and *Spirit*. This means the gospel of Jesus Christ involves his power over the spiritual realm. It involves regeneration and divine supremacy over our twisted inclinations and the supernatural powers that enslave us. The Holy Spirit gives us a new set of affections, making it possible to love our estranged neighbors the way God does. This is the transformative enemy-love of the gospel, not the class struggle of the liberationist.

The Holy Spirit is the umbilical cord connecting us to the living Christ. We realize the communion of the garden not only in a relationship with Jesus Christ, but through *union* with him![22] Perkins has always had a strong sense for the *unio mystica*. Even during his conversion, after quoting "I have been crucified with Christ and I no longer live, but Christ lives in me" (Gal. 2:20), Perkins says, "I could hear [the apostle Paul] say that he had another life—it was Christ's life—in him and that his motivation and his drive were coming from Christ who was in him."[23] Since Christ and his people are vine and branches, head and members of the body, husband and wife, there are profound organic social implications. God's people have deep spiritual communion with other believers, even believers who are estranged. This means reconciliation is at the heart of the gospel.

Ephesus was a multiethnic church, but the newly converted Jews often separated themselves from Gentile believers. But this was at odds with their "common unity" in Christ. Whereas once Gentiles were separate from Christ, "excluded . . . foreigners" without hope, and without God (Eph. 2:11–12), now they are "in Christ Jesus." Once we were all far away, but are now brought near due to Christ's blood (2:13). Jesus himself is our shalom. He has "made the two one." Jesus has made two races—Gentiles and Jews—to be one. Jewish Christians and Gentile Christians, white Christians and black Christians, are united to the same Jesus Christ through the same Holy Spirit. Through Christ's cross, and indwelt by the Holy Spirit, Jesus has put to death all racial, social, and economic enmity and prejudice (2:15–16). We all have equal access to the Father through the *one* Spirit (2:18). We need to live out who we already are (2:19), one building, where God's Spirit lives (2:20–22). It is "the out-living of the in-living Christ!"[24]

The gospel is also *material* and creational. Jesus talks of good news for the poor, freeing prisoners, healing those who are blind, and relieving the oppressed (Luke 4:18–19). The passage quoted by Jesus (Isa. 61) speaks of the Jubilee, a community re-creation event. Jubilee is about development and re-form, which we begin to see in the early church as recorded in Acts. The text speaks about a new world of shalom. This is the good news of the *kingdom* (Luke 4:43). In Luke 7:18–23, John's disciples come to Jesus to inquire if he is the "one." Jesus points them to his deeds.[25] In between the *inclusio* of his pro-nouncement of the Nazareth Manifesto and the inquiry of John's disciples, we find that Jesus drives out an evil spirit (4:31ff.), heals "many" (4:38ff.), heals a person with leprosy (5:12ff.), heals a person who is paralalized, and forgives sins (5:17ff.), preaches the sermon on plain (6:17ff. is a homily that includes hope for the hungry, grieved, and rejected, giving to everyone who asks, and so on), and raises the dead (7:1ff.). This fulfills the year of Jubilee. Here Jesus gives us a brief yet profound eschatological glimpse of the com-munal kingdom, the way life in the garden should be; a kingdom Jesus is beginning even as he speaks, but which will not fully come until the end of this age. God is concerned with material creation, not merely immaterial souls, as with the old evangelical story. He cares about spiritual renewal and bodily renewal in health clinics, that we are clothed in Christ's righteousness and clothed in thrift stores. The divine will is to make whole again the entire creation. This is the both/and gospel: an organic soteriology.

### Forgiveness and Call to a Way of Life

Jesus extends *forgiveness* to the paralyzed man in Luke 5:20. Forgiveness precedes reconciliation, and is made possible by the atoning death of Je-sus Christ. The cross reminds us that unfaithfulness and racism are gross, repugnant, and destructive, that these earn a wage of judgment and death. Many walk about with a stone of guilt in their chests, but the atonement means just satisfaction or payment has been made.[26] The crucifixion of Christ brings reconciliation to God and justification for our guilt, includ-ing our social and economic sins. But the cross also means the Garden of Gethsemane, it mean taking up our own cross, it means both suffering and transformation: the painful road from the degradation of Jim Crow and

•

cotton fields to new birth and restored communities is marked by persecution and abuse.[27] Christ's death is a self-sacrificial love offering to the enemy. In the end, we find transformation and communion and dancing. "When God sets out to embrace the enemy, the result is the cross," explains Miroslav Volf. "On the cross the dancing circle of self-giving and mutually indwelling divine persons opens up for the enemy; in the agony of the passion the movement stops for a brief moment and a fissure appears so that sinful humanity can join in (see John 17:21)."[28] Jesus's body is broken and blood poured out in our place, offered as a gift.

The bodily resurrection of Christ both vindicates his work on the cross and affirms God's gracious plan to redeem us as whole persons, both body and soul. Christ's resurrection grounds our hope; it is an appetizer of a whole new way of being human, a new era, and the promise of full physical restoration.

Before the Ephesians 2:11–22 of racial reconciliation comes the Ephesians 2:8–9 of God's unmerited grace. Evangelicals have been deeply committed to justification by grace alone through faith alone as the grounds for the forgiveness of our injustice and personal transgressions.[29] Perkins himself embodies this grace, consistently granting undeserved forgiveness to the very persons who have oppressed him and his people, to the point of reconciling with a former grand wizard of the Klu Klux Klan.[30] This is no soteriology of control, like the religious right, but a soteriology of embodied grace.

This shows that while works do not save, they must accompany salvation.[31] The grace that saves must then be a lived grace, emphasizing the Spirit living through us and the kingship and sovereignty of the Father in all of life. Jesus calls us to follow him (Luke 5:1–11). Jesus Christ is prophet, priest, and *king*. Our view of the gospel ought, therefore, as a matter of integrity, grasp that Christians are responsible to live their lives in light of Christ's kingdom and lordship. Salvation requires a desire for obedience to the king's good and perfect will and according to his vision for a new heaven and new earth. Where there is no Lord, there is no Savior. Christians are called to repent, put their attitudes, thoughts, and behavior under the lordship of Christ. After Jesus mercifully grants reprieve, he commands the woman to go and sin no more (John 8:11).

Our calling to community *development* shows God's concern not only for conversion, but also *discipleship*. He wants to develop *us!*[32] The both/and gospel is not a works-based salvation, but is rather a candid invitation to the sinner to sacrifice the opium of destructive sinfulness for life-giving fellowship with a holy and sovereign God. Hence the both/and gospel, while never omitting the grace of personal forgiveness, must also involve a distinctive way of incarnated love: reconciling with enemies, feeding the hungry, stewarding the earth, clothing the naked, protection for the weak and vulnerable, and shalom for those in pain and grief (Matt. 25; Luke 4:16–21).

## RESTORED CREATION AND BELOVED COMMUNITY—REVELATION 21–22

### *Back to the Garden*

"Then I saw a new heaven and a new earth" (Rev. 21:1). In the new creation, God remains committed to his good material creation and to the garden. There will be a new heaven and new *earth*! There will be a new America. There will be a new Mississippi. This includes the new resurrection bodies spoken of in Revelation 20 (Rev. 20:11–15). We will not be immaterial spirits floating in space or ghosts in pajamas drifting in the clouds (for example, Plato). Just like the whole creation will be renewed, we will all be bodily resurrected at the end of time.

Cities are communities where people dwell. The New Jerusalem fulfills the eschatological vision of a "beloved community."[33] In the New Jerusalem (Rev. 21:2, 10–21), God will dwell with his innumerable people, as promised to Abraham and his descendants, in the heavenly Jerusalem, as he promised to David. Heaven will be communal, not individualistic. Cities are a place where we find culture and town squares and gardens, music and the arts. *The new earth will be a community garden.*

Its inhabitants will corporately be the bride at the grand and sumptuous wedding feast of the Lamb (Rev. 21:2, 9). This fulfills God's promise of covenant and communion with Immanuel (Rev. 21:3). We will live in the immediate, intimate presence of our covenant God, and sweet, perfect communion is restored. We will be his people, and he will be our God. *The new earth will be a lover's garden.*

For all those who have suffered much oppression and injustice: God will wipe away all their tears. There will be no more death, no more mourning, no more pain (Rev. 21:4). No pettiness, no abuse, no more lies. No cemeteries or hospitals or psych wards. There will be no disease, no dementia. No more predatory lenders or shot-gun houses. For the old order has passed away; the new has come. *The new earth will be a peaceful garden.*

Finally, we will return to the garden, with its tree of life, and there will be no more curse (Rev. 22:1–5). We will be readmitted, as it were, back to the tree of life. We will commune together in the garden *forever.*[34] The new heaven and earth will not be airy-fairy, they will be green. Whatever was beautiful, and refreshing, and good about the old creation, will pale in the light of the new creation for the physical creation "will be set free from its bondage to decay and obtain the glorious liberty of the children of God" (Rom. 8:19–21). The cursed wildernesses of the sharecropper's fields are gone. We will once again enjoy the sweet fragrance of the Edenic trees, with their healing leaves, taste of its succulent fruits, and lie down by the coursing river on its grassy banks. *The new earth will be a cultivated, restored garden.*

## CHRISTIAN COMMUNITY DEVELOPMENT AND ORGANIC SALVATION

Between two gardens lie the lost souls and broken bodies that litter the concrete backstreets of our divided culture, but John Perkins offers the holistic hope of real communion in a new restored garden. Perkins's biblical, organic soteriology is one that resonates with the triune God's holistic work of new creation according to the Father's cultivating providence, by the reconciling works of the Son through spiritual union with his people. Perkins embodies the biblical call that the gospel is consistently concerned with recreating and cultivating the beloved community. It involves reconciliation and communion between both God and other humans, and the whole of creation, both spiritual and material. Thus Perkins, unlike other truncated soteriological alternatives and inadequate accounts of the garden, presents a compelling biblical model for viewing the organic nature of the both/and gospel. What God has joined, let no one tear asunder. There is no red gospel or blue gospel. There is only one gospel, and it is an organic gospel.

### NOTES

1. John Perkins, *Let Justice Roll Down* (Ventura, Calif.: Regal Books, 1976), 15–16.
2. Paul Tillich, *Theology of Culture* (New York: Oxford University Press, 1959).

3. Vatican II was declared in 1959 by Pope John XXIII and convened in 1962. Giuseppe Alberigo, trans. Matthew Sherry, *A Brief History of Vatican II* (Maryknoll, NY: Orbis Books, 2006), 1; Christian Smith, *The Emergence of Liberation Theology: Radical Religion and Social Movement* (Chicago: University of Chicago Press, 1991), 89–100.

4. John F. Walvoord, *The Millennial Kingdom* (Grand Rapids, Mich.: Zondervan, 1959), 134.

5. Perkins decided to move back to Mississippi in November 1959. He and his family would not actually move until June 1960. John Perkins, *A Quiet Revolution* (Waco, Tex.: Word Books, 1976), 22–24.

6. John M. Perkins, *Beyond Charity: The Call to Christian Community Development* (Grand Rapids, Mich.: Baker Books, 1993), 41–43; Perkins, *With Justice for All,* Third Edition (Ventura, Calif.: Regal Books, 2007), 30–31; John Perkins and Charles Marsh, *Welcoming Justice: God's Movement Toward Beloved Community* (Downers Grove, Ill.: InterVarsity Press, 2009), 38–40, 113. Perkins self-consciously presents his theology as an alternative to European "imperialist" theology, "civil rights movement" liberation theology, including black theology, and prosperity theology.

7. Perkins, *Welcoming Justice,* 50, 111. 61–62.

8. Perkins, *Beyond Charity,* 81–82.

9. Perkins, *Beyond Charity,* 36–37.

10. "An Interview with John Perkins and Charles Marsh," InterVarsity Press, 2009, http://www.ivpress.com/title/ata/3453-q.pdf.

11. Perkins, *Welcoming Justice,* 113.

12. Andy Crouch, *Culture Makers: Recovering Our Creative Calling* (Downers Grove, Ill.: InterVarsity Press, 2008), 101–117.

13. "Cultivate," *Oxford English Dictionary* (Oxford: Oxford University Press, 1989); accessed online, emphasis added.

14. John Calvin, *Institutes of the Christian Religion,* ed. Ford L. Battles and trans. John T. McNeill (Philadelphia: Westminster Press, 1960), I.16.1.

15. Martin Luther, ed. and trans. Wilhelm Pauck, *Lectures on Romans* (Louisville, Ky.: Westminster John Knox, 2006), 159. Luther speaks of sin as *homo incurvatus in se* ("humanity curving in on itself").

16. Timothy Keller, "The Gospel and the Poor," *Themelios,* Volume 33, Issue 3 (December 2008): 8–22.

17. This included exhorting, robbing, and oppressing to gain more land (Ez. 22:29; Micah 2:2; Amos 5:11–12). Israel was to repent of economic sin by seeking justice for the marginalized (Isa. 1:17; 61:1; 58:6–7) and be generous in giving resources away (Jer. 9:23–24; Mal. 3:8–10).

18. Gerard Manley Hopkins, "God's Grandeur." In *Gerard Manley Hopkins: Poems and Prose* (London: Penguin Books Ltd., 1985), 27.

19. Lesslie Newbigin, *Mission in Christ's Way: A Gift, a Command, an Assurance* (New York: Friendship Press, 1988), 1.

20. "Relocation," http://www.ccda.org/philosophy.

21. Walter L. Liefeld, *"Luke"* in *The Expositor's Bible Commentary,* vol. 8 (Grand Rapids, Mich.: Zondervan, 1984), 867.

22. Perkins, *With Justice for All*, 17–18.

23. Perkins, *A Quiet Revolution*, 19.

24. Perkins, *With Justice for All*, 18.

25. Perkins, *With Justice for All*, 88–89; Perkins, *Beyond Charity*, 64–65.

26. Perkins, *Beyond Charity*, 81. Perkins intimates that he holds a satisfaction theory of atonement, but does not develop this in detail.

27. Perkins, *Beyond Charity*, 59. Perkins also emphasizes a more subjective exemplary theory, speaking of the "sacrifice made for me" leading to being "transformed."

28. Miroslav Volf, *Exclusion and Embrace: A Theological Exploration of Identity, Otherness, and Reconciliation* (Nashville, Tenn.: Abingdon, 1996), 129.

29. Perkins, *Beyond Charity*, 81. Perkins affirms the view of "salvation by grace" expressed in the 1974 Lausanne Covenant.

30. John Perkins and Thomas Tarrants, *He's My Brother: Former Racial Foes Offer Strategy for Reconciliation* (Grand Rapids, Mich.: Baker Books, 1994).

31. Perkins, *Beyond Charity*, 68–69.

32. Perkins, *Welcoming Justice*, 117.

33. Perkins, *Welcoming Justice*, 113–115. See also Charles Marsh, *The Beloved Community: How Faith Shapes Social Justice from the Civil Rights Movement to Today* (New York: Basic Books, 2005). The phrase derives from a quote of Martin Luther King, Jr offering a vision for a new social order that finds its fruition in the eschaton.

34. Perkins, *Beyond Charity*, 82. Perkins does speak of salvation in terms of future eternity, as well as present reality.

# Religionless Ecclesiology and the Missional Church

*Peter Goodwin Heltzel and Christian T. Collins Winn*

JOHN PERKINS REIMAGINES THE CHURCH AS A MOVEMENT FOR LOVE and justice. In this imaginative proposal, Perkins delivers a challenge to evangelicals to move beyond institutional religion toward a prophetic evangelical faith in and for the world. In this gesture, Perkins's theology has much in common with Dietrich Bonhoeffer's "religionless Christianity." From a prison cell in Germany, he too would reimagine the church without the shackles of institutional religion. While Bonhoeffer articulated a Christological form of prophetic church, Perkins describes the church as a Christ-centered healing movement, more specifically as a movement for community development marked by racial reconciliation and economic justice. Both visions of the church, however, presuppose an eschatological vision of the world, one in which the powers and principalities of this age are passing away. Throughout his ministry Perkins has sought to usher in a new form of evangelical ecclesiology—one that is prophetic, antiracist, intercultural, missional, and transformational. Perkins's vision of a prophetic church is vital for the future of the world Christian movement in the North American context.

## BONHOEFFER'S RELIGIONLESS CHRISTIANITY

In his *Letters and Papers from Prison*, Dietrich Bonhoeffer famously wrote,

> What keeps gnawing at me is the question, what is Christianity, or who is Christ actually for us today? The age when we could tell people that with words—whether with theological or with pious words—is past, as is the age of inwardness and of conscience, and that means

the age of religion altogether. We are approaching a completely religionless age; people as they are now simply cannot be religious anymore. . . . How can Christ become Lord of the religionless as well? Is there such a thing as a religionless Christian? If religion is only the garb in which Christianity is clothed—and this garb has looked very different in different ages—what then is religionless Christianity? . . . The questions to be answered would be: What does a church, a congregation, a sermon, a liturgy, a Christian life, mean in a religionless world?[1]

It is not entirely clear what Bonhoeffer was after when he used the phrase "religionless Christianity," but there is no doubt that he was trying to imagine what the visibility of the church would look like in a world after the Shoah, after the emergence of the so-called world come of age. This would be a public, visible, and concrete faith, but one not articulated in traditional religious categories. In this, Bonhoeffer was attempting to take seriously the secularity of Jesus—that is, that in Jesus the world as such is claimed and therefore the dividing wall between the sacred and the profane is abolished. In this new state of affairs, Jesus stands in redemptive judgment over against the powers and principalities of this world, among whom religion is to be counted. Jesus came for the world and as such calls into question the dichotomy between the sacred (cult) and the profane (world), a dichotomy that is produced by the very category of religion as it has been expressed in modernity. Thus there is, as it were, "no reserve of space or time or concept or aspect of creation outside of or beyond or undetermined by the critical, decisive, and final action of God in Jesus Christ."[2]

This means, then, that Bonhoeffer's attempt to rethink Christianity, and to imagine a "religionless Christianity," is no mere reactionary gesture, a reflexive response to the emergence of Nazism and the horrors of the mid-twentieth century. Rather, the question that Bonhoeffer was asking— though undoubtedly fueled by those horrors—was rooted in a view of Jesus as "he who is to come"—that is, as the inbreaking of God's loving power. The triune God's divine desire is to reclaim and rectify the world. "*In Jesus Christ the reality of God has entered into the reality of this world*."[3] Jesus's entrance into the world heralds the advent of the new world of God. Jesus's incarnation inaugurates a new social order, while the powers and principalities of this world are passing away. As such, all of humanity, not the least being the Christian church, is living side by side with a new state of affairs, living in the midst of the transition from "this age" to the "age to come."

The implication of the incarnation for religion in this new state of affairs is quite problematic. As theologian Christopher Morse puts it, religion is simply an "inadequate frame of reference,"[4] and therefore more apt to obscure and obfuscate, or perhaps even to occlude, the new thing that God is doing in Christ. This is because religion is part of the age that is passing away, part of the powers and principalities that have been subdued by Christ. Thus what is needed is a "religionless Christianity."

The community of God, then, is called to live in the light of the "turning of the ages" that the inbreaking of Jesus has inaugurated. Jesus ushers in a new form of community. In his early theological writings Bonhoeffer spoke of the church as "Christ existing as community."[5] The church, then, takes on an eschatological character in the sense that it refuses to live according the structures and powers of this age. Shaped by Hegel's attempt to name *Geist* in history and Barth's Christocentrism, Bonhoeffer articulated a social ontology of the church that was grounded in the person of Jesus Christ.[6] For Bonhoeffer, the basis and content of the life of the church is Jesus. The church is Christ existing as community.[7] It is a missional community in and for the world.

The Lutheran understanding of Christ as *pro Nobis* is also applied by Bonhoeffer to the church, who, like its master, is called to be a servant in and for the world. The church exists for others because Jesus exists for others. It is Jesus who shows the church what it means to be the church, what it means to be a servant in and for the world. Because Jesus is an earthling, the church is to be for the whole earth. Earlier in *Letters and Papers from Prison*, Bonhoeffer deepens his incarnational theology through an engagement with Irenaeus's doctrine of recapitulation, writing:

> Nothing is lost, that everything is taken up in Christ, although it is transformed, made transparent, clear and free from all selfish desire. Christ restores all this as God originally intended it to be, without the distortion resulting from our sins. The doctrine derived from Eph. 1:10—that of the restoration of all things, *recapitulation* (Irenaeus)— is a magnificent conception, full of comfort. This is how the promise "God seeks what has been driven away" is fulfilled. And no one has expressed this so simply and artlessly as Paul Gerhardt in these words that he puts into the mouth of the Christ-child: "I'll bring again."[8]

God's promise to seek "what has been driven away" begins to be fulfilled as the incarnate Jesus Christ initiates the restoration of all things, what

Irenaeus called *recapitulation*, "a magnificent conception, full of comfort." Because Jesus is fully human, the church is called to affirm humanity, reaching out in attentive, vulnerable love to the whole human family, but especially to those who are poor and hurting. In Christ's identification with suffering humanity—with a humanity ground down under the wheels of the powers and principalities—the church receives its own orientation as those who are called to be with and for the victims of this present age. Bonhoeffer writes, "Christians can and ought to act like Christ: they ought to bear the burdens and sufferings of the neighbor. . . . It must come to the point that the weaknesses, needs, and sins of my neighbor afflict me as if they were my own, in the same way as Christ was afflicted by our sin."[9] That this bearing of burdens is not simply "religious talk" but refers to concrete action is made clear when Bonhoeffer notes: "The hungry person needs bread, the homeless person needs shelter, the one deprived of rights needs justice, the lonely person needs community, the undisciplined one needs order, and the slave needs freedom. It would be blasphemy against God and our neighbor to leave the hungry unfed while saying that God is closest to those in deepest need."[10] The bearing of the sins and burdens of others to which Jesus calls the church is nothing less than a concrete imitation of Jesus's own life, a cruciform life, one that was fundamentally disruptive and that cannot be contained in the categories of religion.

Since Jesus was in full solidarity with the suffering and oppressed throughout his ministry, Christians are to seek solidarity with the suffering. Bonhoeffer calls for a prophetic Christianity that will "see the great events of world history from below, from the perspective of the outcasts, the suspects, the maltreated, the powerless, the oppressed and reviled, in short from the perspective of the suffering."[11] In this, the church should find itself not only in solidarity with those on the underside of history, but standing nearer that place from which "the power comes which will overthrow the world, the wretched, unhappy world."[12] In other words, the church's identification with those who suffer unveils the fact that the current age, in which the few are on top while the many suffer below, has met its end in Jesus Christ. This state of affairs is passing away. The world is being turned upside down, and the church's identification with those who suffer witnesses to this fact in both word and deed.[13]

Christians solidarity with the suffering is a search for Jesus who is hidden in their midst. Bonhoeffer develops the notion of a Christological incognito, the idea that Jesus is hidden in unexpected people and places. The Christological incognito is a new form of the "hiddeness of God" motif that is so prominent in the theology of Martin Luther. Bonhoeffer develops this idea Christologically, connecting the suffering of Jesus Christ with the suffering of the oppressed. Bonhoeffer argues that incarnation in Jesus Christ is not revealed in visible glorification, but is "incognito, as a beggar among beggars, as an outcast among outcasts, as despairing among the despairing, as dying among the dying."[14] The exalted, incarnate one also bears the likeness of sinful flesh, for he is the humiliated, crucified one. Bonhoeffer is not merely interested in the church being in solidarity with the suffering, but calls the church to actively seek to eliminate the suffering of the poor through an ethics of responsibility with two practices of prophetic ministry: unceasing prayer and action for justice.[15]

Though this vision of the church and of a "religionless Christianity" was hammered out through his participation in the "Church Struggle" that occurred during the Nazi era, Bonhoeffer received important initial impulses through his experience of prophetic black Christianity in Harlem. In 1930–1931 Bonhoeffer attended Abyssinian Baptist Church, and there he encountered a vital, enthusiastic faith with a rich and profound theology among the African American Christians who embodied a revolutionary hope in their Christ-centered community, though they lived in a violently segregated nation. In Harlem, Bonhoeffer was baptized into the depths of black suffering and the black freedom struggle. It was not in the great halls of Union Theological Seminary but rather in the black Baptist churches of Harlem that Bonhoeffer found the collective practice of the secret discipline and the ministry of Jesus. What Bonhoeffer encountered in the worship of African Americans in Harlem was the power of hope amid affliction, which he understood theoretically in Barth, but did not fully existentially grasp at that level of intensity. This historical connection, as well as a theology of suffering and hope, makes Bonhoeffer an ideal dialogue partner for the prophetic black Christian tradition of Martin Luther King Jr. and John Perkins.[16]

## PERKINS'S SEARCH FOR THE PROPHETIC CHURCH

Like Bonhoeffer, Perkins has often donned the mantel of a prophet seeking to inspire and equip Christians to join the "this worldly" struggle for love and justice. With a prophetic-apocalyptic imagination, Perkins has reimagined Christianity as a missional movement for community development. Christian faith must make a positive social impact on the local community in which it finds collective expression. Bearing evangelical witness to the transformational justice of God is the mission of the prophetic evangelical church.[17]

Perkins's conception of the prophetic church did not emerge out of a childhood faith. Perkins's Mississippi youth did not include attending church. He grew up around bootleggers and sharecroppers, with good old-fashioned values and economic pragmatism, but not a strong dose of that old-time religion. Thus we can interpret Perkins's life as a search for a church that is relevant to the social and economic context of local community. The longing for authentic community runs very deep in Perkins's soul, as his mother died of malnutrition while she was trying to breast-feed him, and his absentee father died when he was a young boy.

Perkins's subject position on the underside of modernity created the conditions for a prophetic evangelical ecclesiology to emerge from the heart of the Deep South. The racism that Perkins encountered in segregated Mississippi was stubborn white supremacy that flowed through all of the social structures and systems, perpetuating white skin power and privilege. For Perkins, Christianity's this-worldly task always had to include the systematic dismantling of racism that continually inflicted suffering on black bodies in Mississippi.

The deepest source of Perkins's racial lament was the murder of his brother Clyde in 1946. Awarded a Purple Heart for courage on the battlefield in World War II while defending America, Clyde was brutally murdered by a white policeman. A sixteen-year-old boy that night, Perkins became a man as his heart was seared with anger. Scared that he would retaliate, the Perkins family sent John out to California.

It was in Southern California in 1957 that Perkins would find evangelical faith through the ministry of James McArthur at Cavalry Bible Church. It was there that he heard the gospel for the first time, "the fact that Jesus Christ could set me free and live his life in me."[18] Personally, Perkins learned that he could be loved and nurtured by white evangelical men, beginning a process of deep reconciliation in his own life.[19] At Cavalry Bible Church, Perkins was also schooled in a dispensational theological vision that was Christocentric and biblicist, but dualistic, focusing on eternal life in heaven at the expense of "this worldly" realities.[20] It was this born-again individualism with an otherworldly theology that Perkins would take back with him to Mississippi in June 1960 when he returned home with his wife, Vera Mae, and five children.[21]

Encountering the civil rights movement in the 1960s brought Perkins to a theological crisis. Having found economic success working and buying a house in California, where he felt respected and found opportunity, Perkins found life in Mississippi tough. His back was constantly pushed up against the wall because of the racism of the powers and principalities in Mississippi. In Mississippi in the 1960s, African Americans were still struggling with poor jobs, a bad educational system, and a lack of economic opportunities.

Perkins's initial ministry strategy was evangelistic, seeking to convert African Americans to faith in Christ with the idea that the transformation of community would follow. Simply stated, the theology of individual regeneration failed as a social ethic in Mississippi in the 1960s. Perkins writes, "the 'Jesus-saves' only type [of Christian] was not radical enough for the problems that we were dealing with, and that people did need training, they did need skills, they did need jobs."[22] Perkins here identifies the economic inequities that were so pronounced between blacks and whites in the South. If the evangelical gospel was to speak to the realities of African Americans in Mississippi, it would have to speak to the economic and political realities that confronted and deformed the African American community. The gospel would need to be relevant to every dimension of their humanity.

## PERKINS'S SEARCH FOR A RELIGIONLESS ECCLESIOLOGY

Endeavoring to find a form of Christian social existence that could address the challenges his community was facing, Perkins found himself searching for something akin to Bonhoeffer's "religionless Christianity." It would be fair to say that Perkins's own peculiar version of a "religionless ecclesiology" emerged in the fires of the civil rights movement. During the Freedom Summer of 1964, Perkins opened up his Mendenhall Ministries to house civil rights workers from the North and joined the voter registration campaign, viewing it as central to the social witness of the church. In 1967 Perkins served as the state representative of the Federation of Southern Cooperatives. In December 1969 Perkins organized a boycott of white businesses in Mendenhall right before Christmas. A few months later he was brutally beaten in a jail cell in Brandon, Mississippi.

After the beating, Perkins faced a decision: would he respond with righteous anger and react against white racism, or would he courageously move through his anger to love the men and women who embodied the racist spirit of Mississippi? Just as King had prayed at his kitchen table for God's help after the bombing of his home in Birmingham, Perkins prayed from his sickbed for God to give him courage to follow the shalom politics of

Jesus, to be one who did not return blow for blow but boldly proclaimed a new order of peace and justice. Like a Pauline church planter, he started his own ministry called Voice of Calvary Ministries in Mendenhall. Voice of Calvary was more than a church; it was a holistic community center intended to meet the felt needs of the community. Perkins saw the church's primary vocation as meeting the needs of the poor.

Voice of Calvary was a Christ-centered community called to work together to meet the basic human needs of everyone in the local community. The humanity of Jesus of Nazareth and his role as an earthly prophet would be the central motifs of Perkins's ecclesiological vision. Like Martin Luther King Jr., he interpreted Jesus in the Exodus tradition: as Moses led the oppressed out of Egypt, Jesus will lead the oppressed out of their contemporary bondage. Jesus was a liberator of the oppressed. Black evangelical theologian Tom Skinner's famous "The Liberator Has Come" address at InterVarsity's Ninth Urbana Missionary Convention in 1970 had brought national recognition to the emerging prophetic black evangelical theology, of which Perkins's was an exemplar. What is distinctive in this tradition of black evangelical liberation Christology is that Jesus as prophet is directly identified with suffering black folks and their struggle for freedom. Jesus Christ identified with poor people to the point of "equating himself with the poor person," writes Perkins.[23] Within the context of this sacred drama, great African American leaders take on the role of prophets in the struggle for justice. Thus there is often a seamless flow from biblical story to contemporary struggle.

Perkins manifesto *Let Justice Roll* (1976) articulated a prophetic, evangelical theological vision of the whole gospel. Critical to Perkins's theology was the powerful verse from the prophet Amos, "Let justice roll down like waters, and righteousness like an ever-flowing stream" (Amos 5:24). When read through the Hebrew prophets and their vision of justice within shalom, Perkins was able to emphasize what he called "the whole Gospel": Jesus is the prophetic Lord and Savior, the liberator of the oppressed who redeems us from personal and social sin.[24] Following Hendrikus Berkhof and John Howard Yoder, Perkins would interpret the powers and principalities that Paul refers to as "structures and institutions of inequality and oppression."[25] As such, the church and the Christian life in general must be more than an expression of religion. In fact, given the social and racial realities of the South, the Christian life would have to have a "religionless" character to it.

Perkins sought a religionless Christianity because the church in the South was either full of racist whites or oppressed African Americans.

Perkins was frustrated by the ways in which evangelical religion in Mississippi had oppressed his fellow African Americans, writing, "I had always looked at black Christians as sort of inferior people whose religion had made them gullible and submissive. Religion had made so many of my people humble down to the white-dominated systems with all its injustices. Religion had made them cowards and Uncle Toms."[26] The social, political, and cultural processes of white domination did not exclude religion from their domain. In fact, religion in the South played a major role in reinforcing the social order of white supremacy. As such, Perkins saw religion as a shell of cultural corruption hindering the realization of the whole gospel for the whole world, but especially for his corner of the world in Mendenhall.

Like Bonhoeffer, then, Perkins saw religion as part of the old order of the world confronted by Jesus Christ. By leaving religion, Perkins sought to exit "the ways of the world." He seeks to leave the powers and principalities of this age to enter into the new age, or at least to witness to the coming of that new age. Though the new age is coming from the future, it has earthly expression in parabolic ways, and the church is called to reflect the coming of that new age. As Perkins writes, "From coast to coast, city to city, God is building His Church, and consequently, that Church is reflecting His heavenly kingdom on earth. One day, God Himself will establish His own kingdom, a kingdom that is coming. As we are working on earth, we are to let the world know that Jesus Himself is coming again to set up His eternal kingdom. Our lives should give hope to the fact that He is coming again."[27] The church's collective life together then bears prophetic witness to the coming kingdom of God, God's righteous reign that entails provisional embodiment of freedom and justice for all.

In his attempt to embody and cast the vision for this alternative form of Christian social existence, Jesus's teaching of the kingdom of God became especially important for Perkins. From early in life, Perkins had noticed the centrality of Christ's kingdom teaching as central to his own understanding of Christianity. The interconnection of God's kingdom and God's will are captured in the Lord's Prayer, which Perkins's prayed even as a schoolboy: "Thy kingdom come. Thy will be done, on earth as it is in heaven" (Matt. 6:10). For Perkins, "heaven on earth was a key aspect of the Gospel," which implied that Jesus had intended for the Christian community to embody a new form of social existence.[28]

The shape of that new form of community finds its contours in Jesus's own history as suffering servant and messianic prophet. Through these two poles—the one who identifies himself with those who suffer and the one who speaks truth to power—Perkins was working with themes that are at the heart of the black church tradition. He offers a vivid illustration of how the black church sees Jesus as the prophetic Lord and liberator of the oppressed and as the Savior who redeems us from personal and social sin. "If Christ is Savior, He must also be Lord—Lord over such areas as spending, racial attitudes and business dealings. The gospel must be allowed to penetrate the white consciousness as well as the black consciousness."[29] In this, the Lordship of Christ must materialize in the ways in which the community economically orders itself.

The body of Christ becomes especially visible not as it performs ecclesiastical rites, nor as it "rightly administers the sacraments" or performs certain cultic duties. Rather, the body of Christ is evident primarily as it manifests itself among the poor. This manifestation is encapsulated in Perkins's three Rs: relocation, redistribution, and reconciliation. As Perkins writes, "When the Body of Christ is visibly present and living among the poor (relocation), and when we are loving our neighbors and our neighbors' families the way we love ourselves and our families (reconciliation), the result is redistribution."[30] Redistribution is the concrete economic outworking of relocation and reconciliation. Perkins writes of redistribution:

It is when God's people with resources are living in the poor community and are a part of it, applying skills and resources to the problems of that community, thereby allowing a natural redistribution to occur. Redistribution is putting our lives, our skills, our education, and our resources to work to empower people in a community of need. Christian community development ministries find creative avenues to create jobs, schools, health centers, home ownership, and other enterprise of long-term development.[31]

The practices of relocation, reconciliation, and redistribution are constitutive of Perkins's vision of the church. The church is that community marked by witness to the gospel, the whole gospel. The church's most appropriate social location then is among the poor in the abandoned places of empire, a location that places the body of Christ in the ideal situation to witness to the whole gospel, which meets the whole needs of the whole person. The prophetic church, as Perkins's envisions it, is a space in which all people, black and white, poor and rich, can gather and grow from an economy of grace.

This eschatological vision of the church calls for a social existence marked by peacemaking practices and community development; the eschatological horizon reshapes the public discipleship of the community that is at odds with the ways of the world. As such, the Christian Community Development Association (CCDA), the most mature embodiment of Perkins's ecclesial vision, is profoundly discontinuous with the current state of affairs, which places it squarely in the apocalyptic ecclesiology of Bonhoeffer. The "community development" envisioned by Perkins is not merely a secularizing of the church, since the "community" to be developed is not continuous with the current social reality, a reality marked by division, hatred, mutual suspicion, and oppression. It is, rather, a reconciled community, one in which race, class, and gender inequalities are called into question and rendered ineffectual through the practices of relocation, reconciliation, and redistribution. Thus CCDA organizations are also postreligious because they seek to shed the institutional forms of religion that have been so extraordinarily impotent in resisting the power structures of white supremacy. In contrast, problematic institutional forms of evangelical religion like the prosperity church and suburban megachurches distance themselves from the messy work of seeking justice and the end of poverty.[32] And even worse, they sometimes find themselves colluding in propagation of the patterns of racial and economic segregation, as in the use of the homogenous unit principle in church growth circles, which has led to the growth of highly segregated churches, most often white and upper middle class.[33]

Rich white evangelicals are often unsettled by Perkins's vision that calls them to relocate, reconcile, and redistribute. Everyone who seeks to be worthy of the name evangelical needs to ask themselves simple, challenging questions: Do we live with the poor? Are we seeking reconciliation in its intrapersonal, interpersonal, social, economic, and political dimensions? Are we redistributing our talents and resources back into our local community? A Christ-centered community that can answer all of these questions in the affirmative is the type of church that Perkins is after.

## CONCLUSION

While Perkins drew inspiration from Bonhoeffer's vision of Christianity, he also learned from the Bruderhof, a community of German Pietists who sought to collectively live Jesus's Sermon on the Mount. Perkins writes, "When I look back on the church in Nazi Germany, it seems to me that the Bruderhof did as much as Bonhoeffer to interrupt the madness and show another way." Because the Bruderhof live together as an intentional and simple community in exile, their community life provides clues to what the prophetic church could be today. Perkins continues, "When the Civil Rights movement came to Mississippi, a number of Bruderhof people came down to help us. And after the movement moved on, they kept coming. I've always been impressed by their commitment to follow Jesus and live the kingdom out here on earth as it is in heaven."[34]

In *Ethics*, Bonhoeffer writes, "In earlier times the church could preach that a person must first become a sinner, like the publican and the harlot, before he could know and find Christ, but we in our time must rather say that before a person can know and find Christ he must first become righteous like those who strive and who suffer for the sake of justice, truth, and humanity."[35] Charles Marsh writes, "Bonhoeffer was not giving up on Christ and embracing secular humanism. On the contrary, he was moving more fully into the depth and richness of discipleship to Christ."[36] Bonhoeffer's call to public discipleship reaches an apex in the prophetic ministry of Perkins, for Perkins saw that in order for the gospel to manifest in the Deep South, it would require more than forgiveness and interpersonal reconciliation, but repentance by racist whites and systemic transformation through a new intercultural Christian collective. White upper-middle-class existence (as well as black) is interrogated at its deepest level. The gospel of reconciliation demands a giving back of time, talents, and resources to the poorest areas of our neighborhoods. Thus Perkins offers the vision of an apocalyptic-prophetic community that brings to fruition Bonhoeffer's call for a religionless Christianity.

During his imprisonment in Germany for his resistance against Hitler and the Nazi regime, Bonhoeffer imagined what a religionless church would be. It was vital that the church after the war stand with the victims. Likewise, Perkins challenges all who claim to follow Christ to stand with the poor and hurting in our communities. Perkins's vision of community development provides a vision of public discipleship that continues to transform American evangelical Christianity toward a more mature and just end. From his jail cell in Brandon, Mississippi, John Perkins decided to continue his quest for the embodiment of a Christ-centered prophetic community of the disinherited. Through Perkins's consistent and creative perseverance, we have witnessed the emergence of a religionless evangelicalism, in which black and white Christians, and all shades in-between, are now seeking to work together to bear broken witness to a new order of love, justice, and shalom.

NOTES

1. Dietrich Bonhoeffer, *Letters and Papers from Prison*, trans. Isabel Best, Lisa E. Dahill, Reinhard Krauss, and Nancy Lukens, Vol. 8 of *Dietrich Bonhoeffer Works*, 16 vols. (Minneapolis: Fortress Press, 2010), 362–364.

2. Douglas Harink, *Paul among the Postliberals: Pauline Theology Beyond Christendom and Modernity* (Grand Rapids, Mich.: Brazos Press, 2003), 69. See also Philip Ziegler, "Dietrich Bonhoeffer—An Ethics of God's Apocalypse?" *Modern Theology* 23, no. 4 (October 2007), 579–594; and Ry Owen Siggelkow, "The Lamb That Was Slain Is Worthy to Receive Power: Christology, Apocalyptic, and Secularity in the Ecclesiologies of Dietrich Bonhoeffer and John Howard Yoder" (Master's thesis, University St. Thomas, 2009).

3. Dietrich Bonhoeffer, *Ethics*, trans. Reinhard Krauss, Charles C. West, and Douglas W. Stott, Vol. 6 of *Dietrich Bonhoeffer Works*, 16 vols. (Minneapolis: Fortress Press, 2005), 54.

4. Christopher Morse, *The Difference Heaven Makes: Rehearing the Gospel as News* (London: T&T Clark, 2010), 89.

5. Dietrich Bonhoeffer, *Sanctorum Communio: A Theological Study of the Sociology of the Church*, trans. Reinhard Krauss and Nancy Lukens, Vol. 1 of *Dietrich Bonhoeffer Works*, 16 vols. (Minneapolis: Fortress Press, 1998), 189–191. See Charles Marsh, "Christ Existing as Community," in *Reclaiming Dietrich Bonhoeffer: The Promise of His Theology* (New York: Oxford University Press, 1994), 88–100.

6. See Andreas Pangritz, *Karl Barth in the Theology of Dietrich Bonhoeffer*, trans. Barbara Rumscheidt and Martin Rumscheidt (Grand Rapids, Mich.: Eerdmans, 2000).

7. See Dietrich Bonhoeffer, *Discipleship*, trans. Barbara Green and Reinhard Krauss, Vol. 4 of *Dietrich Bonhoeffer Works*, 16 vols. (Minneapolis: Fortress Press, 2003), 225–226.

8. Dietrich Bonhoeffer, *Letters and Papers from Prison*, trans. Reginald Fuller et al. (New York: Touchstone, 1997), 170.

9. Bonhoeffer, *Sanctorum Communio*, 178–180.

10. Bonhoeffer, *Ethics*, 163.

11. Bonhoeffer, *Letters and Papers from Prison*, 52.

12. Christoph Blumhardt, "Jesus among the Wretched," in *Christoph Blumhardt and His Message*, ed. R. Lejune (Rifton, N.Y.: Plough Publishing House, 1963), 190.

13. See Bonhoeffer, *Ethics*, 62–64.

14. Dietrich Bonhoeffer, *Christ the Center*, trans. Edwin H. Robertson (New York: HarperCollins, 1978), 106–107. Bonhoeffer discovers the "incognito" in Søren Kierkegaard, *Philosophical Fragments*, trans. Howard V. Hong (Princeton, N.J.: Princeton University Press, 1974), 37–43.

15. For thoughtful discussions of Bonhoeffer's ethics and Christology, see Larry Rasmussen, "The Ethics of Responsibility," in *The Cambridge Companion to Dietrich Bonhoeffer*, ed. John W. de Gruchy (Cambridge: Cambridge University Press, 1999), 206–225; and Geffrey B. Kelly, "Prayer and Action for Justice," in de Gruchy, *Cambridge Companion to Dietrich Bonhoeffer*, 246–268.

16. Charles Marsh, "Bonhoeffer on the Road to King: Turning from the Phraseological to the Real," in *Bonhoeffer and King: Their Legacies and Import for Christian Social Thought*, ed. Willis Jenkins and Jennifer M. McBride (Minneapolis: Fortress Press, 2010), 123–138.

17. For a theological and social analysis of the rise of prophetic evangelical politics at the turn of the century, see Peter Heltzel and Robin Rogers "The New Evangelical Politics" *Society* 45, no. 5 (September 2008): 412–415. On the rise of prophetic evangelicals, see Peter Heltzel, "Prophetic Evangelicals: Toward a Politics of Hope," in *The Sleeping Giant Has Awoken: The New Politics of Religion in the United States*, ed. Jeffrey W. Robbins and Neal Magee (New York: Continuum, 2008), 25–40.

18. John Perkins, *Let Justice Roll* (Ventura, Calif.: Regal Books, 1976), 57.

19. Perkins became friends with an extensive network of white evangelical men through the Christian Businessmen's Committee of Arcadia-Monrovia. Perkins, *Let Justice Roll*, 77.

20. For an introduction to dispensational theology, see Clarence B. Bass, *Backgrounds to Dispensationalism: Its Historical Genesis and Ecclesiastical Implications* (Grand Rapids, Mich.: Eerdmans, 1960).

21. Perkins, *Let Justice Roll*, 85. Perkins writes of his call to Mississippi: "I couldn't escape a conviction growing up inside of me that God wanted me back in Mississippi to identify with my people there, and to help them break up the cycle of despair—not by encouraging them to leave, but by showing them new life right where they were." Perkins, *Let Justice Roll*, 79.

22. As cited by Charles Marsh, *The Beloved Community: How Faith Shapes Social Justice, from the Civil Rights Movement to Today* (New York: Basic Books, 2005), 168.

23. John Perkins, *A Quiet Revolution: Meeting Human Needs Today: A Biblical Challenge to Christians*, rev. ed. (Pasadena, Calif.: Urban Family Publications with Network Unlimited International, 1976), 141.

24. John M. Perkins, "The Whole Gospel," in Perkins, *Let Justice Roll*, 102–113.

25. Perkins, *Quiet Revolution*, 88. Though there are clear differences, Perkins's thought resonates with Berkhof and Yoder. See Karl Barth, "The Lordless Powers," in *Christian Life: Church Dogmatics IV/4, Lecture Fragments* (Grand Rapids, Mich.: Eerdmans, 1981), 213–233; Hendrikus Berkhof, *Christ and the Powers*, trans. John Howard Yoder (Scottdale, Pa.: Herald Press, 1962); and John Howard Yoder, *The Politics of Jesus* (Grand Rapids, Mich.: Eerdmans, 1972).

26. Perkins, *Let Justice Roll*, 57.

27. John M. Perkins, with Jo Kadlecek, *Resurrecting Hope* (Ventura, Calif.: Regal Books, 1995), 24.

28. Perkins, *Resurrecting Hope*, 17.

29. Perkins, *Let Justice Roll*, 106.

30. Perkins, *Resurrecting Hope*, 22.

31. John M. Perkins, "What Is Christian Community Development," in *Restoring At-Risk Communities: Doing It Together and Doing It Right*, ed. John M. Perkins (Grand Rapids, Mich.: Baker Books, 1995), 22–23.

32. John Perkins, "A Time for Rebuilding," in Charles Marsh and John Perkins, *Welcoming Justice: God's Movement toward Beloved Community* (Downers Grove, Ill.: InterVarsity Press, 2009), 108, 113.

33. Perkins critiques the homogeneous unit principle of church grown throughout his writings. See Perkins, *Resurrecting Hope*, 22; and Perkins, "Time for Rebuilding," 108.

34. John Perkins, "The Cultural Captivity of the Church," in Marsh and Perkins, *Welcoming Justice*, 51.

35. As quoted by Charles Marsh, "God's Movement in the Twenty-First Century," in Marsh and Perkins, *Welcoming Justice*, 101.

36. Marsh, "God's Movement in the Twenty-First Century," 101.

# "Lady, Give Me a Drink"

## Reading Scripture, Shaping Community Development

### Kelly West Figueroa-Ray

IN 2009 JOHN PERKINS, AN AFRICAN AMERICAN EVANGELICAL CHRIS-
tian and civil rights activist, gave a presentation on the Christian Community Development Association (CCDA) as part of an academic conference hosted by the Project on Lived Theology at the University of Virginia. When I sat down, I expected to hear a few minutes of background
information and an outline of the organization's core principles. Instead,
following a brief introduction, Perkins began his presentation by saying: "I
am primarily a Bible teacher."[1] In the talk that followed, Perkins exhibited
a strong tendency to unite his explanation of John 4 or the text's explica-
tive sense with both the text's historical referent (Jesus's encounter with the
woman at the well) and its present applicative sense or meaningfulness for
Perkins's community of believers. In this chapter I argue that this tendency,
found more generally in African American hermeneutics, is a form of what
Hans Frei terms "literal-realistic" interpretation. Additionally, I demonstrate that the prevalent mode of acculturation of African Americans into
the biblical world, as described by Allen Callahan in *The Talking Book: African Americans and the Bible*, guarded African American hermeneutics
from experiencing "the eclipse of biblical narrative" that Frei laments. This
particular community's habits of scriptural reading, therefore, provide resources—apart from precritical interpreters, such as the Christian church
fathers and the Jewish rabbis—for postliberal theologians to explore literal-
realistic scriptural reading tendencies as *living habits*, expressed not only
within African American worshipping communities but also in the midst
of pluralistic publics.

# LITERAL-REALISTIC INTERPRETATION IN AFRICAN AMERICAN HERMENEUTICS

First, it is useful to explore three criteria of "literal-realistic" readings in light of African American hermeneutics. African American hermeneutics fit Frei's criteria in the following ways: biblical narratives are understood literally, as if they actually happened in history; the biblical world is understood as the real world; and it is a real world in which present-day readers and hearers of the Bible are active members. Therefore just as precritical interpreters based their understanding of sin, for example, on the ostensive referent of the particular narrative of Adam and Eve's sin in Genesis, a similar tendency to define the concept and realities found in the world through the narratives of Scripture is found in African American hermeneutics. Yet African American hermeneutics do not depend on an exclusively linear and futuristically oriented understanding of history requiring that "the several biblical stories narrating sequential segments in time must fit together into one narrative."[2] This is a difference that makes it possible for African American hermeneutics to function within a modern context and produces a distinct interpretation from the one developed in the Western precritical context.

Figural interpretation was one of the main tools of interpretation that held biblical reality together for the precritical interpreter. "Figuration was at once a literary and a historical procedure, an interpretation of stories and their meanings by weaving them together in a common narrative referring to a single history and its patterns of meaning."[3] Figural interpretations always keep the integrity of the first event as an event that happened in history, while at the same time understanding that event as a prefiguring of another future event. In other words, figuration helped to sequence all biblical narratives and present-day life experiences into one temporally linear story encompassing all of reality from creation until consummation. For a precritical interpreter, this was just as much a part of literal interpretation as was assuming the text related events that had occurred in history.[4] On the other hand, for a "modern" interpreter, figural interpretations are not literal at all:

> Literal readings came increasingly to mean two things: grammatical and lexical exactness in estimating what the original sense of a text was to its original audience, and the coincidence of the description with how the facts really occurred. . . . Figural reading . . . was now

bound to look to historical-critical eyes like a rather preposterous historical argument, and it rapidly lost credibility.[5]

Frei portrays this loss of credibility in figural interpretation as a sort of linchpin, whose removal ensured the collapse of the biblical temporally sequenced metanarrative, and therefore of the traditional reading of biblical narrative. Frei does not argue for a return to the precritical dependence on figural interpretation, but yearns for a hermeneutic that understands biblical narrative as realistic and as having "bearing . . . in its own right on meaning and interpretation."[6]

African American hermeneutics provide a model of biblical hermeneutics that is not dependent on figural interpretation and yet continues to read Scripture with similar literal-realistic tendencies found in precritical interpretation. African Americans' unique history and development of a biblical worldview made this phenomenon possible. Allen Callahan, in *The Talking Book*, describes African Americans' first encounter with the Bible as slaves:

> It was through the human voice . . . and not the printed page, that the Bible came to inhabit the slave's inner world. The slaves' Bible became musical, even as the slaves' music became biblical. . . . Through the peculiar liturgies of the Peculiar Institution, slaves could become biblically articulate without the benefit of letters.[7]

This particular type of acculturation into the biblical world—through human voice and song—resulted in a hermeneutic heavily dependent on the biblical narrative for meaning. Stories for African Americans were literal in the precritical sense, since they were taken at face value, but they were not literal in the modern sense. When this culture was forming, the actual words on the page, the exact sequence of narratives, and even which book or testament of the Bible they were found in, were not readily accessible to slaves.[8] Therefore biblical narratives were not understood to form a temporal sequence that constructed one overarching metanarrative, but instead produced more of an organic storied world in which biblical characters and events exist simultaneously:

> In the Negro spirituals, the New does not supersede the Old. The two Testaments, Old and New, are correlated to each other. Moses is not a "type" of Jesus. Both bear witness—eternally, equally valid witness— to what God has done and is doing in the world. They are placed side

by side with others in the Bible, that "great cloud of witnesses," as the writer of the Epistle to the Hebrews puts it, who corroborate each other's testimony. Thus the remarkable juxtaposition of Moses, Mary and Martha, even Joshua and Jesus, in the earliest African-American folk songs.[9]

In this understanding of the biblical world, the process of figural interpretation, although a tool that can still be used hermeneutically, is not vital to maintaining the integrity or viability of that world.[10]

## JOHN PERKINS AND SCRIPTURE-SHAPED ACTION

Perkins demonstrates this form of literal-realistic interpretation by engaging and enrolling the audience in a worldview of Scripture through a guided reading of Jesus's encounter with the woman at the well in John 4.[11] Although described as Scripture study, this engagement begins with a description of his personal faith crisis in the 1960s: "My two white friends . . . pastors . . . had just committed suicide. . . . And I began to see some of my black friends . . . have emotional breakdowns, because the way they had packaged the truth. . . . They had taken this wonderful God and they had put into that racial culture."[12] Beginning in crisis and doubt, Perkins then moves to the text in search of some way to heal or repair the brokenness he sees before him. I will point to two especially important features of the narrative for Perkins. First, Jesus leaves the territory of the Jewish people and goes into Samaria, the territory of the woman. I do not have the time to explain the complicated relationship between the Jews and the Samaritans at this time, but suffice it to say that Jews and Samarians did not get along. So not only did Jesus enter hostile territory, but then he also asks a Samaritan woman for a drink. These two moments shape Perkins's community development philosophy. In the following excerpt, he begins by quoting Scripture, and then he sees, and demonstrates to his audience, through the narrative a new logic of community organizing unfolding before him:

Now look what happens here *"then comes a woman of Samaria to draw water. Jesus said to her, 'Give me a drink.'"* Give me a drink.
He met that woman and he loved her; he called her a Lady. He said, "You got something that I don't have. You got a bucket, and you

can get some water, and I can drink some out of your bucket." She couldn't believe that, she couldn't believe that.

So I began to see this significance: how do we do that? And out of thought came the whole idea of the three Rs of Christian Community Development.

This living among the people.

This going to the people.

This incarnated God is in her village, is in our village.

God didn't send no angel to tell us, he came himself "*and the Word was made flesh and dwelt among us.*"

We are his missionaries.

Go to the people. Live among them. Love them. Learn from them. Plan with them. Start with what they know. Live on what they have.

And the best leaders, when all is said and finished, when our task is done, we want the people to say we've done it ourselves so they have dignity. The people can solve their own problems, but they need our help, they need our technology, they need our presence; they need us there in the village with them.[13]

Literally, Perkins reperformed the process that led him to form the organization, which became and continues to be a living token of his reading habit of Scripture. He did not make disclaimers, apologize, or ask permission, but gently enjoined his audience, regardless of their own beliefs about Scripture or even Christianity, to inhabit the Scripture with him as a necessary process in order to understand the community development organization.[14] Moreover, Perkins does not depend on the use of figural language to make sense of either the coherence of Scripture or Perkins's own place within the biblical world. Instead, he shares the context of his first encounter with the text and proceeds through the narrative line by line, interacting with the text the entire time. He interjected with thoughts, filled in the gaps of the text, pointed out significant verses, and touched upon experiences in his own life. Perkins demonstrates a playful flexibility with the text, and yet this is the same text that continues to fund the logic of the community development model he put into place over fifty years ago. The text's meaning became the interaction between the words on the page and Perkins's commentary. And yet Perkins fully engages with Scripture, and this engagement shapes his habits and the habits of those in his community, of which the audience has temporarily become a part.

# AFRICAN AMERICAN COMMUNITIES OF FAITH AS LOCI FOR LIVED POSTLIBERAL THEOLOGY

Through both historical warrants and the contemporary example of John Perkins's presentation, this essay provides evidence that literal-realistic reading tendencies exist within the African American hermeneutics tradition. It is my understanding that one criticism of postcritical scholarship is that although scholars in this field desire to transform reading practices and therefore overall habits of the Christian church, it has remained mainly an academic endeavor. And yet even though Frei's colleague George Lindbeck recognized the classic pattern of reading as most likely occurring in black churches (based on the testimony of his students, not his own experiences), most efforts to locate literal-realistic scriptural reading habits have been in Western primordial scriptural reading traditions.[15] The argument of this chapter is not to replace the efforts to study classical reading habits, but to consider adding to this inquiry the study of African American hermeneutics. I hope postliberal scholars will accept my modest proposal that inquiry into this tradition would be not only beneficial for their reparative project within the church but also serve as a resource for modes of *faithful* and *public* engagement resulting in living tokens of scriptural reading habits such as community development programs that ultimately work for the repair of the world.

## NOTES

1. John Perkins, "John M. Perkins: American Evangelicalism and the Practices of Peace (From the Spring Institute for Lived Theology, April 23, 2009)," *The Project on Lived Theology*, http://www.livedtheology.org/silt2009.html.

2. Hans W. Frei, *The Eclipse of Biblical Narrative: A Study in Eighteenth and Nineteenth Century Hermeneutics* (New Haven, Conn.: Yale University Press, 1974), 2.

3. Frei, *Eclipse of Biblical Narrative*.

4. Frei, *Eclipse of Biblical Narrative*.

5. Frei, *Eclipse of Biblical Narrative*, 7.

6. Frei, *Eclipse of Biblical Narrative*, 16.

7. Allen Dwight Callahan, *The Talking Book: African Americans and the Bible* (New Haven, Conn.: Yale University Press, 2006), 12.

8. Callahan, *Talking Book*, 11. Callahan states: "Slaves were rarely introduced to the Bible through the medium of the printed page. For many slaves biblical literacy began with spontaneous aural memorization and oral recall. Slaves mimicked what they heard

in sermons from white preachers and readers, and in repeating what they heard they often improvised on it."

9. Callahan, *Talking Book*, 189.

10. I am not making the claim here that a basic function of figuration, or of relating two situations or figures between two separate narratives, is not essential to the establishment of a larger narrative web or organic worldview, but rather what is not crucial to African American hermeneutics is the idea that a later event somehow is a fulfillment of an earlier event and *therefore* fills out the meaning of the first event more completely based on chronological ordering and a futuristic bias.

11. I am not making the claim that John Perkins is the "perfect" or only representative of African American hermeneutics. In fact, I would expect others who would claim an African American hermeneutic practice to have a different take on John 4. The greater point is to offer one example of African American hermeneutics, that of John Perkins's reading of John 4, and its strong literal-realistic tendencies, thereby making the case through evidence that inquiry into African American hermeneutics is worth further study for those interested in facilitating more the growth of postliberal scriptural reading habits in Christian communities.

12. Perkins, "John M. Perkins."

13. Perkins, "John M. Perkins"; "CCDA Philosophy, Christian Community Development Association," n.d., http://www.ccda.org/philosophy.

14. The context of this presentation was not a religious service. Although most of the members of the audience would hold some Christian affiliation, this was not a homogeneous gathering. The group was made up of people from a variety of denominations with a diversity of beliefs regarding Scripture and Christian faith.

15. George Lindbeck, "The Gospel's Uniqueness: Election and Untranslatability," *Modern Theology* 13, no. 4 (1997): 431.

# Prophetic Ministry, the Prosperity Gospel, and Gentrification

*Cheryl J. Sanders*

THIS IS AN EDITED TRANSCRIPT OF A PUBLIC PRESENTATION AND DIS-
cussion that took place at the University of Virginia on April 23, 2009, as
part of the Spring Institute for Lived Theology.

## A RECONCILIATION TRIUMVIRATE

There is a book that I think many of you are familiar with: *Divided by Faith*.
In that book, Christian Smith and Michael Emerson designate John Perkins
as one of the founding fathers of the reconciliation movement in evangelical
Christianity, and he is named as one of three black evangelical leaders who
formed what I would call a reconciliation triumvirate: those three men are
Tom Skinner, Sam Hines, and John Perkins.[1]

As I address my topic, which is John Perkins and the social witness of
the African American church, I want to begin by locating Perkins within
this reconciliation movement. Tom Skinner was from New York; Sam Hines
was from Jamaica by way of Washington, D.C.; and John Perkins was from
Mississippi. These were three prominent black leaders who participated in
what Smith and Emerson regard as a failed experiment to convince white
evangelicals to practice reconciliation. Skinner was the evangelist; Hines
was the pastor; Perkins was the witness, the storyteller, the Bible teacher,
the community organizer. Perkins is the only one of the three who survives
and continues to thrive in reconciliation ministry. Tom Skinner died in his
fifties; Sam Hines died at the age of sixty-five. In both cases I think we can
say they died prematurely, but all the more reason to be thankful for the
fruitful longevity of John Perkins, because he has lived long enough, I think,
hopefully to outlive the verdict of Smith and Emerson: that the reconciliation movement failed.

I knew all three of these men, but I knew Sam Hines the best, because he was my pastor for twenty-five years, and I succeeded him when I assumed the pastoral leadership of the Third Street Church of God in Washington, D.C. I knew Tom Skinner to be a gifted evangelist, one of the few preachers I've ever known who can hold an audience for two and a half hours of preaching, with people at the edge of their seats, as opposed to falling off of their seats or vacating their seats. He addressed the claims of the gospel of Jesus Christ in evangelistic crusades and conventions. He specifically addressed the relevance of the gospel to the call to Black Power and liberation. His testimony was that he had been a gang member—a gangbanger—and he had a conversion experience, and he preached the gospel out of that journey.

Hines brought preaching and pastoral care to the work of reconciliation and the context of the local congregation. He excelled. He was an excellent exegetical preacher, but he also excelled in forging relationships and acquiring resources to support urban ministry partnerships. The hallmark of his ministry at Third Street was the urban prayer breakfast, which was a daily program of ministry and outreach among the poor and homeless residents of Washington, D.C. The church is located right in the center of the city. Washington is shaped like a diamond, with the Capitol in the center. We are about one mile north of the Capitol, so we are right in the middle of the city. And there, for about twenty-five years or more, we would have a breakfast outreach ministry from Monday through Friday. At 7 A.M. there would be praise and worship; there would be proclamation of the gospel, a call to discipleship that specifically reached out to the poor. Because the street population ministered to far exceeded the small membership of the congregation, sometimes we had so many people that we would have the fellowship hall on the lower level filled with chairs, and then we would have the sanctuary full of people waiting to come down and be served.

There is one thing I can commend: honor the memory of President Ronald Reagan, because during the Reagan years (that was the high-water mark of our ministry), so many people were turned out of mental institutions and other places that had been their place of safety. They were turned out to the streets, and those were the years when we had the highest attendance. It is still a mystery to me how President Reagan gets to be the hero of evangelical Christians, but that is one thing he contributed to our ministry: through his policies, he gave us more people to feed.

We fed more people than we had members, and the only way to do that was to enter into ministry partnerships. We fed about 5,000 people over a three-week period. We had to have ministry partnerships in order to sustain the day-to-day tasks of preaching, leading worship, cooking, cleanup, security. We had people from far and near who came; they saw what we were doing, and they would come and participate.

Pastor Hines began this ministry on the basis of a friendship. Perkins has spoken about an important first step, if you're serious about the ministry of reconciliation, which is to get into an interpersonal relationship with someone in another group. For Hines, it was Pastor Louis Evans, who died not too long ago. He pastored the National Presbyterian Church in Washington, D.C., which was, shall we say, on the "other part of town." To this day, the National Presbyterian Church remains a valued ministry partner in terms of volunteers and resources to support our outreach ministry.

In the summer of 2007 we had to suspend the breakfast. It became too expensive, and it was really demanding for our limited number of volunteers, not to mention the fact that our church had undergone a renovation. Our kitchen was torn out in 2003, and we are still trying to rebuild and expand to reestablish: if you can imagine a church without a kitchen, that is who we are. So you are hard-pressed to do this kind of ministry if you don't have a kitchen. We do have a full-time social worker on staff, and we do have a drop-in center, a basement apartment, and a townhouse that we own on the block. Our social worker's salary is paid in part by the National Presbyterian Church. He is able to do support groups, Bible study, and referrals for the poor on a drop-in basis during the week. We also sponsor community dinners at Thanksgiving and Christmas, with volunteers and contributions from a broad range of denominations and races coming together to celebrate the holidays with the homeless and with our neighbors who are housed in the community.

Our latest endeavor is a Sunday morning community worship service, which we just started on Easter Sunday, a one-hour service from 8:30 to 9:30 A.M., where we serve a light continental breakfast—coffee, fruit, and pastries—and we invite people to participate in the worship, to listen and respond to the preached word in a relaxed atmosphere. The work that Hines started at Third Street does continue, as we are still endeavoring to make a difference in the community. Tom Skinner's legacy lives on in Washington, D.C., in the work of Barbara Williams-Skinner. Barbara is also an alumna of the Howard University School of Divinity; after Tom's death she enrolled in the Master of Divinity program and went on to earn her Doctor of Ministry degree. She runs the Skinner Leadership Foundation, with a significant campus ministry presence at Howard University, including a chaplain and a staff of assistants who are doing leadership development with Christian students at Howard.

I also wanted to mention a person whose story is told in *Divided By Faith*, and that is Curtiss Paul DeYoung, who wrote an autobiography entitled *Homecoming: A "White" Man's Journey through Harlem to Jerusalem.*[2] Curtiss's sojourn includes receiving an undergraduate degree from the Church of God University in Anderson, Indiana. The son of a Church of God pastor, he came to Washington, D.C., to work in urban ministry under Pastor Hines. He fell in love with a young black woman on the first Sunday that he came to church, and he decided he was not going back to Indiana. He transferred to Howard, earned his Master of Divinity degree there, and did his field education internship at Third Street Church of God.

Curtiss has written a number of books on reconciliation, and he has established a department of reconciliation studies at Bethel University in St. Paul, Minnesota, where he is professor of reconciliation studies. I would just say that Curtiss's emphasis, his focus, his stamina in this reconciliation ministry are largely credited to these three men: Skinner, Hines, and Perkins.


## PROPHETIC MINISTRY, THE PROSPERITY GOSPEL, AND GENTRIFICATION

As the focus for my presentation today, I'd like to speak about the impact John Perkins has had on the social witness of the African American churches with respect to three specific concerns: prophetic ministry, the prosperity gospel, and gentrification.

I have been intentional about using the term "churches" rather than "church." There's a book entitled *Your Spirits Walk Beside Us: The Politics of Black Religion*; the author is a historian at the University of Pennsylvania, Barbara Savage. The subject of the book is black religion and politics.[3] In that book, Savage makes a case for always referring to the black or African American church in the plural, in deference to the diversity of traditions, practices, and denominations represented among black Christian congregations. In her book, Savage analyzes the Jeremiah Wright/Barack Obama controversy, when Senator Obama had completely denounced and severed his ties with the Trinity United Church of Christ. Savage makes the point that Jeremiah Wright does not represent the black church in the singular, and that as scholars, we need to think a little more broadly about the black church when we speak about who is included in the black church, or who represents the black church, or what is the voice of the black church, or what kind of preaching goes on in the black church.

I want also to affirm the language I have heard from Perkins this week when he speaks of the "so-called black church." I like that. "So-called." It reminds me of the Honorable Elijah Muhammad, back in the 1960s, who used to write and speak about the "so-called Negroes." But what I hear from Perkins is that there's really no such thing as the black church, or the white church, because the real church belongs to God. We bring ethnicity and culture and denomination and all these distinctions to our corporate Christian witness, but I'm not sure we want to privilege our race or color or culture or history as categories by which to name our churches. Should the church be named for the God who rules it, or for the people in it? And who does the church belong to? To God, or to certain categories, or groups, or classes of people?

Let me say a word about the prophetic ministry, the prosperity gospel, and gentrification. By *prophetic ministry*, I mean the proclamation and the implementation of the spoken Word of God. That assumes that the prophet has heard from God, in order to speak from God, but prophetic ministry is not just proclamation, it is implementation. Certainly John Perkins models this in his stories, his testimonies, his books, and his life as a community organizer. The Christian Community Development Association (CCDA) gatherings equip, empower, and encourage people to do transformative prophetic ministries. And when people say—and I hear this all the time—that the black church is silent on the issues of the day, they are not hearing what John Perkins is saying every day. I have already mentioned Jeremiah Wright. It is like when the black church does speak, it is saying the wrong thing. But it is one extreme or the other: either the black church is saying the wrong thing and cursing and saying all this terrible stuff about our nation, or it is saying nothing. Then all the rest of the discourse that goes on in-between goes unheard. But John Perkins implements, proclaims, and illustrates prophetic ministry.

In thinking about the prosperity gospel, Perkins's own narrative of his ascent from poverty to purposeful prosperity has been focused on giving and empowering others. I wrote a book back in 1995, *Empowerment Ethics for a Liberated People: A Path to African American Social Transformation*, which was my effort to give a constructive intellectual response to black theology.[4] In that book I argue that you have not really helped or transformed an individual until that individual is positioned to give back. You can feed them, you can get them a job, you can get them a place to stay, you can get them to join your church, you can get them a life-changing encounter with Jesus Christ, but until they are giving back, you have not closed the loop. So that ought to be our goal in our transformative ministries: that we empower people to give back.

Perkins is critical of black pastors and televangelists who wrongfully divide the Word. The Bible says you are supposed to rightfully divide the Word of truth (2 Tim. 2:15). The Word is still true, but they wrongfully divide it, in terms that maximize profit rather than prophecy, and they promote consumerism over the cross. Prosperity is biblical. Perkins is correct in his condemnation of white and black evangelicals whose own endorsement of materialism and excess leaves them no leverage for addressing the current economic crisis, not to mention an understanding of its root causes. If you seek to analyze or respond to something, you need to get at the root causes, but some of us as Christians cannot get to the root causes because that mirror shines too brightly for us to see our own reflections. And there's a mirror down there when we're digging. There's a mirror, and we don't want to see that image in the mirror, and we just decide to stop digging, because we're going to undermine our own value system in order to responsibly bring a critique of where we are and where we're headed.

We can agree that we do not want the prosperity gospel. But what are you doing with your wealth? How are you reinvesting? How do you go about doing that? I think we get these questions from John Perkins, and I thank him for that.

Third and finally, I want to say a word about *gentrification*. At the Third Street Church of God, we are on Gentrification Boulevard. The Capitol is on a hill in Washington, D.C. As you would expect, the senators, the congresspeople, and the lobbyists have nice condos and row houses in the area. It is not a huge residential area, because there are a lot of federal buildings as well, but you expect it to be an upscale area. Georgetown, all the way to the far west edge of the city, has a reputation of being very affluent, with shops. If the president does go Christmas shopping—see in Washington, we are obsessed with media coverage of the president, so when the president goes to buy a Christmas gift, it is a press event—well, the president is going to go to Georgetown to get a nice boutique gift for his wife.

Fifty years ago Georgetown was a ghetto. Today the only vestiges of black presence in Georgetown are a few little black churches just barely hanging on. Other than those churches, Georgetown is completely gentrified to the point where even the memory is erased. Gentrification moved from

Georgetown, east to Dupont Circle, then Logan Circle, and then Capitol Hill. The last thing in the space from Capitol Hill to Georgetown that would prevent an unbroken corridor of gentrification is Shaw, the community in which we live. Now Shaw is rapidly gentrifying. Once the Shaw community becomes completely gentrified, there will be a solid corridor of gentrification from Georgetown to Capitol Hill. What does that mean? Where do those people, who are renters for the most part, go? Well they go to the suburbs, or some other neighborhood, but they are not going to be able to afford to stay.

We commend the notions of relocation, redistribution, and reconciliation, as we ought to do, but because of where I sit as pastor of a small Holiness congregation in the middle of a rapidly changing neighborhood in the center of the city, I must ask myself the question: what entitles anyone to relocate to our neighborhood? I have to ask that of anybody. If you are white, if you are Asian, if you are black: what entitles you to relocate yourself to our neighborhood?

The most obvious manifestation of transformation in the Shaw community is the renovation of row houses by the moneyed gentry. Gentrification is done by the gentry. The gentry are the landowners, the people who have the resources, who have the intelligence, who have the connections to buy property, to renovate property, and fix it as they want it to be, so that they can live in it. The affluent, highly educated, professionally employed or comfortably retired, gay or straight couples and individuals who have decided that Shaw is a desirable place to live. So they purchase and rehab their houses. They all seem to have dogs and blogs. And they fight crime through the neighborhood associations. Today in Shaw, we have—it is almost like the old days of racial segregation—the white community association, and we have the black community association. I try to go to both of them.

What does it mean for a black congregation to be a good neighbor in a changing community? That is a question that I have to live with and wrestle with every day. How do we preach the gospel to affluent white people who do not think they need to hear about salvation? And if they do, they certainly do not need to hear it from somebody who looks like me. What kind of good news do we have to offer to white people who move into our community? Can we speak their language? Can we comprehend their values? Can we reinvent ourselves as a church to meet their demands without offending their cultural and intellectual sensibilities? What does it mean to meet them as they are? That sounds good; when you are trying to evangelize people, don't you meet them as they are? But what does that mean when we're talking about white people, to meet them as they are? Do the principles of mutuality and reciprocity that we see demonstrated in Jesus's outreach to the Samaritan woman apply to them?

Read John 4 about Jesus and the Samaritan woman, particularly the part where Jesus is tired and he's hungry and the disciples go into town and he sits at the well and he asks the woman for a drink of water. Who was ministering to whom? He was the one that was thirsty, not her. Their whole conversation grows out of Jesus asking her for a drink. However, for many of us, our mindset is that we are the ones that have the glass of water. And the people we're trying to minister to, we're trying to offer them our glass of water. But if you are trying to put yourself in the place of Jesus (of course we all want to do that), then you are the one who is thirsty. And you're the one who's asking for an intervention.

That is what I mean by the principle of mutuality and reciprocity. I think if you are going to relocate, if you're going to reconcile, if you're going to redistribute, you have to have a consciousness of mutuality and reciprocity. You have to be conscious that those people you are helping are not your mission project; instead, they are *people* who have lives and aspirations, and they just might have the glass of water that you need if you will acknowledge the mutuality in ministry. I have more to say about that in my book *Ministry at the Margins: The Prophetic Mission of Women, Youth & the Poor.*[5]

The Samaritan woman represents for me one way of answering all these questions. I know I have raised more questions than I have given you answers, but that is why we are here, to have a conversation. In the face of this gentrification and its social impact on the black churches, how do we make our way? I know for a fact that there are many black congregations in our city that have made the decision that we are just going to move to the suburbs. In Washington, the move to the suburbs generally means a move to Prince George's County, because Prince George's County is home to the largest and the most affluent megachurches in the country, maybe rivaled by the suburbs of Atlanta. So it is like, "Let's just forget about the city, and go to the suburbs." I have a ministry colleague who attempted to do that and ended up congregationally homeless because the financing failed on the new $31 million construction in the suburbs, and they sold their church in Logan, so now they are just renting space in a school to worship. So it is a real crisis for us in the city. Our church has been located in that community since 1927. So we have a long-standing presence in the community, and we have an ongoing commitment to be good neighbors in that community. I am just trying to figure out what that means given gentrification and the changing demographics of our city.

**Audience member:** Bob Lupton in Atlanta has a chapter in one of his recent books called "Gentrification with Justice," where he talks about the fact that gentrification is something that we need to recognize as a reality.[6] Those with power and influence are now returning to the cities. Lupton says on the one hand we do need to recognize the gravity of this and the fact that it is threatening to the poor, but at the same time, gentrification could be a boon, as resources pour back into these long-abandoned city centers. He says, let's not throw gentrification out altogether; let's talk about how we can harness it and use it justly, that's his phrase, gentrification with justice. What would gentrification with justice look like in your neighborhood?

**Cheryl Sanders:** That is an important question. I think that gentrification is probably inevitable. I mean you can rant and rave, but you cannot stop it, I will acknowledge that. I don't see eye to eye with Bob Lupton on the whole project, but I do agree that there ought to be some way to recapture or inject a justice formula into gentrification that would include things like requiring some kind of balance of affordable housing. If a developer is going to come in and do a condominium, or a row of houses, a certain percentage could be sold or valued at $75,000 versus $300,000.

Another aspect in Washington is the notion of historic preservation. Historic preservation is a good thing, but it can be the devil if you are the one whose property is on the historic register, because it restricts what you can do. In our case, neighbors put our church building on the historic register without our knowledge as an aggressive act against us. That just complicates the challenge of being a good neighbor, when you know that your neighbors have done those kinds of things. After all, they are gentry, so they are intelligent, connected, and resourceful. I am not sure where the justice discourse gets you in this situation, but I am not going to fight fire with fire. If there are dirty politics, to me it is not a solution to try to do the sort of old school, old boy kind of political strategizing. Although I have people saying, "Well you know you can't get anything done in Washington unless you do this, that, and the other thing." My response is, "Can we just have a system that's fair and square? Where everyone gets treated not based on who he or she knows, but on the merits of the project?"

I think there are a lot of places where a consciousness of the importance of justice as central to the Christian agenda is a way that we can be good neighbors. My issue with Lupton's approach is that he still leaves unanswered the question: who entitled you to relocate there in the first place? And that entitlement thing, you know that's a race thing still.

**Audience member:** I sense a tension between the message to move in with the people, and at the same time the necessity of questioning entitlement. Arnie Graf, who is one of the founding members of the Industrial Areas Foundation (IAF), suggested to me that one of the paradigms they use in community organizing is that you look at the world as it is, and then you look at the world as it ought to be, and what negotiates that tension is justice. Am I hearing correctly then that the real word for Christian witness is discernment? And that simply means our capacity to sense entitlement from a calling and not just trading places—with white folks moving out of the city and into the suburbs, and vice versa—but a sense of calling among ourselves, where this sense of beloved community is literally being put together by this Spirit of God?

**Cheryl Sanders:** Dr. Perkins answered that question very eloquently this morning when he said that relocation is a calling, not a mandate. So don't do it, don't even try it—at least that's what I heard him say—unless you are specifically called. You cannot argue with calling. I think you are right. It does require discernment, but discernment does not always have to be an individual gift. Discernment can occur in conversation and dialogue and in community, and even in community with the people who will become your new neighbors, if you decide to relocate. That is if you are relocating with purpose. Most of us pick a place to live based on the schools or the cost or the proximity to other things that we have to do, but if you're being intentional about relocating to a community with the intention to transform it, then you just have to tread very lightly. Jesus passed through Samaria; he did not move in. He discerned he was not called to move in, but while he was there, he had his impact. But some of us might have missed the calling, and we should be passing through instead of moving in. Others of us need to stay where we are. But it's a calling. So you are exactly right, discernment is an important part of that.

**Audience member:** I am trying to figure out how John Perkins's life and the three Rs relate to your very different but also challenging ministry context, and also trying to think about the story of Jesus at the well. I think I understand how Perkins is using it in his context, but I'm trying to understand if the way he's using it translates to your context. One of the things that strikes me is the commitment to reconciliation. If Perkins can be reconciled to folk who nearly beat him to death, you can be reconciled to your neighbors who have attacked you with a historic preservation registry. Also, relocation: Perkins relocated, you are also being relocated. That is to say your location is changing, but you're called to stay there so that's a kind of relocation. So how do you "be" the gospel, how do you "be" Jesus in that context? The way Perkins uses the story of Jesus at the well is that, rather than approaching the woman and saying, "I've got water for you," Jesus goes to her with his need. Will that translate to your situation? What would that mean in your context?

**Cheryl Sanders:** Well, first let me say that I am not John Perkins. I have bent over backwards in some cases, trying to work things out with our neighbors, but I really wrestle—and I am not just talking about me personally—with the extent of our flexibility as an institution. In my experience as an African American, why is it that we are the ones who always have to adjust to what white people want to do? I have to incorporate that question in order to respond to what you are saying. That is the history of my people. We always have to adjust to what white people want to do. So I say, when is it my turn, to tell them, "Can't y'all just adjust a little bit to what we're trying to do?" Or can we work together, can we inhabit this space together, or is it always that you are entitled and I'm the one that just has to figure out, "Oh, how can I sacrifice myself so that they can be happy and we can live together?"

Some of them have been very amenable; I don't want to generalize. Some of our neighbors have been very graceful and gracious and we have worked together, and others have been a pain in the neck. I don't want to generalize, but I also have to be very careful to protect the self-esteem of the people that I represent. I'm not talking about pride or ego; I'm saying that if people have been accustomed to being run over by other people who feel they're entitled, justice says to me I'm not going to take that anymore.

I will give you an example of a situation I had just to illustrate the dynamics of reconciliation: I went to a community meeting at another church, and while we were at the meeting there was a man (he was a gay white man), and when he found out I was the pastor at Third Street, he just launched into this tirade. He got in my face in this meeting room full of people, saying, "Your church did this, and you did this, and when Pastor Hines was there . . ." and so forth, and he just went on and on, and I just sort of sat there and took it. Being a Christian, right? I ran out of cheeks to turn.

As it turned out the next day there was a meeting about HIV/AIDS ministry, a whole other meeting. I was sitting at a table and then this same guy came in the door and said, "May I sit with you and have lunch?" And I was like, "Oh, sure." The first thing that came out of his mouth was, "I want to apologize for the way I spoke to you yesterday, but I need for you to understand the anger that we felt when such and such a thing happened twenty years ago, and my partner was dying of AIDS." Because I did not respond to him at the time, I did not match my anger and my tone of voice with his, we were able to come to an understanding. We are flexible to a point, but we have to maintain some sense of dignity and presence, and not just say, "Okay, you're the ones that have what we need, so just tell us what you need for us to have."

I will say this: I continue to look for different ways to communicate. For example, I said already: we have a white—it's not lily-white—gentrified neighborhood association, and we have worked very hard to build relationships with them on their own turf. We come to the meeting because we're in the neighborhood, and we share information, when we had a community day year before last, we had a dog show, because they all have dogs. So we said let's have a dog contest. The dog that was most obedient, the prettiest dog, the ugliest dog, and we gave out prizes. And you know, it was an amazing thing—the dogs all got along! The dogs had the best time. And the people brought their dogs, and the dogs had so much fun, so we said this is a good thing. We had fun with the dogs. So when I say dogs and blogs, I'm not just joking, that's their life. Those things are important to them.

So I say, if that's important to you, then let's try to incorporate that, because that's not something—you know, we don't bring our dogs to church, but some of our members brought their dogs to be in the contest, and we had a lot of fun with that. So we try to find places for conversation and to establish rapport, but to have them in a space where we can preach the gospel—that's what I'm trying to figure out how to do. Because they don't relate to the way we worship or the message that we preach. When I have some of them who will come to the church—I have a few of them, they'll come, but they kind of stay at the margin, they don't come in and get too deeply involved in what we're doing. But we try really hard at least. I think every church, regardless of whether it is urban, rural, black, or white, ought to have an open door; so that anybody who comes there, even if they don't understand your worship or your language, doesn't feel when they walk through the door, "Oh, you made a mistake when you came here, you meant to go to the church around the corner." And so we try to maintain an open door, but that's not enough.

## NOTES

1. Michael O. Emerson and Christian Smith, Divided by Faith: Evangelical Religion and the Problem of Race in America (New York: Oxford University Press, 2000), 52–54.

2. Curtiss Paul DeYoung, Homecoming: A "White" Man's Journey through Harlem to Jerusalem (Minneapolis: Jezi Press, 2009).

3. Barbara Dianne Savage, Your Spirits Walk Beside Us: The Politics of Black Religion (Cambridge, Mass.: Belknap Press of Harvard University Press, 2008).

4. Cheryl Jeanne Sanders, Empowerment Ethics for a Liberated People: A Path to African American Social Transformation (Minneapolis: Fortress Press, 1995).

5. Cheryl Jeanne Sanders, Ministry at the Margins: The Prophetic Mission of Women, Youth & the Poor (Downers Grove, Ill.: InterVarsity Press, 1997).

6. Robert D. Lupton, Renewing the City: Reflections on Community Development and Urban Renewal (Downers Grove, Ill.: InterVarsity Press, 2005), 119–130.

Part III

# RECONCILIATION

*Continuing the Journey*

†

# Communities of Resurrection and the Transformation of Bodies

*Chris Rice*

MUCH HAS BEEN MADE, AND RIGHTLY SO, OF JOHN PERKINS AS A GRASS-roots prophet of justice for the poor and marginalized. Yet whose justice? Reaching toward what end or purpose? During the American civil rights movement, Will Campbell argued in *Race and the Renewal of the Church* that in a world of racism and poverty, the church had adopted a largely humanitarian approach around freedom, justice, and democracy. "These things are good," said Campbell, "but are they the most basic, most distinctive concern of the church?" To be true to the church's own nature something "far more radical" was needed. "The sin of the church is not that it has not reformed society, but that it has not realized self-renewal," wrote Campbell. "Its sin is that it has not repented. Without repentance there cannot be renewal."[1]

In this chapter I illuminate the significance of John Perkins's life and ministry for answering this challenge of something "far more radical"—namely, that the true end of justice across social divides is a call to conversion toward becoming new people in a community of friendship, how this happens through a deeply embodied life of repentance and grace that is local, and what this has to say about the mission and ministry of the church in a divided world. I discuss Perkins renowned three Rs (relocation, reconciliation, and redistribution) as spiritual works of bodily conversion across social divides to unlearn habits of division, self-sufficiency, superiority, and inferiority toward a new future of mutuality and friendship. This is, I argue, not only a more radical but a more beautiful vision of our identities, loyalties, and habits being reformed into God's "new we." Seeing this "new we" as the end of justice in bodily and communal form offers a powerful new local and global missional paradigm for a U.S. Christian church that (in Perkins's words) has "over-evangelized the world too lightly."[2]

# JP AND THE SIGNIFICANCE OF JESUS-SHAPED PHYSICALITY

"JP" or "Grandpa." That's what my wife, Donna, our children, and I affectionately call him in the Rice family. I met him in 1980 when I was a student at Middlebury College in Vermont. After hearing his strange Mississippi story, matched by the lines in his face and earthiness of his manner, my life was never the same. At the end of his Vermont visit I drove JP and his assistant to the airport. It was early morning, and I had just rolled out of bed. It was February, it was freezing, and my car had no heat and a hole in the floor. JP was undeterred. He flipped open his Bible and did a spontaneous, energetic devotional. It was as if he was preaching to 2,000—not two. The powerful *physicality* of JP's presence over those days made a profound impression on me.

That day in 1980, social justice was at the margins of American evangelicalism. It isn't anymore, and JP's teaching and ministry were at the heart of that transformation. Today a whole new generation of restless young Christians take for granted what was fresh and new to me as a young Christian.

Two years after that airport drive, I was in Jackson, Mississippi, at JP's Voice of Calvary Ministries, volunteering for six months with no inkling that I would stay seventeen years. The community there had been abandoned by the white church when black folks moved in. It was abandoned by the black church when many black folks moved up and out. What JP said—what he's kept saying all these years—is that a particular kind of infected American Christianity, a virus that does not discriminate racially, is captive to individualism, selfishness, and greed. This captivity can only be unlearned over time. One place of conversion is abandoned communities at the margins, and that little inner-city zip code in west Jackson was a testing ground for a Christian antidote. That's where we would learn a new kind of Christianity, a hope hammered out through a deep and intimate kind of *physicality* shared with strangers and with God—locally, daily, eating together, singing together, worshipping together, working together across deep divides like race and class.

What I learned is that this vision was in fact a very big idea, because in light of our peculiar American Christian virus—what Martin Luther King Jr. called America's "giant triplets" of racism, materialism, and militarism[3]—this was an antidote with power to break the virus. It had power not only *against* but power *for*, to form people into the likeness of the body of Christ in this history *here and now*.

JP's son Spencer told a critical part of the story JP doesn't tell, which adds to the chemistry of the antidote. Many know about JP's beating in 1970 by white state police in a jail cell in Brandon, Mississippi. What Spencer described was how in the long months after the beating—after JP's daughter saw him in the hospital room and ran out saying, "I hate white people, I will always hate white people"—JP wrestled with God. Those days of spiritual pain matched his physical pain. Why bother? Why not give up on white folks? Why not just work with black folks and turn nationalist? We easily forget how many who are oppressed understandably do just that, how many of those scarred by injustice and the difficult struggle for change end up bitter, angry, in despair, or mimic the way of the oppressor as they gain social power.

In other words, the "quiet revolution" of beloved community is grounded in a *conversion*, a conversion through an inseparable relationship between a physicality of hope and a physicality of suffering that is shaped by an encounter with the physicality of the crucified and forgiving Lord. On a hospital bed after the beating, it was a vision of seeing the *body* of Jesus on the cross crying out, "Father forgive them; for they know not what they do" (Luke 23:34), that became JP's critical turning point toward the new vision that birthed the interracial Voice of Calvary community.[4]

If a vision of the Lord of history forgiving the unforgivable is what ultimately turned JP toward his unique prophetic voice within American history, it was the apostle Paul's startling claim about Jesus's body that sustained JP's ministry over the next forty years: "who for the *joy* set before him he [Jesus] endured the cross" (Heb. 12:2). If JP is anything in the midst of his tireless activism living in America's most marginalized communities for over fifty years, he is joyful. Just watch him bust into a fresh watermelon, or tend his roses and tomatoes. He loves few things more than overseeing the rehabbing of a house, striding through the rooms and telling you his plans. We once sent a young Duke Divinity graduate student to work with JP for a summer. His first morning someone said JP wanted to see him, so he quickly changed into nice clothes and went outside. As soon as JP laid eyes on him he said, "Boy, get out of those clothes! We gonna build a fence today!"

JP's witness, with the scars of Brandon still on his body, calls us to remember the wounds of Jesus's own resurrected body, wounds that did not disappear (John 20:27). The peace of the crucified, risen Christ tore down the dividing wall of hostility, turning power upside down. True peace disturbs the power of the way things are. We prefer ending poverty without repentance. World peace without carrying a cross. In JP's body and story is a deep intimacy between dying and resurrection. We cannot choose between the two. His life and his body demand our response. To be a Christian is a constant showdown between our shallow desires and God's deeper vision of transformation, beauty, and joy.

## THE THREE Rs AS A TRINITY OF DISCIPLINES OF CONVERSION

The profound mixture of sacrifice, hope, and joy in JP's journey is a physicality that illuminates the DNA of his "far more radical" witness. A danger today is sexiness about social justice. In many circles justice and ending poverty have become popular, even cool. But without his costly, local, deeply embedded story of daily life and conversion shared with other companions over time, there *is* no JP, no new reality of beloved community, and no powerful social alternative that the communities of the Christian Community Development Association (CCDA) embody.[5] His popular "three Rs" must not be sentimentalized or abstracted from his explicit story of pain and hope within the Mississippi narrative.

Something far more radical is at stake with the three Rs than a strategy to address poverty and injustice. These are not techniques or how-to's with the "privileged" as the subject and solution, and "poverty" or "the poor" as the object. The new world created is not one of helpers and beneficiaries but of sharing life and sharing power. It is a world of deep enough relationship to extract the residues of pain and privilege from one another, and to also extract a deeper joy and gratitude.[6] Seen this way, these are three social disciplines with abundant power over time to bring communion and kinship between what is fragmented, to alter participants at their core, and through this to birth transcendent social signs of what a deeper hope looks like in contexts of historical division.[7] Yet to go further, these are three *spiritual works of conversion* through which captivity to King's trinity of sins could be gradually broken. Relocation as a shared life between "relocaters" and "remainers" at the socioeconomic margins;[8] reconciliation expressed in a shared social space pursuing truth and hospitality between hostile groups; redistribution as gifts willingly exchanged in mutuality between rich and poor—these became transformational practices that gradually detached desires away from the viruses of ethnocentrism, privilege, endless individual consumption, and the default mode of violence for addressing difference

*dense, but well said.*

and conflict. This is how the three Rs become works of conversion that, over time, put racial hostilities to death and form people who gradually unlearn cultural self-sufficiency, division, superiority, and inferiority.

This unlikely way of formation (or catechesis) evokes what theologian John Swinton has described as a process of "transvaluation" in relationship to support people working with people with disabilities:

> As we have spent time with careers and support workers, one of the things that has struck us is the way in which *people's lives and world-views have been radically transformed through their encounters with people who have profound developmental disabilities.* In encountering people with profound developmental disabilities in friendship, *people's lives are changed, their priorities are reshaped and their vision of God and humanness are altered at their very core.* What we are discovering is the occurrence of a process of transvaluation within which personal encounter with people with profound developmental disabilities initiates a movement towards a radically new system of valuing.[9]

*Transvaluation* describes nothing less than a journey of deep transformation that occurs through a profound new encounter across a line of deep difference, with an openness to hope and surprise. Such an encounter thus becomes a gift where we come to understand how little we know, see how shallow our desires are, and are formed into something like what the apostle Paul calls "a new creation" (2 Cor. 5). Through this a miracle in everyday life occurs: deep common journeys with strangers are transformed into a school of conversion, and we discover that *there are some things God can teach us only by relocating our bodies to strange ground and fresh encounters there.* Again it is crucial to not romanticize such a profound altering of lives, priorities, and worldviews. L'Arche founder Jean Vanier once described how the closer he came to people with disabilities his own anger and desire to control intensified, calling him to deeper conversion. Vanier went on to speak of a "spirituality of loss," which is necessary for such a transformation. "What are we willing to lose in order to gain the 'better' that God's new creation is? Those who come to help the poor only stay when they become poor themselves."[10]

This is a very different tonality from versions of peace and reconciliation without physicality and sacrifice. The African American and white cofounders of what became New Song church and ministries in inner-city

Baltimore became convinced a "fourth R" was needed, *repentance*, and that this "R" should in fact precede the others.[11] They eventually discovered that their shared history in their neighborhood had become ground for seeing, naming, and confessing their own sin and the sins of a city that intentionally created excluded neighborhoods, and for creating a life of forgiveness and redemption. Whether remaining in or relocating to the abandoned community that is the fifteen blocks of their Sandtown neighborhood, in uniting their ordinary lives they experienced the power of the New Testament Greek *metanoia*, a profound personal and social turning from old racial and economic desires toward new ones shaped by God's desires. And they experienced a movement from illusions of success as upward mobility to one of joining the Jesus who "taking the form of a slave . . . humbled himself and became obedient to the point of death—even death on a cross" (Phil. 2:7–8). These new desires were knit into brick and mortar over nearly thirty years in birthing a health center, school, arts center, and 300-plus new Habitat for Humanity homes, all anchored in shared congregational life. Repentance became embodied in new institutions of community service, in physical, material reality. They testify that their very sanctification and the salvation of the neighborhood are at stake: tasting the reign of God, the incoming kingdom of shalom, the peace of Christ, both now and not yet, here and now.[12]

## CONVERSION TOWARD WHAT: GOD'S "NEW WE"

Yet a critical question remains unanswered, what might be called "the *telos* test": the three Rs *toward what vision of the future*? Without being located within a larger story, the three Rs as such fail to provide an answer.

JP often preaches, "I don't believe in a black, white, Latino, or Asian church." Here he speaks out of multiple convictions grounded in his reading of Scripture,[13] his companionship with a strange collection of people, a particular social location, and his understanding of life with a particular God. Together these factors altered him and many others (in Mendenhall and Jackson, Mississippi; Pasadena, California; and the CCDA) at their very core. One ultimate result was the formation of a "new we" in the world bearing witness to who God is.

A biblical image that best captures this "new we" is Paul's account of "new creation" in 2 Corinthians 5:

Therefore, if anyone is in Christ, the new creation has come: The old has gone, the new is here! All this is from God, who reconciled us to himself through Christ and gave us the ministry of reconciliation: that God was reconciling the world to himself in Christ, not counting people's sins against them. And he has committed to us the message of reconciliation. We are therefore Christ's ambassadors, as though God were making his appeal through us.

The biblical scholar Richard Hays notes the significance of the Greek word for "reconciliation" in this text; it is not a religious, but a political term. Paul's exhortation, says Hays, is this: "We don't just announce reconciliation. We embody it." Hays contends a key phrase is often mistranslated:

> Paul certainly does not write, "If anyone is in Christ, *he is a new creature*." Rather, he blurts out, in a burst of wonder, "If anyone is in Christ . . . *New Creation!*" The background of this text is Isaiah 65:17, where Israel's God declares: "for I am about to create new heavens and a new earth; the former things shall not be remembered or come to mind." So Paul is proclaiming the transformation of the world, and summoning us to see all things made new in light of that transformation. Note: "God was reconciling *the world* to himself" (2 Corinthians 5:19). Not just individuals. The frame of reference is cosmic and corporate. Paul is not just saying, "Look at me, my sins have been forgiven, and so I'm now a new creature." He is saying that the whole world is being made new by the cross and resurrection and that all our relationships have to be re-evaluated in light of that transformation.[14]

The "new we" is thus divinely enacted; it is *God's* "new we." It is not abstract but a new *social* reality and interruption that demonstrates that the way things are is not the way things have to be. In reference to Native American history in the United States, Cherokee scholar Jake Weaver argues that through an intentional, ongoing process of de-colonization we can collectively work toward what he calls a "we-hermeneutics."[15] The theological significance of such a hermeneutics is described in a rich essay by theologian and missiologist Andrew Walls about the letter to the Ephesians and its powerful image of Christ overcoming "the dividing wall of hostility" between Gentiles and Israel (Eph. 2:14). Walls describes the letter as emerging from an unprecedented historical moment. In a real place called Ephesus, in a small, fledgling church community, Greeks and Jews dared to share social life together over a period of time, which altered them forever—their ways of seeing the world, their core identities, their vision of following Christ. Walls writes:

> Only in Christ does completion, fullness, dwell. And Christ's completion, as we have seen, comes from all humanity, *from the translation of the life of Jesus into the lifeways of all the world's cultures and subcultures through history. None of us can reach Christ's completeness on our own. We need each other's vision to correct, enlarge, and focus our own; only together are we complete in Christ.*"[16]

This "Ephesian moment" makes a startling claim on the lives of all Christians: "The very height of Christ's full stature" (Eph. 4:13), writes Walls, "is reached only by the coming together of the different cultural entities into the body of Christ. Only 'together,' not on our own, can we reach his full stature."[17] Seeing the end, or telos, of justice as God's "new we" in bodily and communal form illuminates a vision not only far more radical but, I contend, more beautiful than civil rights or social equality. There is much more going on here than the gift of diversity. They are impoverished and diminished without exchanging their gifts. They are becoming something more virtuous and, I dare say, *even more holy* than what they were apart. We see here stories of strangers and enemies growing into a surprising interdependence, becoming a new reality, even a new mestizo of in-between people whose supposedly "fixed" cultural identities (Asian American, African American, Anglo-American, "middle class," "poor," and so forth) are further hyphenated and confused toward a transcendent end:[18] tasting the new creation, greater Christ-likeness. These changed people and transformed identities beg for a new language.[19]

## HOW JP'S STORY CAN BECOME OUR STORY

In his book *Resurrection: Interpreting the Easter Gospel*, Rowan Williams describes an "ecclesiological blandness" that characterizes much of the church in the West. Williams argues that a crucial factor in renewing this church life is the witness of what he calls "communities of resurrection." He describes these as communities that are "deliberately created in response to an overwhelming failure in the society around—multi-racial 'cells' in a racist society, or communities in which the disabled, the mentally or physically handicapped or the marginal are accorded a place of security." Such groups, he contends, are "vivid images of the Church" that "judge very eloquently; they do not speak of possible transformations but enact them."[20]

JP's witness speaks a very similar beauty to blandness. How does his witness "eloquently judge" our standards of excellence in our own stories and contexts? We are speaking here of a way of dying and being raised into new life, of something being created that requires traveling with Jesus into Gethsemane to learn to say "not my will but yours be done" (Luke 22:42). There is usually not one "Gethsemane moment" but many. For JP, the turn toward the forgiving Christ after the 1970 Brandon jail beating was decisive in surrendering his desire to get as far away from white folks as he could and welcoming God's call to form an interracial ministry only twenty miles away from the site of violence. We see here the strange scandal that mercy (and beauty!) is, not unlike the one named by the South African narrator who took our pilgrimage group to the limestone quarry on Robben Island where Nelson Mandela was jailed for twenty-seven years. Here, he said, was where they humiliated the inmates by making them pound rocks in the beating sun. "This is where the vision of reconciliation in South Africa was birthed."

Both JP and Mandela illuminate an inseparable link between truth and mercy in welcoming "something far more beautiful" into our stories of division, injustice, and brokenness. For me and fellow companions in that Voice of Calvary zip code, over twenty-odd years together there were two critical moments that defined whether or not we would become a "new we."

The first was a racial crisis in 1983 that almost split the church. For me and other whites, it was our first reckoning with our privilege, the reality that we could walk away and never have to engage "race" again—unless we chose to. We were happy at Voice of Calvary as long as it didn't mean losing power, innocence, or swallowing the black anger that erupted. Becoming a "new creation" cost black folks a great deal as well, letting go of their power of not forgiving, or of throwing the race card when it didn't fit. All of us embraced a vision of something better than "give me equality and leave me alone": an exchange of gifts, the best we could offer in pursuit of a common mission. But the truth of our trauma and deformity, our pain and our privilege, had to be seen, named, and taken head-on in order to get beyond it.

The second Gethsemane moment came fourteen years later. By 1997 John's son Spencer and his family, my family, and other families had lived over ten years in an intentional Christian community called Antioch, one gift on the other side of surviving the racial conflict. But after the ups and downs of intense life and ministry our Antioch gospel had largely become one of trying harder and doing more. And that is not good news in a "gospel" sense. Make no mistake, Antioch was "on the move," taking on more and more projects (a day care, hospitality ministry, law office, national magazine, reconciliation ministry, active church membership, singing in the choir, raising children!). But the life was sucked out of our hyperactivity. We ran out of resources and wisdom to "solve" that moment. Furthermore, Spencer and I stood at the verge of splitting up as we stood before a long list of grievances about each other. The journey to a breakthrough is too long to tell here, but we in the Antioch community eventually came to understand that while God's story in Scripture is full of stories about loving one's neighbor and loving God, the far more important story is God's love for us. As a mentor put it at the time, "If you don't get God's love into your bones, and extend that love to one another, you will become very dangerous activists."[21]

Once again, yet differently from 1983, our desires and habits were in need of radical repair. The truth that needed to be learned this time was not the power of race but the power of God. Suffice it to say that when Spencer preached this message of "playing the grace card" at what turned out to be the last conference we led, the room was absolutely still, soaking in the cost of pursuing social justice through undeserved grace across divides.[22] Without both the truth of 1983 and the truth of 1997 there *was* no beloved community, no "new we." Both crises had to be resolved in different ways to renew us and hold us together.

Spencer had entered profound new territory here. The son stepped into his own identity by standing on his father's broad yet fragile shoulders and reaching still higher. You see, Spencer, too, was in that 1970 jail the morning after JP's beating. He saw his father's bloody ripped shirt, the humiliation on his face. Spencer's movement to the "grace card" was not about amnesia but about seeing the profound difference between a human community and one that is shared with God, a community that holds together both the truth about sin and the truth about divine grace.

This is why Mark Gornik's claim that the three Rs are fundamentally an *ecclesiology* is so important. Ecclesiology requires worship of the triune God and God's presence for its existence, whereas a strategy to address social problems alone does not. The mentor who exposed our blind spot put it this way: "The most important person in your community is not any of the poor in West Jackson, or Spencer, or Chris, or any of you. The most important person is Jesus. And the question is, how do you keep Jesus at the center?"

If God's love in spite of human sin is the central story of the world, of all human life, and if God is the central actor in saving the world, then authentic Christian activism must give an account of its relationship to God's unique prior action. Within this reality of God as the central actor in bringing about peace, the three Rs are not only a profound way of bearing witness to who God is, they are *a means of grace*. To put it this way is to fully embrace the physicality that JP's understanding of Christianity is: bodies seeking to cross divides and histories of injustice ultimately and fully matter only as they come into intimate relationship *with the body of Jesus*. The equation of peace is not "us" and "them" becoming a "new we" but "us," "them," and *God*. America's virus and King's trinity of sins are resisted through a trinity of social disciplines that only reach their full power and meaning in a trinity of social actors—the self, the other, and the God of truth of grace.

It is out of this journey of holding together the turning point of 1983 (the power of the social trauma) with the turning point of 1997 (the power of grace) that I formed an axiom that expresses what JP and Spencer together taught me about reconciliation: "Reconciliation is as big as engaging the race problem in America and genocide in Rwanda. Yet reconciliation is never bigger than the person nearest to you who is most difficult to love. And the greatest force in pursuing this is not our love for God or the other, but God's love for us." I believe this axiom is true to JP's witness. He would candidly admit to anyone two realities about the "near." First, that there would be no JP without his wife, Vera Mae, and that loving Vera Mae especially in his last years of growing older has become a central calling and gift for him. Second, that one of his greatest places of struggle has been learning how to love his own children. There is no JP without both the one who birthed the CCDA in all its growing collective power and the one who owns up to his own fragility in trying to be faithful to those who are nearest.[23]

Yet why would this surprise us? If JP is anything, he is always so fully human. The very nature of being a creature and not the Messiah, the critical understanding Antioch came to see, is that all is gift, and we do not and cannot order and control our lives. 2 Corinthians 5 depicts the church's mission in the beautiful language of new creation and being ambassadors of reconciliation, yet the chapters before lay out the spirituality that makes ambassadorship possible: God's gift of new creation is not carried in smooth and sturdy containers of power and control but in "jars of clay," earthen vessels of fragility and gentleness (2 Cor. 4:7–12). There is no work of conversion, no transvaluation, no beloved community, no "new we," without the central, prior action of the resurrected Jesus whose wounds did not disappear. There is no JP without his belief in such a God. We cannot welcome the fullness of such a God without becoming gentle and weak ourselves.

If the physicality of the three Rs counters the gnostic theology that characterizes so much of American Christianity in pursuing a purity of the soul detached from bodily captivity to social realities, there is also a Pelagian character to contemporary evangelical ministry that is just as great a danger: over-busyness, hyperactivism, and the loss of the Sabbath as a day of ceasing, desisting, and being still before the God who is the only indispensable One. To see the three Rs as means of grace that allow the grace of God to flow and the gifts of God's people to be used means that we do not control the final product. This is to live within the Acts narrative where the disciples are continually being surprised by a larger vision that keeps unfolding more of who God is, and where the central actor in the story is not Peter or Paul but the Holy Spirit.

## A NEW GLOBAL MISSIONAL PARADIGM

One challenge facing the academy regarding peace and reconciliation was expressed by the Jewish peace-building scholar Marc Gopin: "Academics kills practice. It makes the theoreticians the experts. The genius of a Ph.D. does not require a Ph.D."[24] A danger at the other extreme is practitioners becoming obsessed with metrics driven by business models versus theological reflection. (For example, how does the "C" in Christian community development shape CCDA ministries differently from humanitarian organizations?)[25] Overcoming the often-fragmented worlds of theory and practice is exactly the intersection the Duke Divinity School Center for Reconciliation has sought to engage. The challenge of forming students well for faithful ministry in a divided world lies in both cultivating deep theological thinking and scriptural imagination, as well as seeking to illuminate, learn from, be changed by, and nourish "communities of resurrection."[26]

As the center's work has expanded from Duke to Durham, North Carolina, to the United States, to international regions, I have become convinced that JP's unique witness is a sign of a story far bigger than JP. If something new is possible in one place, suddenly the possibility opens of a larger pattern. This is exactly what we encountered under the radar screen in the east African Great Lakes region.[27]

One country there, Burundi, is a place of intense beauty as well as poverty and historical conflict. There we stumbled across the community-based ministry of Maggy Barankitse, a woman whose work has to be seen to be believed.[28] In the village where she grew up, was almost killed, and was forced to watch loved ones killed because of their ethnic identity, Maggy refused the knee-jerk solution to bring in non-governmental organizations (NGOs) to help. "Love made me an inventor," she says, and so she planted Maison Shalom (Home of Peace). Their answer to war is a cinema to re-shape community imagination. Their answer to poverty is not handouts but farms and businesses. They believed children of war needed not orphanages but *homes*. Their answer to health care is not only one of the finest hospitals in Africa but a nursing school. Yet in talking to villagers transformed within this community of resurrection, it is clear that all these ministries are ground for people of warring groups to be "messed up" into a "new we" with the power to break their categories of exclusion and violence.

Add to Maison Shalom places like New Song in Baltimore, other CCDA ministries, as well as Jean Vanier's L'Arche communities across the world, and a larger pattern emerges—perhaps even a movement of the Holy Spirit—which enlarges our vision not only of what the church *is* but what it *is becoming and needs to be* in our time: *the carrier of a new paradigm of mission as mutuality toward a new creation.*

The growing problem is that "over-evangelizing too lightly" will become the dominant mission mode not only in America but throughout the global church. A new paradigm is surely needed for this global time of unprecedented migration and immigration, of increasing traffic of missions groups and initiatives from the United States to Africa, of post-Christian European nations struggling with who will be in and who will be out, of a U.S. crisis seen in growing political polarization and animosity and a broken immigration system, of a southward shift in the vitality of Christianity.[29] This is why Andrew Walls's claim is so significant: the "Ephesian moment" is now the crossroads of Christian history in the twenty-first century. What a paradigm of mission as mutuality toward new creation offers is a fresh and faithful presence within a world of intensifying conflicts over land, water, oil, religion, and power. The church can only bear hope in such a world by repenting and becoming renewed itself, by growing into the full stature of Christ.

What is at stake in Maison Shalom, New Song, L'Arche, and the physicality of JP's witness are powerful, concrete realities and patterns of something profoundly new breaking in that is somehow carried in fragile jars of clay. The significance of such a paradigm of mission was well expressed to me by my friend Glen Kehrein about his thirty-plus years living as white community developer and innovator in inner-city Chicago with his companions at Circle Urban Ministries and Rock of Our Salvation Church: "I believe in racial reconciliation because it's the best way I know of for white males to die to self." The clear implication was how this long journey not only drew Glen closer to God but also released innovative power to create something new with a neighborhood and people Glen had once considered not his own, and them with Glen. The divine mystery revealed in Glen's life, and JP's life, and communities of resurrection is that the authentic Christian mission is a participation with the body of Christ in both dying and resurrection that releases not mediocrity into the world but excellence, hope, joy, and power.

This is something far more radical and more beautiful than what we often settle for. JP has not settled for less, and neither should we.

### NOTES

1. Will Campbell, *Race and the Renewal of the Church* (Philadelphia: Westminster Press, 1962), 3–4.

2. Charles Marsh and John Perkins, *Welcoming Justice: God's Movement toward Beloved Community* (Downers Grove, Ill.: InterVarsity Press, 2009), 37.

3. "Beyond Vietnam: A Time to Break Silence," Riverside Church, New York City, April 4, 1967, http://www.hartford-hwp.com/archives/45a/058.html.

4. Charles Marsh, *The Beloved Community: How Faith Shapes Social Justice, from the Civil Rights Movement to Today* (New York: Basic Books, 2005), 172.

5. The CCDA's growth has been explosive, remarkable for a loose network of Christians committed to incarnational, holistic life, and ministry with the poor. From the first annual conference in 1989 with 150 participants, there were as many as 3,000 at the 2012 conference. The creation of the CCDA is arguably JP's greatest legacy, which goes beyond a network of mutual encouragement to sustaining a particular theology, set of practices, and deeply embedded ways of life. A great challenge for CCDA is developing ongoing practices of reflection to keep the vision grounded in a distinctly Christian and theological imagination. The temptation is always a more and more pragmatic approach.

6. This conversion process is a journey that often begins with intense idealism for the one who comes to the place of need from a place of privilege to help. It is what I have called the "caseworker" posture. I came to see that the journey from helping to mutuality was one of becoming "comrades." See "Chris Rice on Voice of Calvary," Theology and Race Workgroup Meeting, Oxford, Miss., February 24, 2001, 6, http://www.livedtheology

.org/pdfs/crice.pdf. See also Chris Heuertz and Christine Pohl, *Friendship at the Margins: Discovering Mutuality in Service and Mission* (Downers Grove, Ill.: InterVarsity Press, 2010).

7. By "deeper hope" I mean the unfinished business in many so-called postconflict societies where funders disappear and faithful initiatives diminish after new peace accords are signed, legal integration is enacted, or regime change occurs. This has been the case multiple times from Northern Ireland, to South Africa, to Rwanda, to the United States.

8. A powerful account of a theology of place is provided in Jonathan Wilson-Hartgrove, *The Wisdom of Stability: Rooting Faith in a Mobile Culture* (Brewster, Mass.: Paraclete Press, 2010).

9. John Swinton. "The Body of Christ Has Down's Syndrome," Centre for Spirituality, Health, and Disability, 2004, http://www.abdn.ac.uk/cshad/TheBodyofChristHasDown Syndrome.html.

10. Talk by Vanier at Duke Divinity School, November 2008.

11. Mark Gornik, *To Live in Peace: Biblical Faith and the Changing Inner City* (Grand Rapids, Mich.: Eerdmans, 2002), 169.

12. To put it another way, theologically, what is at stake with the three Rs is not a strategy but a soteriology.

13. JP's 5 A.M. group Bible studies are famous. When he is not leading them, he is up himself early in the morning reading and wrestling with Scripture.

14. Richard Hays devotion, Duke Summer Institute, June 2010, http://www.faithand leadership.com/sermons/the-word-reconciliation.

15. "From I-Hermeneutics to We-Hermeneutics: Native Americans and the Post-Colonial," in *Native American Religious Identity*, ed. Jace Weaver (Maryknoll, N.Y.: Orbis, 1998), 1–25.

16. Andrew F. Walls, *The Cross-Cultural Process in Christian History: Studies in the Transmission and Appropriation of Faith* (New York: Orbis, 2002), 79.

17. Walls, *Cross-Cultural Process in Christian History*, 79. The book of Acts is an account of the story of the formation of the church toward this new way.

18. Virgilio Elizondo offers a profound account of mestizo as the existence of a mixed people that is not only richer sociologically and historically but is the goal of Christian existence as seen in Revelation. See Virgilio Elizondo, *The Future Is Mestizo: Life Where Cultures Meet* (Boulder: University Press of Colorado, 2000).

19. This is exactly what happened in the city of Antioch in the book of Acts, where the first truly interethnic congregation took form. The mixture of Jew and Greek, slave and free, male and female was so strange and new that the external society came up with a new description for them—"Christians" (Acts 11:26).

20. Rowan Williams, *Resurrection: Interpreting the Easter Gospel* (Cleveland: Pilgrim Press, 2002), 48

21. See the full story in my book *Grace Matters: A True Story of Race, Friendship, and Faith in the Heart of the South* (San Francisco: Jossey-Bass, 2002). The mentor was John Alexander, a pastor at Church of the Sojourners in San Francisco.

22. Spencer died of a sudden heart attack three days later. This last message was included as a new chapter, "Playing the Grace Card," after Spencer's death in a new edition of

our book *More Than Equals: Racial Healing for the Sake of the Gospel* (Downers Grove, Ill.: InterVarsity Press, 1993), 238–247. It was also published in *Christianity Today*, July 13, 1998, http://www.christianitytoday.com/ct/1998/july13/8t8040.html.

23. One particularly moving moment in my past ten years with JP was a 2010 visit with him and Vera Mae in Jackson. As I sat by Vera Mae's bed hearing her weak voice describe the painful journey of declining health, JP stood quietly and tenderly listening, then went and prepared her breakfast just the way she liked it. Of course the typical, down-to-earth banter continued between the two of them.

24. Marc Gopin, keynote address, Consultation of Educators in Theology and Religion, Boston University, August 9–11, 2010.

25. Peter Dula and Elain Epp Weaver of the Mennonite Central Committee offer a fresh theological critique of humanitarianism as sin, contrasting the dominant imagination and practices of NGOs to the implications of the incarnation. See Peter Dula and Elaine Epp Weaver, "MCC, Intervention, and Humanitarianism," *Mission Focus, Annual Review* (2005): 13:68–82.

26. Founded in 2005, the center's work across the theory-practice divide has resulted in a Resources for Reconciliation book series with seven books coauthored by a practitioner and a theologian; the Teaching Communities program, which places divinity students in ten-week apprenticeships with exemplary communities of practice; and a summer institute, which serves as a theological fueling station for Christian leaders and institutions.

27. What Charles Marsh does in *The Beloved Community* in terms of highlighting the significance of the witness of John Perkins and the CCDA, Emmanuel Katongole does by telling the stories of Maggy Barankitse as well as Paride Taban of Sudan and Angelina Atyam of Uganda in *The Sacrifice of Africa: A Political Theology for Africa* (Grand Rapids, Mich.: Eerdmans, 2011), 166–192.

28. See the online video about Maggy Barankitse and Maison Shalom called "Opus Prize" on YouTube, http://www.youtube.com/watch?v=Dxz9yEoO-Sk.

29. My friend David Kasali, founder and president of a Christian university in the conflict-torn Democratic Republic of the Congo, puts this well to the U.S. church: "Missionaries came and baptized my father. That was one age, and we are grateful for that time. Yet I now have a Ph.D. in theology from the U.S. You can't come to Congo the same way you came before. Before anything else, I want you as a friend."

# Love, Reconciliation, and the Solidarity of Pain

*Mae Elise Cannon*

I FIRST MET JOHN PERKINS WHEN I WAS ON STAFF AT WILLOW CREEK Community Church. Willow Creek is one of the most influential mega-churches in the United States and the world. While at Willow Creek, I was responsible for some of the ministries that were involved in compassion and justice in the city and around the country. We invited Perkins to be our spiritual mentor and teacher on a weeklong experience called the Justice Journey. On the trip, a group of mostly whites and blacks traveled on a spiritual pilgrimage through parts of the South that played important roles during the civil rights movement. We visited Atlanta, Selma, Birmingham, and Montgomery, and ended our journey in Memphis at the Lorraine Motel where Martin Luther King Jr. was assassinated. The mission of the trip was to "experience the past, understand the present, and embrace hope for the future." Traveling alongside brothers and sisters of a different race, we learned about the historical and present-day realities of the African American experience in the United States. We entered into the spiritual process of transformation through repentance and forgiveness. Through Perkins's example and teaching, we sought to understand how our Christian faith calls us toward love and reconciliation.

John Perkins has given the world a theological legacy deeply rooted in love. It is a love embedded in the biblical truths of Jesus Christ—love that manifests itself in leadership, civil rights work, community development, teaching, preaching, advocacy, and great sacrifice. Following in the stead of other powerful leaders of social reform movements such as Martin Luther King Jr., Perkins's life example, leadership, and model of discipleship incarnate King's notion of *beloved community* and the quest for justice through nonviolent means. Perkins and his legacy continue the unfinished work of the civil rights movement as he leads people to make a difference through reconciliation and love. Perkins has said time and time again, "The task of a leader is to enter into the pain of their people." He has chosen to live his life on behalf of others—even those who have caused him and others around him great pain. John Perkins has willingly entered into the pain of my own family experience, extending healing love while walking alongside as both a mentor and friend.

The personal narrative of John Perkins's life story is wrought with painful memories that began at birth with the loss of his mother to a nutrition deficiency. He grew up surrounded by white-dominated systems of injustice in rural Mississippi. Perkins suffered profound loss with the death of his brother Clyde, who, after returning from World War II, was brutally murdered in New Hebron by a Mississippi deputy. Perkins writes in his memoir, *Let Justice Roll Down*:

> Dead! My brother dead. All that army stuff about making the world safe for democracy. All that fighting some place off in Europe didn't get him killed. He had come home safe from the white man's war only to be shot down six months later by a white man in his own hometown.[1]

Shortly thereafter Perkins moved to California to leave behind the burden of being a black man in the Jim Crow South. He lived for a while seeking personal satisfaction and economic prosperity, while taking advantage of opportunity for social mobility in California.

Although he achieved material success in California, Perkins was discontent and began to be led by a deep spiritual conviction. He says, "God began to show me the unimaginable. And He began it in a quiet way."[2] His son Spencer had been going to Sunday school and began to share Bible verses with the family before mealtimes. John describes what he saw in Spencer: "I watched our son. I could see something was developing in him that was beautiful, something I knew nothing about. I'd had no real experience before of seeing Christianity at work like that in a person's life. At work in a way that was beautiful—and good."[3]

At Spencer's urging, John began to go to church. Through his son's persistence, and the encouragement of a Christian friend at work, Calvin Bourne, Perkins began to read the Bible. He eventually committed his life to Christ. Previously looking down on religion, Perkins saw black Christianity as "gullible and submissive"—just another way for the African American community to enter into their inferior role in white-dominated society. Perkins saw white Christianity as particularly irrelevant: "To me it was a part of that whole system that helped dehumanize and destroy black people; that system which identified me as a nigger."[4] Perkins's conversion transformed his personhood and redefined his understanding of the world. God equipped him to enter into the execrable brokenness of racial injustice, grapple with people and institutions abusively using their power, and prophetically use his voice to speak truth against many horrors wrought throughout the Christian community in the South.

Compelled to return to Mississippi in order to evangelize and improve biblical literacy in the African American community, Perkins desired to live out his faith amid the ravages of southern white racism.[5] Blacks in the South were still expected to adhere to social codes of deference to whites. The African American community had limited (if any) access to education and health care; even working blacks were caught in an endless cycle of poverty. In the mid-1960s, blacks came face-to-face with many restrictions on and requirements for voting, including poll taxes and literacy tests.[6] Afraid that black voters would upset the system, Perkins became a visible target for "Klan types," whites in the community who wanted to keep the black population under their control. Perkins writes, "The southern white doesn't want the blacks *removed*. What he wants is to have blacks under his control, in a special relationship to him. So one of the greatest sins in the eye of the typical southern racist is for someone to take away control of 'his' niggers."[7] One of the ways blacks were "kept in their place" was through police brutality, beatings, and arrests.[8] Perkins regularly experienced taunting, threats, and other pressures from whites in positions of power. The culmination of these abuses occurred when Perkins and other civil rights protestors were brutally beaten and tortured, almost to death, in the Rankin County Jail in Brandon, Mississippi.[9] This event largely shaped Perkins and his understanding of his Christian faith, leading him on the road to forgiveness and forcing him to wrestle with Jesus's words, "Love your enemies and pray for those who persecute you" (Matt. 5:44).

When beginning the painful process of healing, the verses in Matthew came to mind over and over again. Perkins was continually reminded: "If you forgive others when they sin against you, your heavenly father will also forgive you" (Matt. 6:14–15). He says: "As I lay in bed and thought and prayed about his forgiveness and what it meant to me, I began to apply his forgiveness to the faces of the men who had beaten me and to other white people."[10] Coming to terms with his faith, Perkins questioned if the reconciling power of Christ's love could be strong enough to overcome the hatred of whites toward blacks in rural Mississippi. Perkins wrestled with this and came to the realization: "Somehow, God's forgiveness for me was tied up in my forgiveness of those who hurt me."[11] Perkins realized that he, too, was guilty—guilty of hatred and anger and bitterness. Feeling strong conviction and realization of his own depravity, the Lord led him to a place of personal repentance, which allowed him to begin the process of forgiveness.[12] Perkins came to a new understanding of God's justice and mercy: "I saw how my bitterness could destroy me. The Spirit of God had a hold of me and wouldn't let me sidestep his justice. And his justice said that I was just as sinful as those who beat me. But I knew that God's justice is seasoned with forgiveness. Forgiveness is what makes his justice redemptive."[13]

God's justice was not only about righting the wrongs within Perkins's own community, it was also about righting the wrongs in his own heart. Perkins experienced the reconciling power of the gospel through the recognition of his own sin. A movement of the Spirit of God brought about the redemptive power of justice in his own life. Perkins knew that he could not be healed unless he could forgive those who beat him in the Brandon jail.[14]

After the beating, Perkins continued in his civil rights work. He had another encounter with a Mississippi policeman. He describes the policeman as the epitome of the stereotype, a "big fat white guy."[15] After the beating, Perkins struggled greatly whenever he saw a man dressed in a police uniform; this occasion was no different. But this policeman was different. He pursued a friendship with John and became a servant of John's work and ministry. He did anything Perkins asked. He provided police escorts to make sure that John and others got home safely. When there were tent meetings, he surrounded the tent with his police force and ensured the participants' safety. Perkins says of this man: "He drew out of me some hatred with his own love."[16] This policeman manifested the incarnational power of God. He came alongside and embraced the work of God in John Perkins's life. Perkins says, "His love for me . . . bore some of my pain."[17]

The task of a leader is to enter into the pain of his or her people. John experienced healing as that policeman loved him and came alongside his ministry. The love of Christ drew out the hatred that could have taken root in John's soul. Instead, he entered into repentance and forgave those who had hurt him the most.[18] Still, Perkins could have chosen to leave the white community behind. Some time later he told a friend that he felt called to preach the good news to black people. But, his friend challenged him, "Maybe God is calling you to preach the gospel to everybody." God continued to lead Perkins, and he heard God saying, "Maybe you can't free one without the other. Maybe what frees blacks frees whites too."[19]

John Perkins continued in his call to the ministry, extended his teaching and discipleship beyond the black community, and welcomed whites along on the journey. This is how he came to be leading a group of blacks and whites from Willow Creek in Chicago through the battlegrounds of the civil rights movement.

On one of the first days of that trip, Perkins and I were having a conversation about a phone call he had received a few days earlier from the White House. He had been invited to meet with the president of the United States to talk about his ministry and work in Christian community development. He turned down the invitation. He told the president he was not able to meet because the trip he was leading was more important. When I asked him why he made that decision, he said, "I told them 'no,' because it is more important that I be here with all of you. This is the work of the gospel." While on that journey, and the many others he has been on since, Perkins continued to leave his legacy—a legacy that says "no" to presidents and says "yes" to the work of reconciliation, mercy, and justice.

Prior to leaving for that first Justice Journey, I told my family about the trip. After hearing about it, my mother told me she wanted to go, too. I was surprised! My mother does not go to church, and I do not think she particularly likes things that involve prayer and Bible study. For some reason, the purpose of this experience intrigued her, and she joined our team. Some of my favorite memories of that trip include long stretches of highway from Birmingham to Montgomery, with Perkins sitting in the front seat sipping his Diet Coke, and he, my mother, and I talking into the late hours of the night. On one such evening we had a conversation about pain and suffering. My mother asked where God is when horrible things happen in the world.

My mother knows a lot about suffering. The greatest loss in her life came when she was a young mother. Before my parents had children, they had a conversion experience. My parents were introduced to Christ through a college professor who had been a student of Francis Schaeffer and his teaching. My parents' new belief was so significant that their lives were turned completely around. They became a part of a Christian community, studied the Bible regularly, and attempted to faithfully live out their new beliefs. A few years later they had their first child, and they named him Daniel, after the person who had led them to Christ. About a year later I was born. Daniel and I spent the first few years of our lives with parents who were doing their very best to love us, care for us, and raise us in a way that would honor God. In September 1978 our family went through a terrible tragedy. My cousin, a four-year-old girl named Shana, had a severe heart defect. She was born with holes in her heart. The doctors told her parents that unless she had a very risky surgery, she would die. Her parents elected to have the surgery. Shana died on the operating table. The entire family was devastated. My mother, still a young believer, began to question. From the moment of my cousin's death, my mother prayed every night for God to "keep her children safe." Less than a month later, my brother was killed in a hit-and-run car accident.

On the Justice Journey, that late night on a highway somewhere in Alabama, my mother shared her story with Perkins. She told him that she did not understand or believe that God could love her and still allow such horrible things to happen. She poured out her heart and told about her anger toward God. She couldn't make sense of her suffering, the pain and loss she knows so intimately. As he listened, Perkins entered into my mother's pain. He told her about his own son's death. He talked about the pain he experienced and still carried with him after Spencer's passing. We cried together. As Perkins took my mother's story into his heart, he listened to her and loved her. He loved her not only with his own love, but with the love of God. In the car that night, the anguish of such deep loss was palpable. As Perkins shared his own grief, he and my mother transcended into the heart of their pain together. Together, not alone—and Christ was there with them. Perkins could have been with the president that night; instead, he chose to be with my mother.

Many times I have heard John Perkins say that love is entering into people's pain. Love is walking alongside someone in the midst of their suffering. Perkins knows God to be the God of comfort and compassion, the one "who comforts in all our troubles, so that we can comfort those in any trouble with the comfort we ourselves receive from God" (2 Cor. 1:2–4). God expresses his love in the world through the compassionate acts of his people. Perkins says: "To love people is the basic requirement for anyone who leads people. Only through love can I really come to know my people, their problems and failings and deep weaknesses—and not lose my energy. . . . Only love will take me close enough to the people to share their real needs and to make them my own."[20]

I have seen this truth lived out in John Perkins's life. I now see him a few times every year. Each time I see him, without hesitation, sometimes without even saying hello, he asks me the same question. He asked me this question time and time again, before he even knew my name. The most recent time we were together, I thought he might not ask. We spoke of many things—ministry, life, passion, and opportunities. There were people all around and a million things happening all at once. Just when I turned to leave, he stopped me, and he asked, "How is your mother?"

John Perkins understands the gospel as an inspiration for how love must be lived out in community. Once you understand the pain of people, love compels you to action. Love is not only about comfort for the soul but also about meeting the physical and material needs within community. After returning to Mississippi to work among the poor, Perkins was overwhelmed by the conviction to meet people's physical needs:

> The whole community was suffering. And we realized that it would take more than a verbalization of the gospel and token action in our spare time to be effective. God was allowing us to take the blinders off our methodology we were using to present the gospel long enough to love people. Meeting physical needs was going to have to be right at the center of our evangelism and ministry.[21]

Ministry could no longer focus only on the condition of a person's soul; it also had to extend to meeting their physical needs. As Perkins and others grappled with the poverty that surrounded them, they came face to face with the "hostile forces of hatred and racism" that limited their ability to respond to the needs they witnessed.[22] Reconciliation became a critical part of their ministry. For Perkins, God's words had to be applied to the sins of both blacks and whites, because of the deeply embedded racial damage found in communities around the country.[23] Reconciliation could only occur when whites moved beyond their guilt and blacks moved beyond their blame. Poverty would be overcome through black indigenous leadership and white contributions of technology, working together "to create beautiful evangelistic, social, and economic alternatives in the poor community."[24] Thus, as a means of pursuing justice, "*reconciliation* became the most important ministry, the most relevant impact the gospel could make for reaching the poor."[25]

One of the greatest driving forces in Perkins's life was the desire just to be loved.[26] In reflecting about the importance of relationships in his life, Perkins shared these words: "One of the greatest driving forces in my life has been because of true friendship. In gratitude, that gets me up in the morning. That pushes me. Absolute grace. My friends have not let me down. My friends have allowed me to persevere—and have both freed me and restrained me—because of their love."[27]

The love of others provided John Perkins with great strength, sustenance, and motivation to keep working diligently on behalf of justice and reconciliation. Over the course of his life, he experienced the love of God most profoundly through friendships and relationships. Through this intimate connection of relationship and sharing of one another's pain, God reveals his love.

NOTES

1. John Perkins, *Let Justice Roll Down* (Ventura, Calif.: Regal Books, 1976), 22.

2. Perkins, *Let Justice Roll Down*, 67.

3. Perkins, *Let Justice Roll Down*, 68.

4. Perkins, *Let Justice Roll Down*, 57.

5. Perkins, *Let Justice Roll Down*, 80.

6. Perkins, *Let Justice Roll Down*, 115.

7. Perkins, *Let Justice Roll Down*, 119.

8. Perkins, *Let Justice Roll Down*, 135.

9. Perkins, *Let Justice Roll Down*, 156.

10. John Perkins, *A Quiet Revolution: Meeting Human Needs Today: A Biblical Challenge to Christians*, rev. ed. (Pasadena, Calif.: Urban Family Publications with Network Unlimited International, 1976), 192.

11. Perkins, *Quiet Revolution*, 191.

12. Perkins, *Let Justice Roll Down*, 9.

13. Perkins, *Quiet Revolution*, 191.

14. John Perkins, "Let Justice Roll Down," conversation with Charles Marsh at Spring Institute for Lived Theology, University of Virginia, April 22, 2009, transcribed by the author from the recording available from http://www.livedtheology.org/silt2009.html.

15. Perkins, "Let Justice Roll Down."

16. Perkins, "Let Justice Roll Down."

17. Perkins, "Let Justice Roll Down."

18. Perkins, *Let Justice Roll Down*, 10.

19. Perkins, *Quiet Revolution*, 192.

20. Perkins, *Quiet Revolution*, 125.

21. Perkins, *Quiet Revolution*, 64.

22. Perkins, *Quiet Revolution*, 74.

23. Perkins, *Quiet Revolution*, 193.

24. Perkins, *Quiet Revolution*, 196.

25. Perkins, *Quiet Revolution*, 194.

26. Perkins, "Let Justice Roll Down."

27. Perkins, "Let Justice Roll Down."

# Only Love Wins

## Justice and Public Policy

### Lisa Sharon Harper

I FOUND JESUS AT A SUNDAY EVENING CAMP MEETING IN ERMA, NEW Jersey, in August 1983. After listening to the preacher bellow a hell-fire and brimstone message that lit up aged trees surrounding our tent meeting, I sat planted in my seat wondering if I should uproot myself and walk forward. When my friend tapped me on the arm and asked if I would walk forward with her during the altar call, I said, "Yes." I was the only African American in this multichurch, community-wide gathering in this small town of about 300 residents on the outskirts of Cape May, but I felt no different than anyone else. I just felt loved. I knelt at the altar with my friend. She wept. I wept. The elders swarmed us both, and I entered the kingdom by proxy on that day.

In those days, the gospel was simple to me. I was a sinner, and I needed God's forgiveness in order to get into heaven. Jesus died so that I could be forgiven, and there was no other way to have relationship with God, except through Jesus. That was the good news . . . well most of it.

Soon after I entered the kingdom, I was told I had to switch political party allegiance and become a Republican. Mind you, I wasn't of voting age, but if I was a Christian, I had to join the Republicans in their fight to elect Ronald Reagan for a second term. I did it, and I tried to convince my parents who were active in the civil rights movement that Reagan was their man. My mom looked at me like I was an alien with an antenna sticking out of my head, and her eyes were filled with anger. Her first and final answer was "No."

Mom knew something I didn't. She knew that in 1983 President Ronald Reagan was in the middle of carrying out a massive economic agenda: the wholesale redistribution of wealth and power in America. Money and power were siphoned from the poor, the working class, and the middle class and were redistributed to rich individuals and corporate empires. Reagan declared upon entering office his intent to usher in a new economic era in the United States. That new era was defined by an economic system the United States had never seen before—neoliberal free-market capitalism. The three pillars of basic capitalism are private ownership, profit motive, and the competitive market. Free-market capitalism places its trust in the forces of market supply and demand to maintain economic balance and prohibits government intervention in the process. Economic neoliberalism calls for the transfer of control from the public to the private sector.

During Reagan's reign basic public services that poor, working-class, and middle-class communities depend on were slashed or burned. The U.S. education budget had been increased under every president since Lyndon B. Johnson. In his first term, Reagan cut the education budget by 18.6 percent. Likewise, Reagan is the only president to date to cut the Housing and Urban Development (HUD) budget since its creation under President Johnson in 1965. He cut HUD spending in his second term by almost half—40.1 percent. To boot, Reagan cut the Department of Labor budget by 33.4 percent in his first term and another 17 percent in his second term.[1] Meanwhile Reagan instituted the deepest tax cuts in American history. In 1954 the top-tier marginal tax rate was 91 percent. When Reagan entered office it was 70 percent. By the time he left office in 1988, the top tier marginal tax rate was only 28 percent.[2] My mother said "No" because under Reagan's reign she saw the poor getting poorer while the rich got the hook up.

Another reason my mother wanted no part of my newfound faith came to light on a day that started out no differently than any other, I attended my first church board meeting at Tabernacle United Methodist Church, where I was an active member of the youth group. My best friend, Joanna, and I represented the church youth at the board meeting. The discussion that day was focused on evangelism and outreach: "How could Tabernacle exercise its mandate to go out and preach the good news to Jerusalem, Samaria, and to the ends of the earth?" We talked about sending buses out to pick up children in The Villas (a low-income white community), in North Cape May and Cape May Point (middle-class white communities), and up to West Cape May and Cape May (where middle-class whites and blacks lived). When I pressed for the need for African American children (many of whom were in my extended family) to be bused to our church so that they might also hear the gospel, the board's first and final answer was: "They have their own churches." That was my first conscious brush with systemic racism in the heart of the church. Jesus's direct command to make disciples in Jerusalem, Samaria, and to the ends of the earth made no impact on the invisible racism in the hearts of elders—a matter-of-fact kind of racism. Like air, it was undetectable to those who depended on it for the survival of their (way of) life.

They say the books children read make imprints on the soul that last a lifetime. I wasn't a child, but it was the first time I ever read a book on social justice from a Christian perspective. *With Justice for All*, by John Perkins made an indelible mark on me. Perkins's three Rs (reconciliation, redistribution, and relocation) and their biblical foundations introduced me to a Jesus I had never known, and it was liberating to make his acquaintance.

I was introduced to Perkins's works during the 1989 Here's Life in the Inner City Summer Project, a ministry of Campus Crusade for Christ. Our mostly white group of evangelical students and staff were deeply affected by Perkins's own story of triumph over southern racism through love. We were moved to practice redistribution of resources through the very act of offering the resources of our very selves in service to and partnership with typically underresourced communities. And we were challenged to uproot ourselves and relocate from cloistered suburbs to the inner city. Many of us did. In fact, several moved to New York City the very next year upon graduation from college. But what we didn't get were the roots of Perkins's message. Yes, we got "love": we got the fact that love breaks down racial barriers between people. We got that love compels us to offer our personal resources in service to others. We got that love moves us from safe, controlled lives into closer proximity with those in need—that we might taste from their cup, walk in their shoes, and experience the chaos that tosses lives from bliss to blank stares in the blink of an eye. We got that. But it never occurred to us to challenge the systems that caused the racial, economic, educational, health, and social disparities in the first place. It never occurred to us to challenge our neoliberal free-market fundamentalist economic system. We were woefully silent, blissfully ignorant, or our politics compelled us to justify the very system that exacerbated the need for the three Rs in our times.

In Mendenhall, Mississippi, in the 1960s and 1970s the systems Perkins fought were overtly racially biased systems of economic and social oppression. Perkins also fought systems of thought, or worldviews, within the evangelical church. One that he names is the belief that "spiritual manipulation alone" can effect justice.[3] He explains in his book *Let Justice Roll Down* that the white evangelical church believed focusing on the salvation status of individuals would bring about a more just world. Perkins's encounter with the southern systems of political and economic oppression made him acutely aware of the need for both spiritual and "human manipulation" to lift oppression.[4] So in 1964 Vera Mae Perkins began a child care center that became a Head Start center in 1966. In 1965 Perkins's Voice of Calvary (VOC) ministry engaged in voter education and registration campaigns. Then the week before Christmas in 1969 Perkins's nascent theology of reconciliation, which required both personal and systemic reconciliation, led him to cry out from behind the bars of a Mendenhall County jailhouse window to a crowd that had gathered on the street to protest his wrongful arrest. He called them to "take a stand." This was an economic stand. He called for the equitable redistribution of good jobs in Mendenhall businesses. He called for paved streets and better living conditions for the black community. Then he called for an economic boycott of all Mendenhall stores for the entire week before Christmas.[5] Later, during the boycott, a list of demands were made, including the demand that police obey the U.S. Constitution and the orders of the Supreme Court; the demand that police have sworn warrants of arrest for any person, house, or car they search; the demand for the adherence to paying the minimum wage—especially for domestic workers. They also demanded the desegregation of all public facilities.[6]

Within two months of Perkins's and VOC's demands, he and three colleagues were beaten to within inches of their lives by white police officers who targeted Perkins for being an "uppity nigger." After a recovery period, he suffered a relapse and found himself lying on his back for weeks in a hospital bed in Mound Bayou, Mississippi, staring at a ceiling and fighting with God. Perkins wanted to give up—not his fight for justice, but rather his fight for racial reconciliation. He didn't know if reconciliation was possible. Then he remembered Jesus.

Jesus was wrongfully arrested and thrown in jail by his religious enemies. He was beaten to within an inch of his life by his ethnic and political enemies. His people were economically and socially oppressed by the same Roman occupying enemies. He was nailed to a cross by all of us, and yet he said: "Father, forgive them" (Luke 23:34). Perkins reflects: "When [Jesus] looked at that mob who had lynched Him, He didn't hate them. He loved them."[7]

In Perkins's mid-twentieth-century context, the dictates of modernity ruled the rubric that defined reality. For centuries, reality had been defined by domination of the powerful over the weak. This *either/or* worldview was gasping its final breaths in the era of the Cold War when Americans were *either* Communist *or* capitalist, or in the era of racial segregation when the players were *either* racial oppressors *or* oppressed, and in the century-long battle for the domination of *either* the liberal social gospel *or* the fundamentalist gospel of personal salvation.

The first hints of postmodernity challenged the hegemony of domination in the 1950s and 1960s with the fall of colonial powers in Africa and the rise of the civil rights movement in the United States. Into this fractured context Perkins called forth "the whole gospel."[8] He united the evangelical/fundamentalist personal gospel with the modernist social gospel and communicated the good news of *both* personal holiness *and* social and economic reform. This gospel had been preached for more than a century by the historic black church, but it was disregarded and labeled "Communist" by white evangelicals of the day because they didn't believe Martin Luther King Jr. was a Christian. Perkins, whose own evangelical faith was born in the context of the white fundamentalist church, was uniquely able to translate the gospel that fueled the civil rights movement—the whole gospel—into terms white evangelicals could understand. At the heart of Perkins's *both/and* gospel is the call to love our enemies as Jesus loved us. It is relational. It is personal, but it is not only personal; it is also structural and systemic. "If sin can exist at every level of government and in every human institution," Perkins explained in his first book, *Let Justice Roll Down*, "then also the call to biblical justice in every corner of society must be sounded by those who claim a God of Justice as their Lord." Here he identifies with Mordecai and Esther, who were compelled by their faith to fight against earthly powers whose policies and systems did earthly harm to whole people groups.[9]

Rooted in a firm belief in systemic reform and political engagement, Perkins's work took a turn after the beating. I believe this context—the solidly racialized South, where whites had the political power and blacks didn't—led Perkins to shift focus. Mound Bayou showed him in this brutally racialized post–civil rights movement context where every system was set up to protect white power and where most whites claimed to be followers of the same Jesus as blacks—in this context, political engagement was tantamount to beating one's head against a stone wall. The problem was spiritual. Thus the keys were the heart and the soul. The key was love. The hearts and souls of both whites and blacks could only truly learn to love like Jesus loves in the context of transformational community. So Perkins's three Rs called for love exercised through *relocation* of whites, blacks, and others into underresourced segregated areas; interpersonal and communal racial *reconciliation*; and the equitable and costly *redistribution* of personal and systemic resources from rich to poor in order to begin to level the unjust slanted playing fields impoverished people face every day. The three Rs sprang from Perkins's own life experiences, yet after his Mound Bayou revelation, Perkins's practice of the three Rs shied away from civic transformation of policies and systems in favor of the kind of transformation that would be unhindered by the thick white wall of political power. Perkins's work focused on personal, interpersonal, and communal transformation, and transformation of the systems they could control within the black community through the development of education, housing, and health care cooperatives. Thus the goal of the three Rs was always to fully realize the image of God within oppressed communities by lifting all forms of oppression, but Perkins's lasting legacy will likely be the fruit of his work in community development, not the transformation of broad-reaching civic policies and systems.

In our post-Reagan, neoliberal, free-market capitalist society, racial disparities of the civil rights era have been exacerbated and reinforced by President Reagan's deeply rooted and sweeping economic agenda, which resulted in the widest wealth gap in U.S. history. The gap between rich and poor in the United States is the greatest it has been since 1928—the year before the Great Depression. The wealth gap between blacks and whites has been uniquely exacerbated by Reagan's economic policies. According to a 2010 report by the Institute on Assets and Social Policy at Brandeis University, in 1984 the average white family had $20,000 more than the average black family in assets. By 2004, the gap had more than quadrupled to $95,000 for the same families.[10] Perkins's call to love as Jesus loves still stands, and that love still calls for personal, interpersonal, and communal reconciliation, redistribution, and relocation. Yet, ultimately, America's entrenched poverty and yawning wealth gap were created by public policies and must be addressed on the level of public policy if justice will ever roll down like water.

Thus Perkins's call for evangelicals to exercise Jesus's sacrificial love through racial reconciliation, relocation, and redistribution of resources is even more relevant today than it was when he demanded justice from a jailhouse window. In the context of the greatest recession since the Great Depression, the struggle is against poverty. In my current work leading New York Faith and Justice, I am witness to a new generation of evangelicals who are choosing to love sacrificially. They are relocating into the most underresourced corners of our city. They are living in multiethnic Christian communities and intentionally seeking to partner with their neighbors to address injustice in the community. And they are walking Jesus's love right back into the public square where it first took root in Perkins's own life. White, black, Latino, Asian American, and Native American evangelicals are calling for just policies, including health reform, immigration reform, tax reform, environmental justice and climate change legislation, and education reform.

In December 1969 the Holy Spirit rose up in John Perkins and compelled him to cry out from a Mendenhall County jailhouse window. His cries galvanized a local movement for economic justice and modeled evangelical engagement for generations to come. His Mound Bayou breakthrough informs present-day evangelical community organizing and political advocacy for just economic policies. Protest, organizing, and advocacy without love for "our enemies" are as clanging cymbals. They may make a lot of noise, but ultimately only love wins.

## NOTES

1. Veronique De Rugy, "President Reagan: Champion Budget Cutter," American Enterprise Institute for Public Policy Research, http://www.aei.org/paper/20675.

2. "Federal Income Tax Rates History: Income Years 1913 to 2011," January 1, 2011, http://www.taxfoundation.org/publications/show/151.html.

3. John Perkins, *Let Justice Roll Down* (Ventura, Calif.: Regal Books, 1976), 104.

4. Perkins, *Let Justice Roll Down*, 103.

5. Perkins, *Let Justice Roll Down*, 141.

6. Perkins, *Let Justice Roll Down*, 149.

7. Perkins, *Let Justice Roll Down*, 205.

8. Perkins, *Let Justice Roll Down*, 103.

9. Perkins, *Let Justice Roll Down*, 195.

10. Rich Blake, "Skin Color Wealth Gap: Whites Average $95K Richer than Blacks," ABC News, May 18, 2010, http://abcnews.go.com/Business/study-finds-wealth-gap-blacks-whites-quadrupled/story?id=10670261.

# Moving toward the Next Evangelicalism

*Soong-Chan Rah*

SEVERAL YEARS AGO ON A FRIGID JANUARY EVENING I FOUND MYSELF IN the back of a Boston police squad car. Just to be clear, I was not under arrest. I was part of an effort by the Boston Ten-Point Coalition to curb gang violence in our city. Armed with my clerical collar, I was teamed with a police officer to visit at-risk youth in the community. We would visit the home of a youth whose name had appeared in the school police blotter. The student had gotten into a fight, been caught with weapons, or sported gang colors or signs at the school. A local pastor(s) and a police officer(s) would team up to visit the youth and his family. It was the classic bad cop, good pastor routine.

A typical visit would begin with the police officer knocking on the door and the lights being shut off inside the house. The pastor would then knock on the door, the door would be opened, and the pastor would be invited in with the police in tow. The officer would threaten the full measure of the law if the youth was caught involved in gang activity. The youth was now on their radar. They would be on the lookout for him and making sure that the safety of the school was maintained. There were strict laws about gang activity, and they would not be shy about enforcing those laws. The bad cop routine was followed immediately by the good pastor. The pastor would offer the student and his family all the love and support that they needed. He or she would offer to take the troubled child to a movie or offer to have folks from the church come by to help with the family. Our shared goal was to keep the young man from joining the national gangs that were attempting to infiltrate our city. Law and grace were working together for justice.

Sitting in the backseat of the police car that evening, I realized that neither my theologically conservative immigrant church upbringing nor my evangelical seminary education had prepared me for this kind of civic engagement. I had no theological lens to understand this act of pastoral care. The seemingly singular focus on personal evangelism among many evangelicals did not give me the grid to see how riding around in a police car could actually be an integral part of the work of the church. Evangelical-ism's lack of understanding and involvement in matters of social justice is rooted in both an inadequate theology and the impact of twentieth-century American church history.

For those who grew up in immigrant churches, this divorce is exacerbat-ed by a marginalization from the larger American culture and larger evan-gelical subculture, coupled with a desire to assimilate to and be accepted by that same culture. Asian American churches, therefore, often lack the theological, historical, sociological, and ecclesial role models and examples to navigate through a healthy engagement with the world. This community has been held captive by the norms of Western forms of Christianity that can hinder the formation of a healthy social justice engagement. Ironically, the great promise of the Asian American Christian community is that the experiences of immigration and the subsequent transition to the second generation generates a triple consciousness that provides the necessary balance to combat the individualistic and consumeristic evangelicalism of the twentieth century. Furthermore, by looking beyond the white forms of evangelicalism for role models like John Perkins and the Christian Com-munity Development Association (CCDA), the Asian American church can find a positive example of social and cultural engagement. My personal hope for the Asian American community is that this nascent community would begin to embrace the theological legacy of John Perkins in order to move toward a more holistic biblical community for the next epoch of American evangelicalism.

## THE GREAT DIVORCE

For most of the twentieth century, among evangelical Christians, there was a conspicuous divorce between social justice and personal evangelism. The historian David Moberg describes this divorce as "the great reversal"[1]—an unbiblical separation between justice and evangelism that occurred in the twentieth century, in contrast to the integration of the two streams in the nineteenth century. In the twenty-first century, many Christians are at-tempting to reverse "the great reversal." More and more Christians are seek-ing to integrate justice into the life of the church.

While this desire is noble and well-intentioned, even the best of inten-tions can go awry. The renewal of interest in justice should not be rooted in a political correctness that comes from the trendiness of justice issues in the world (even Walmart can now claim to be "green"). Instead, justice needs to be situated in our biblical-theological reflection—leading to an authentic sociocultural engagement by the church leading to God's justice. In other words, our justice needs to go deeper. Out of this twenty-first-century context of the reemergence of a justice and compassion ministry, the life, work, ministry, and theology of John Perkins takes on a greater significance.

In the early part of the twentieth century, the fundamentalist/modernist contention yielded a growing rift in how Christians viewed the church's relationship to the larger culture. Fundamentalists viewed the world as a hostile and evil place, worthy only of rejection and damnation. Spurred by a growing mistrust of the world as well as being driven by a dispensational eschatology, fundamentalists rejected the trappings of modern culture. In the language of H. Richard Niebuhr,[2] fundamentalists took on the posture of Christ against the culture. Meanwhile, the modernist branch of American Christianity saw culture through a more optimistic point of view, believing that Christ could be *of* the culture. This disparate framework of how the church relates to the culture yielded the creation of two camps: the social justice camp and the personal evangelism camp, the Christ against culture camp and the Christ of culture camp. The hardening of the line between these two camps tended to exclude other ways that the church could relate to the culture.

American evangelicalism continued this disproportionate emphasis on personal evangelism inherited from fundamentalism. Many evangelicals continued the belief that involvement in social concerns would distract from the important work of personal evangelism. As American evangelicalism emerges out of the rubble of the fundamentalist versus modernist controversy as well as the mainline versus evangelical divide, there is a growing awareness of the failures of a personal evangelism-only model of engaging the culture. "There was a deep, deep individualism that lay at the heart of the evangelical project. This individualism is best exemplified in the doctrine of personal regeneration. . . . When translated into a social ethic, this meant that the conversion of individuals led to the transformation of society."[3] Both fundamentalism and evangelicalism failed to integrate a healthy and just engagement with the culture and displayed an inability to move beyond the strictly individual expression of the gospel.

Where this divorce was not as evident in American Christianity was in the black church. The African American community living in the context of racial and socioeconomic injustice did not experience the great divorce to the extent experienced by the majority culture fundamentalist and evangelical churches. The black church engaged the injustices of American society with the gospel of Jesus Christ on both the level of individual salvation and social justice. Part of the restoration of a holistic gospel may be the bridge that connects the separatist tendencies of white fundamentalism and evangelicalism with the socially conscious and engaged expressions of the African American church. "Today black and white evangelical Christians are coming together in a post–civil rights moment. Prophetic black Christianity that had been tucked away within a white evangelical modernity gradually emerged to redirect evangelicalism to its deepest prophetic roots."[4] The hope of twenty-first-century evangelicalism is that what had once been unjustifiably divorced may now be restored—through the integration of black and white Christianity.

Another group that did not experience the divorce between personal evangelism and social justice would be the recent immigrants who arrived on the shores of America after the change in U.S. immigration laws in 1965. Recent immigrants to the United States would not have the deep history of fundamentalist separatism found in the majority culture Christian community or the long history of a corporate struggle against social injustices evident in the black church. This recent (last forty-plus years) wave of immigration produced churches that were not directly involved in the controversies of the early twentieth century that resulted in the great divorce. The first-generation immigrant church and the emerging second-generation church, therefore, provide an intriguing case study of the potential intersection of personal evangelism and social justice. The possibility of bridging this gulf is the example set by the life and ministry of John Perkins. The theological legacy of John Perkins, therefore, may prove to be of great importance and could have a significant impact on the developing story of the immigrant Christian communities in the United States.

## IMMIGRANT CHURCHES AND AMERICAN CHRISTIANITY

My involvement with the CCDA and my appreciation of John Perkins's theological legacy did not begin in the context of the immigrant church. Growing up in a Korean American immigrant church context, we didn't hear much about the words, wisdom, and work of John Perkins. Our immigrant community was too preoccupied with surviving in a hostile environment, preventing the Korean church from engaging in the needs of the larger community. In addition, immigrant churches were also trying very hard to assimilate into the majority white evangelical subculture, failing to recognize the work of one of the most important American Christian voices of the twentieth century. However, the life and practice of the Korean immigrant church often mirrored the challenges raised by John Perkins, even if Korean immigrants lacked a specific understanding of the connection of the teachings and impact of John Perkins with the everyday life of the Korean immigrant church.

The Korean immigrant church has consistently placed a high value on evangelism and evangelistic efforts. While a significant percentage of Korean immigrants have some sort of Christian background before coming to the United States, the conversion rate of Koreans after immigration is substantial. Estimates place conversion growth in the Korean immigrant church as high as 40 percent, which would place the Korean immigrant church as one of the more successful evangelism stories in the twentieth century.[5] Evangelism has had a significant role in the life of the Korean immigrant church. Interestingly, the type of evangelism employed by the Korean immigrant church expanded beyond the simple sharing of the facts and truths of Christianity.

Korean churches were proactive in reaching out to other Koreans through social services and outreach ministries.[6] The Korean immigrant church is active in providing educational services to the younger generation through Korean-language programs or after-school tutoring. One of the Korean immigrant church's key roles is to provide the social service of youth ministry, providing de facto child care for immigrant families. Korean churches also provide relational support that results in the provision of social services. Job training and placement, senior citizen care, social and psychological support for the alienated immigrant, and the availability of the church leadership to provide a wide range of social services for newly arrived immigrants are direct ways that the Korean church employed social service ministry resulting in successful efforts at evangelism.

Inadvertently, the Korean immigrant church has been an expression and embodiment of the principles of John Perkins and the CCDA. The bulk of these social services, however, are directed inward toward their own community. These CCDA-type ministries ultimately served the high level of social and economic need found in the immigrant community. Immigrant churches have been active in providing community development and social services to their own communities. The work of John Perkins and the CCDA is the necessary theological and ecclesiological bridge that connects the existing work of the immigrant church to the Scriptures. Furthermore, the work of Perkins and the CCDA needs to become a more explicit example and model for the emerging second-generation immigrant community.

In the Korean immigrant church and its second-generation progeny, the models of ministry have focused on white evangelical leaders. Growing up in the immigrant church, who were our spiritual heroes? One such hero was Billy Graham, the symbol of effective evangelism and the unifying figure of evangelicalism. His passionate focus on evangelism and the salvation of souls provided a locus for twentieth-century evangelicalism. Graham's prominence results in the justifiably high reverence afforded to Graham by the Korean Christian community. For example, a friend of mine in seminary was named after Billy Graham. His legal name was actually "Billy," not William. His first-generation pastor father had named him after the highly admired American evangelical, but did not know that Billy was a nickname for William.

In more recent years Korean evangelicals have become enamored with other prominent white American evangelicals, such as Bill Hybels, Rick Warren, Tim Keller, and John Piper. Attendance at conferences sponsored by their churches and their organizations will typically have a high level of participation by Asian Americans. Books written by Piper and Keller are placed at the top of the reading list for second-generation Korean Americans. The worth and value of these individuals' contributions to American Christianity are to be affirmed. However, it seems that in the Korean immigrant community, there appears to be gravitation toward expressions of white evangelicalism more than nonwhite expressions of Christian faith.

Asian American attendance at national conferences that are dominated by white evangelicals (both in terms of the percentage of participants and the roster of speakers and workshop leaders) can be assumed. More surprising is that conferences like Sojourners' Mobilization to End Poverty or the National Christian Community Development Association Conference—organizations that champion racial diversity—only see a trickle of attendees and participants from the Asian American community. While notable efforts are made by the organizers of these conferences to attract Asian Americans, the level of participation pales in comparison to conferences that are held exclusively for the Asian American community or conferences that arise out of the majority culture context.

The disparity between the elevation of the majority culture's expression of individualized Christianity and the lack of connection with the expression of social justice–focused Christianity may have two different explanations. The first explanation arises out of the desire for acceptance by second-generation Korean Americans. In short, many Asian Americans operate under the mistaken notion that to be accepted as Christians in America, we must operate as honorary white people. Similar to the ways that many nonwhite Christians both domestically and globally have co-opted American culture to become Christian, Asian American Christians feel the need to put on the clothing of Western, white Christianity in order to fit into the ethos of American Christianity.

There is a desire to fit in with the in-crowd of white evangelicals. Most Asian American Christians will be familiar with and have the highest respect for successful ministers with best-selling books and successful megachurches. Code words like entrepreneurial leadership and cutting-edge ministries became the mantra for Asian American churches. Typically, these types of leaders and ministries would be found in the white evangelical megachurches—leading to the pursuit of success in many Asian American churches being framed by the dominant culture's definition of success.

The second explanation is connected to the first reason in that just as the majority culture's expression of Christianity has focused on an individualized faith, so, too, the imitators have fallen into the same patterns of faith. Asian American Christianity's inability to grasp the importance of a holistic gospel message may trace back to white evangelicalism's inability to move beyond the fundamentalist/modernist controversies of a previous generation. The immigrant church and the second-generation church are following the patterns laid down by the dominant culture's brand of American Christianity. The great promise of the twenty-first century is that Asian American Christians who latched onto the dominant culture's expression of faith would have the capacity to move toward a more holistic faith. That transition needs the teaching, ministry example, and life story of a John Perkins to be a guide in that process.

## THE POWER OF STORY

We're taught from an early age to appreciate the stories of the Bible. We're taught in Sunday school to be moved by the stories of missionaries. We are taught in the Sunday worship to be inspired by the personal stories and illustrations of the preacher. We are taught to share our personal testimony stories at every opportunity in order to communicate the gospel message. When in doubt, share your story.

John Perkins's story has been a particularly impactful and significant story in my own life. In many ways, I am both a typical and an atypical product of the Korean immigrant church. My introduction to faith and the fostering of my personal relationship with Jesus was nurtured in the context of the Korean immigrant church. My convictions about the need for a passionate personal piety come from years of worship services, Sunday school classes, Friday night youth group meetings, Saturday fellowship gatherings, early morning prayer meetings, summer youth retreats, winter youth retreats, summer revival meetings, fall revival meetings, and spring revival meetings. My experience in the immigrant church gave me a healthy respect for the importance of individual salvation. Growing up in a Southern Baptist church to boot meant that altar calls were commonplace. Not only were frequent altar calls issued at our church gatherings, it seemed that I answered every single one of them. The importance of coming to Christ on your own and receiving Christ as your personal Savior (sometimes repeatedly, just to be sure) was central to the life of our church.

Like any good twentieth-century evangelical, I learned to share my personal testimony not too long after my conversion experience. A key component of evangelism training was learning how to share your testimony. There were templates and samples that would guide the process of formulating the perfect personal testimony. Sharing your testimony at a campfire or at a sharing night replaced the answering of the altar call as the way to publicly demonstrate your spirituality. My very first public proclamation at my church was the sharing of my personal testimony at a Sunday evening church service. I became very adept, even prideful about being able to share my personal testimony.

In contrast to most of my friends at church, I came from a single-parent home. The shame of coming from a broken home was more pronounced in a cultural setting where deviation from the norm was generally considered unacceptable. However, once I started sharing my story, the shame of coming from a broken home was replaced by the pride of having an exciting story to tell. I came to recognize the power of stories in the immigrant church. Our senior pastor demonstrated that power. He would frequently share stories about his years as a drug-addled dealer at a nearby college. Instead of shame, his story of overcoming addiction helped him to gain credibility and even a sense of awe from his congregation. The use of a well-placed and emotional moving story can transport an expository sermon to new emotional and spiritual heights. To this day, I am quick to share my story because I know that my story can inspire others to repentance and action.

A key contribution of John Perkins is the power of his story. When consideration is given to who are the role models for the younger generation, those with powerful life stories will rise to the top of the list. Knowledge of the propositional truths of the Scriptures in order to engage in an academic apologetic of the gospel message held much sway in the twentieth century, but an increasingly postmodern ethos leads to a greater appreciation of narratives. Personal testimonies already held a place of great importance among evangelicals, but they are elevated to an even more prominent position in the twenty-first century. A life lived will have more to say than simply words spoken. John Perkins's story is an important aspect of his impact on twentieth-century American Christianity.

Perkins's story is familiar to many. Just poll those that have even met John Perkins once and hear how that onetime meeting and the hearing of John's story and the real presence and engagement of John has irrevocably changed thousands of individuals. One of John Perkins's key theological contributions is the power of his story lived out in the face of great trials and tribulations. There may be other evangelical leaders with a great testimony, but no one rivals the lived theology and embodied story of Jesus's redemptive power than John Perkins. Among twentieth-century evangelical leaders, no one has done more with less. No one has overcome as many obstacles as John Perkins.

Hearing John Perkins's story has been a source of great inspiration to me. To hear of someone who has overcome so many obstacles encourages me to face the obstacles that I have experienced in my own life. Perkins's willingness to speak of his pain and struggle emboldens me to share the stories of my pain and struggle. Perkins's ability to rise above the struggle and speak a strong prophetic word encourages me to rise above and speak the truth, no matter what the obstacles. Very few evangelicals have the depth of testimony of John Perkins. For the Asian American community, the power of John Perkins's story calls us as a community to rise above our struggles and contribute to the greater good of American Christianity and the larger society. If John Perkins could overcome racism, economic injustice, and social inequality and become a source of inspiration and an example to many, continuing to do good works in Christ, then the Asian American Christian community can also rise above, overcome, and do good works. His story becomes the story of our community as well.

## CHRIST AND CULTURE, PERKINS-STYLE

Perkins's impact on twenty-first-century Christianity is not limited to his ability to relate to a broad audience through his personal story. His sermons, books, and teachings have had a prophetic impact as well. As mentioned above, the majority culture's expression of Christianity has often displayed a dysfunctional relationship with the surrounding culture, whether that's an antagonism toward the world or an overacquiescence to the world. Perkins's context necessitated his voice being raised against the injustices of our society. But his connection with fundamentalist and evangelical Christianity also gave him a deep passion and appreciation for the work of personal evangelism.

In the early years of his ministry, John Perkins would be aligned with Bible outreaches that would have warmed the hearts of even the most fundamental of fundamentalists. The formation of Perkins's early Christianity was steeped in the personal evangelism of fundamentalism and evangelicalism. These roots, however, did not prevent him from engaging the social structural evils of his time. John Perkins's context determined that he would not only be an advocate and practitioner of personal evangelism, but that he would be one of the most significant advocates and one of the most articulate voices of social, cultural engagement by the church in the twentieth century.

Perkins's personal story comes into play here. Because of his ministry context and because of his personal experiences arising out of the African American experience, Perkins raises issues that were not broached by majority culture Christians. Perkins would speak on the need for racial reconciliation because he lived under the oppression of racial unrighteousness. He had personally experienced racial persecution. Perkins's theological expression, therefore, arose out of the context of the African American community but with a broader impact on majority culture evangelicalism. In this dual context (growing up as a black man in the South, while connected to the larger context of majority culture Christianity), Perkins could speak prophetically out of a real life experience while understanding the language of majority culture Christianity.

The context of twentieth-century Christianity demanded a voice like John Perkins's. The vacuum of biblical social justice could not be sustained. The great reversal needed to be reversed. John Perkins became the theological corrective necessary for the full gospel to rise up. John Perkins remains a prophetic necessity and corrective to a dysfunctional relationship between church and culture. The impact of John Perkins upon American evangelicalism is the beginning of the acknowledgment that racial and social justice is an integral part of the gospel message. John Perkins was able to bring this message out of his own life experience and out of his own cultural context. His courage to bring this message provides inspiration for succeeding generations.

As an Asian American, I struggle with my particular contribution to the larger movement of God in American Christianity. Are my experiences valid? Are the unique contributions that arise out of my particular social context applicable to the larger context of American Christianity? John Perkins shows that a prophetic voice is a necessary part of the move of God. Perkins provides the possibility that prophetic voices emerging from the margins can have a significant theological and ecclesiological impact on the larger movement of American Christianity.

## BUILDING BRIDGES

John Perkins has made this significant prophetic impact by traversing the difficult territory of reconciliation. Perkins's ability to transcend the restrictions and limitations of being exclusively in the context of the white church or the black church has allowed him to be an important bridge across dividing lines. The theological context of the white church vis-à-vis the black church has different originating points. One emerges out of the context of majority culture and dominant power. The other emerges out of oppression and suffering. Walter Brueggemann distinguishes between a theology that arises out of celebration versus a theology that emerges out of suffering. To Brueggemann, a theology of the "haves" is not the same as a theology of the "have-nots."[7] Different worldviews and priorities emerge when one perspective seeks to maintain the status quo and the current power dynamic, while the other perspective seeks to challenge the status quo and seek redress for injustice.

An uneven power dynamic characterizes the relationship between the two perspectives. Those in power have no incentive to hear from those outside of that power. Those who hold the political power and control the material assets have the power to dominate the conversation. The division exists because the ones who have the power are usually not willing to hear from those without the power. There are numerous methods by which the powerful can shut out the powerless. The powerful can set up educational structures that determine who are the experts within that system. The powerful dictate who are the representative voices of the community. The powerful are able to determine what is orthodox thinking versus thinking that is considered to be on the margins. John Perkins's ability to gain a hearing in the dominant culture's expression of Christianity is, to some extent, a miracle. Despite being a voice from the margins, Perkins has been acknowledged as an important leader among American evangelicals. Perkins still needs to receive a wider reading among evangelicals, but he remains one of the few ethnic minority leaders who have been able to receive a hearing in majority culture evangelicalism.

Furthermore, with the changing face of American evangelicalism, more and more ethnic minority voices need to be brought to the forefront. In the latter part of the twentieth century, nonwhite evangelical voices of leadership were few and far in-between. Perkins never compromised the prophetic edge of his message, nor did he deny the context from which his message and story arose. Yet his story and ministry, which appear to be atypical of the twentieth-century evangelical narrative, have built a bridge between the haves and the have-nots, between the celebrants and the suffering. Perkins provides the possibility that an ethnic minority can be himself or herself in one's unique cultural and racial identity and still exhibit leadership in the context of majority culture evangelicalism. This dualistic worldview emerging out of a personal experience in two seemingly disparate worlds provides hope for the Asian American Christian community to bridge the gap between personal evangelism and social justice.

The Asian American community stands in a unique position in twenty-first-century evangelicalism. Specific needs in the context of the immigrant community required the formation of an immigrant church concerned with meeting those needs. At the same time, many of these communities were marginalized from majority cultural expressions of evangelical faith. The second-generation children of the immigrant generation straddled both worlds—the world of their parents attempting to build a new life in the context of a foreign and sometimes hostile world and the world of majority culture, which provides both an enticement and a sense of rejection. The reality of this duality yields a triple consciousness identity for the second-generation immigrant.[8] Triple consciousness individuals feel like insiders and outsiders in both their culture of origin and in their adopted culture. In straddling the world of their parents and of the majority culture, second-generation Korean American Christians are poised to develop an understanding of reality that allows for multiple consciousness and liminality.

Initially, this liminality may be viewed as a disability and a hindrance. However, the story of triple consciousness is the story of an extraordinary ability. It is the ability to understand both sides of the equation, to empathize with two different worldviews, and to form a third worldview without compromising or acquiescing to the worldview of origin. It is the ability to bridge the seemingly disparate motivation and trajectory of evangelism and justice. John Perkins's contribution to twenty-first-century American evangelicalism is his ability to be a bridge between the different communities of faith that are evident in a multicultural America. John Perkins's story is one of triple consciousness identity. He has successfully navigated different worlds and disparate worldviews to emerge with a testimony and a theology that speak to both worlds.

For the Asian American community that has typically been absorbed into the majority culture's expression of Christianity, Perkins stands as an example of the possibilities of the next evangelicalism. Perkins's story resonates with those that emerge out of the context of suffering and struggle, while challenging an individualized and consumerized evangelicalism. Perkins's prophetic teachings never compromised the truths of biblical social justice, yet received a hearing from the dominant culture. Perkins's ability to transcend the dividing walls of hostility serves as a model for being able to enter into a dialogue in the inevitable multicultural Christianity of the twenty-first century.

## NOTES

1. David O. Moberg, *The Great Reversal: Evangelism versus Social Concern* (Philadelphia: J. B. Lippincott, 1972).

2. H. Richard Niebuhr, *Christ and Culture* (New York: Harper & Row, 1951).

3. Peter Goodwin Heltzel, *Jesus and Justice: Evangelicals, Race and American Politics* (New Haven, Conn.: Yale University Press, 2009), 138.

4. Heltzel, *Jesus and Justice*, 4.

5. Soong-Chan Rah, *The Next Evangelicalism: Freeing the Church from Western Cultural Captivity* (Downers Grove, Ill.: InterVarsity Press, 2009), 166–167.

6. Rah, *Next Evangelicalism*, 173–179.

7. Walter Brueggemann, *Peace* (St. Louis: Chalice Press, 2001), 29.

8. See Eldin Villafane, *The Liberating Spirit* (Grand Rapids, Mich.: Eerdmans, 1993); and Rah, *Next Evangelicalism*.

# APPENDIX A.

## Let Justice Roll Down: A Conversation with John Perkins

THIS IS AN EDITED TRANSCRIPT OF THE EXTENDED CONVERSATION BETWEEN theologian Charles Marsh and John Perkins that took place at the University of Virginia on April 22, 2009, as part of the Spring Institute for Lived Theology.

**Charles Marsh (CM):** Good evening, ladies and gentlemen. It's so nice to have you here for this extraordinary event, one that I'm very excited about; a conversation with an activist, a writer, a pastor, a civil rights hero and a very close friend of mine, Dr. John Perkins. Welcome to all of you.

**John Perkins (JP):** Well, I'm really honored to be here. Outside of my coming to faith in Christ and marrying Vera Mae and her giving me this heritage of eight children and thirteen grands and two great-grands, my friends—I live at the mercy and thanksgiving and the gratitude of my friends. I would consider you folks here to be some of those friends. So I consider being here with you a great honor. You honor me and I like all these other honors, I have to tell the truth about that, but the real honor goes to my friends. It's been that quality of friendship that has caused me to persevere, that has both freed and restrained me because of their love, so I just thank you for being here and having me.

**CM:** Dr. Perkins, you were born in 1930 as the sixth child to Maggie Perkins, the fifth child to survive, and you were raised on cotton plantations in Simpson County. You wrote in your memoir, *Let Justice Roll Down*, that your earliest memory is of a winter afternoon, a close gray sky and a small house on a dirt road. In the memory, your grandmother sits inside the house sewing a quilt to keep the children warm. You're standing in the front yard chopping wood for the fire, occasionally carrying small bundles of sticks to the porch. Your family farmed on halves, moving from plantation

189

to plantation with the changing seasons according to the shifting demands for cheap labor. And like most rural African American children, you were put to work in the fields picking cotton alongside your grandmother, aunts, cousins, and sisters, waking up before first light and returning home after sunset. From September through November, riding to and from work in large, open-body trucks, as you wrote in the memoir, "just like hogs and cattle." Can you share with us a sense of what the world looked like to you as a child coming of age in this brutal and oppressive society?

**JP:** Let me see where to start here. I love hot weather; I could have lived in the California desert. I think it's because of the harshness and the kind of shacks that we lived in. The plantation-type houses that had one board over another board, and when that board would come off the house the ice chickers in the winter would be on the inside of the house as well as the outside of the house, and the misery of being cold, and the misery of standing by the fireplace, all of those things are still vivid to me.

When I was writing *Let Justice Roll Down*, I was talking to an old lady who had been living in the community when I was born. She said my mother died of a disease that had to do with nutrition deficiency and I was sucking her breast, right up until she died. I was probably taking the nutrition she needed for her own survival.

When my mother died, a lady down the street who had a milk cow—we didn't have a milk cow because the plantation owner would not allow his people to have milk cows on the plantation—started bringing a quart of milk for me. I was nothing but skin and bones, and she began to see me recover. We were doing the research, and I said to the old lady, "What happened to her?" And she told me a story about my hometown, about this lady dying a slow death because they didn't have a doctor, and there hadn't been a doctor in twelve years in my hometown of New Hebron. I said, "That will come to an end" (because we built a health center there).

One of the things that confronts me each day of my life is that I have a funny feeling of looking forward to heaven, but I've never seen a picture of my mother, and then of course with Spencer [Perkins] being there, I don't see it as a bad deal. But what drives me too is, I imagine my mother is going to say to me, "What did you do for other people like me?" So this idea of the poor is so deeply rooted. I'm not poor; I haven't been poor since I was an adult. I was bent on breaking out of that, but I think that question is a big driving force, because I would like for her to say too, "Well done." Naturally, I want Jesus to say it, but I would like for her to say it too.

**CM:** Dr. Perkins, the folks that created this evil system called Jim Crow were by and large white folks that called themselves Christians. And I'm wondering as a child, and as a young man, if you thought about that. When you passed a white church, did you think "What's going on in that place?" And how did you come to terms with that fact?

**JP:** My family, while we were sharecroppers, we were also bootleggers and gamblers. We were not religious people, so early on I did not see religion as relevant to society. I could not understand why black folk were Baptist because all the white folk were Baptist. And I would see all these signs, "revival tonight," these revivals at all these white churches, "everybody's welcome" ... well if I had gone there there would have been a riot.

I did not get the virtue of religion, nor did I see the meaning of it until after I came to Christ when I was twenty-seven. So I didn't think of it in terms of religion; I saw it in terms of black folks struggling for emotional dignity and [church as] an outlet for their pent-up emotions, [and] white folks using it to affirm their plantation ownership, so I did not see the virtue in religion.

I saw [religion] about the same way as Karl Marx saw it—I didn't know about Karl Marx at the time, I learned about that later.

**CM:** In 1947 your brother was murdered by a police officer in the town of New Hebron. A decorated war veteran with a Purple Heart, he returned home from World War II after surviving extensive combat wounds, and yet he died in your arms from a gunshot wound as your uncle searched for a hospital that would treat African Americans. You said in your memoir, *Let Justice Roll Down*, that your mind was frozen into a numbed blankness, and after that there was rage and anger, with which you resolved to leave Mississippi once and for all. You ended up in the coastal town of Southgate, California, found work at the Union Pacific foundry, and after the Korean War, you and Vera Mae settled in Monrovia, giving yourself fully to your twin ambitions: making money and forgetting the bad memories of life in the Deep South. You got a job as a janitor in a supermarket chain called Shopping Bag, and you so impressed the company owner with your work ethic that you soon moved up to the welding shop and eventually to equipment design. Settling into the comforts of the black middle class and a spacious new home, you tried not to think too much about Mississippi and the life you had escaped. So why on earth did you and your family move back to Mississippi in 1960?

**JP:** That's a good question. You need to know a little bit about how I was raised—growing up without a mother, growing up without a father in my life, growing up in a big extended family—my grandmother had been the mother of nineteen children. We were not influenced by Christianity, so many of my cousins would have three brothers or sisters with different fathers—they would have different names—but at least they had their mother. And my mother was dead, and my daddy dropped the five of us there. My grandmother wound up giving away three of my siblings because she just had too many in the family. On the plantation, when they would ask somebody to go get water, or do something, I would always run because I liked the affirmation you would get for obedience. And what I discovered the morning I came to faith in Jesus Christ, I discovered what was missing in my life, and what was my driving force: I was designed to be loved.

I think my driving force in life was to be loved. And that Sunday morning, of course I'm not a very religious guy, so I don't say like "The Holy Spirit told me," I don't use that kind of language—that Sunday morning though, I know it was God who did that. It was that Galatians passage that just [revealed] to me the good news of the gospel. When Paul said, "I have been crucified with Christ, nevertheless I live. Yet not I, but Christ lives in me, and the life that I now live in the flesh I live by the faith in the Son of God, who loved me." By this time, I recognized that Christ had died, of course for the sin of the world, but it wasn't necessarily for me. But that morning, I realized that there was a God in heaven who loved me, and it felt like to me that that God embraced me.

And I was afraid of this God because I was so contaminated and so sinful and he loved me.

He loved me.

He gave himself for me.

The longing I felt—what I had been missing—[now] I felt that I was loved by the Holy God. I think that affected me in every area of my life.

After my conversion to Christ, there were some businessmen in town who I got connected with at a crucial time. See, I was converted in 1957, when there was a pivotal revival going on in Southern California. In fact, that's where Billy Graham struck it rich, there in Southern California in the midst of that revival. It was after World War II; the missionaries had gone back to Africa and all over the world, and I was converted during the time of their furlough. In that environment, there was this passion among the missionaries for the black people in Africa. When I was converted, and coming from my background, I thought that's what it meant to be a

Christian: to be one in Jesus Christ. It was a pivotal time; it was a moment; it was an environment; it was a people. And they embraced me. It was like they were sensing that there were no blacks in their environment, and for me I thought, I'm living in the black community, and this is what it meant now to be a Christian in society.

These businessmen would go up on a Sunday morning to the prison camps in the San Dimas mountains out there in Southern California. They asked me to come and give my testimony. I shared my background. And right as I got to the end of my talk, I realized there were too many black people there. I was in a suburb of LA—Arcadia, Monrovia—that was a wealthy area of town. I saw that 80 or 90 percent of those people were young black people. That horrified me. As I was speaking and sharing my testimony, two of those young black people, boys in the back, they must have been about thirteen, they began to cry and to shake. I went back there and sat between them and I asked them, "What's wrong?" And they said, "When you were sharing your testimony, you were describing my own life. I grew up without a father." And here they were in prison, and here they were speaking my language. I could hear that, they were family from the South, like me, speaking Ebonics like me, and I realized then that I had lived in Mississippi all these years, not hearing this good news that Christ could deliver. It was the first time in my life that I realized that in sharing the gospel, it was possible that God could transform, and take what I had shared and affect other people's lives.

I think, too, that when you're striving for something all your life and discover that you have found it—I think you need a new challenge. I think that this idea of Jesus saying "If anyone come after me let him deny himself and take up his cross and follow me," I think that's part of a built-in challenge. I think it was a combination of a burden and passion—passion is putting yourself in the same situation that other people are in. So I think those boys did it that morning. That was the call of God upon my life; I didn't go back with any civil rights ambition. I went back really to share Christ, to see whether the transformation that had happened to me and to those boys—could I go back and live among the people and see that transformation happen? So that was my call.

CM: I am very interested in your vision for faith and justice when you returned in 1960 to Mississippi. Spencer [Perkins] told me in a conversation one time, "When we returned to Mississippi in 1960 we weren't trying to raise any ruckus." Yet by 1963, and of course, 1964, Mississippi was becoming the spotlight of the civil rights movement. Bob Moses and others in the Student Nonviolent Coordinating Committee said that "our mission is to crack the iceberg of Southern segregation, and Mississippi was the solid-most core of the iceberg of Southern segregation," so the movement came south for that amazing 1964 Freedom Summer project. You once said that when you came back to Mississippi, you didn't have a holistic gospel. You found it some time after you got back. I'm very interested to know what is a holistic gospel, and what influenced your move to that gospel.

**JP:** I went back to Mississippi thinking that the gospel could burn through those racial barriers. Then I faced the harsh reality. I became a friend of the First Baptist pastor, Dr. Odenwald, in town, and by this time in about '64, and this was the hottest time—the three civil rights workers had been killed, the voting rights thing was . . . long hot summer and all of that. I was working in segregated public schools, doing chapel programs. They would gather in the gym, and that was a big thing back there in Mississippi. I began to watch and to see the behavior of our people, and the fact that my people had developed—given the misery and the poverty, I want y'all to understand, and the hopefulness of our people, they tied education to leaving Mississippi and going off and getting a job. They didn't tie education to their economic condition in Mississippi. You would go to somebody's house, and they would have all these graduation pictures of these kids on the mantle over the fireplace. You looked down in the house and the pigs and the chickens and the cracks and the cold was there, but they would be bragging about the fact that their children were now in Chicago, New York, or somewhere else. Education wasn't tied to the reality of the now. As you went north, education became tied to how you could look when you came back to Mississippi, what kind of car you were driving. It was symbolic of success; it was not concrete ownership of any assets within a community and was in no way tied to economic development. It was tied to consumerism and the way things looked, and the way you looked, and if you looked like you was prosperous in society. So that was a short trip, then, to prosperity theology.

I began to see what was happening, and I remember I said to Vera Mae, "I'm worried about these kids that I'm working with. They're going to succeed, but they're going to leave and I'm going to have to keep doing this over again, keep doing this over again." I said to my wife, "Honey, if we're going to make a difference in Mendenhall, then this is what we're going to have to do: We're going to have to stay in town long enough to win some of the young people to Jesus Christ. We've got to disciple them in our faith; we've got to help them get a love for God, a love for themselves, and a love for the community that's a bigger love than consumerism and materialism. We're going to help them stay in school, go off to college, get some skills, and bring those skills back to the community."

Vera Mae went to crying, and she said, "I will never have another house." She saw the significance of that commitment. First thing I did then was, with the guys, we built her a house, a nice house in the community. We got a framing company to come and develop the shell and we built the rest of it: the only two-story house—still—in the black community of Mendenhall.

Around that same time, I had this idea, I met a [white] Presbyterian pastor in another town, and I began to talk to the Baptist pastor in Mendenhall, Dr. Odenwald, about what I was going to do. He was born in the Mississippi Delta, so he could relate to me, and he had been off to university and probably had a master's degree in theology. And what made us friends, because that's the big hurdle—the greatest hurdle in the South was that imperialism and racism were so tied together that whites could not think that a black person could be equal enough with them to assume the foundation of a friendship, that would always be a patronizing situation. Reconciliation assumes equality. Everything else is patronizing. The first truth is that we're created in the image of God, each one of us. So somehow, we became friends. I think this is what happened: because I had been discipled in the biblical foundational truth, I think I might have been the first black he'd ever listened to theologically, because you [whites] don't listen to black preachers for what they say—that was brought out in the Jeremiah Wright deal. White folk, that was the first time they ever listened to a black preacher. They don't go to black churches to hear what they say; they go there for the music and some other reasons. But in this case, with this friend, I was the first person that he probably ever met that understood theology as well as him, and that sort of shocked him.

This gave us a friendship, an emotional friendship, but it was also a friendship in terms of mission (and that's what ought to be the end of friendship, for Christians: the end of friendship ought to be mission together). He wanted to help me, and he was so passionate that he began to go back to his church, like any good pastor would, and try to get his people softened up for it. But they heard him too clearly, and they rejected him, and he committed suicide. A few months later, my Presbyterian friend also committed suicide. That's when I began to see that slavery and segregation and racism had destroyed white folks too.

White people had taken this precious gospel, this love of God, this gospel that's supposed to reconcile people to God and to each other, across racial and social barriers. We had taken that gospel and put it into our racial culture in a way that the gospel had lost its power. We had accommodated racism and bigotry within the church. We had accommodated the very central truth of the gospel: that God was in Christ reconciling the world unto himself. And it was the pain, then, of me losing the hope that I realized could be realized. Because in California I had experienced that for a little while, for three and a half years after my conversion. So my passion became not just for those—and of course I'm passionate, and you'll hear about that later, about the socioeconomic conditions—but now I'm passionate about this force, the blindness of this force that's holding us there. And it was the church that was holding us there.

Now these kinds of things test your faith. Then you begin to talk about what to do with it, and what forces you want to join. Some of the dynamics of the civil rights movement . . . of course there was John Lewis, of course there was Bob Moses, all the kids who dropped out of university and gave up their lives to the movement. [Among their number were] the young Jewish people. They weren't bringing their Jewish faith; they was bringing their deep social commitment. They didn't have any Christian faith. Most of them was young atheists—wonderful people, wonderful Jewish people—I probably would have been an atheist too, if I had been a Jew over there, and seen what had happened there and that Catholic church accommodating to that Holocaust.

Those guys would come, but they didn't have any faith, and to a certain degree it was undermining the historical faith of those young, black, talented young folks who was joining with them. I was motivated deeply by my faith; I was motivated by their commitment. I'm overly competitive, I guess you know that, so I thought that Christianity could be as good as those wonderful Jewish people. I thought my Christian faith could be as good as those Black Muslims. I thought my faith had to be involved as much as their faith.

I was trying to maintain my faith that brought me there, that motivated me, that gave me my meaning, that freed me from my own individual prosperity and success and put me in the midst of that; I was to keep that in life. Then there was the morality of it: these young men would fight for civil rights all day and sleep with somebody's wife during the night. So all of those kind of realities were part of my struggle, but I wanted my faith to be the compelling element. It was the compelling element, because I think I had found my meaning—I had found love and I knew what it was, and that love was in Jesus Christ and that love was for each other. So I think that's what drove me to the sense of wholeness. You know I always tell the story about me working for fifteen cents, when I really began to discover that justice was an economic stewardship issue. It was trying to maintain my faith, and of course later, when I got locked in jail and beat up I had to struggle with my faith again. So I've had my faith come to crisis, and in the midst of crisis—I haven't found a lot of contradictions in the Word of God. You have to go stretch it hard to find racism as the reality within the New Testament. It's not there.

**CM:** By the late 1960s the shape of your ministry in Mississippi had now sort of included the double punch of salvation and social justice, salvation as personal faith in Christ and engagement in the world for justice. At one point you said, "Social action fleshes out the Lordship of Christ. The grace that frees is the grace that forms." And then in the fall of 1969 you organized a selective buying campaign, a boycott, in the town of Mendenhall against white businesses that were discriminating against African Americans.

And you paid a price for that courage. In February of 1970, as you mentioned, you were tortured and beaten nearly to death by a mob of white racist police officials in a jail cell in the town of Brandon, Mississippi. And while recovering from these injuries in Mound Bayou, at the Tufts Medical Center, you had a kind of vision of Jesus on the cross, and you said, "I might go so far as to say I experienced a second conversion while I lay in that hospital bed. It was a conversion of love and forgiveness." I wonder if you would be so kind as to talk about the transformations in your life that followed from your arrest and your beating and your recovery.

**JP:** When my two white friends committed suicide, I committed myself to work for reconciliation. The months following [their suicides], I neglected that for the development of Dolphus [Weary] and Artis [Fletcher] and those kids in the community, and I left the racial thoughts out. I think it was that night in that Brandon jail, when we was being tortured, that it came back to me again. When I saw the behavior of those people, they looked like monsters. They looked like horror out of the night as they tortured us. And as people torture people the Abu Ghraib comes out—they always torture them sexually—and so they tortured us in that jail. And that's when I said to God, "If you allow me to get out of here alive," which I didn't think I would, "then I want to preach a gospel that is stronger than my race; I want to preach a gospel that is stronger than my economic interest; I want to preach a gospel that can reconcile black and whites together."

As soon as I got out of that jail, I wanted to forget about that. I didn't want to hear that anymore. When I was recovering in the Mound Bayou

Hospital, I wanted to read my Bible but I couldn't. And almost every time I would open my Bible, it would come to this place in Matthew, "Unless you can forgive those who trespass against you, how do you expect your heavenly father to forgive you?" And that haunted me.

I can feel like I'm a hero now, but I am not. A few years later, we moved from Mendenhall to Jackson where the crime was severe in our neighborhood. It was the period when blacks were moving in and whites were moving out. You know they call that the time of integration—the period from when the first black moved in until the last white moved out!

What I did was, I got a tent, and began to put the tent in people's yards. The police all heard about that, and one of these policemen was a big fat white guy. He looked like everything that was stereotyped, and he wore a police suit—and that was the hardest thing, after being beaten, is to see a . . . to make a long story short, he made a relationship with me. He did anything I would ask him to do. He would send the policemen to escort the people home. He surrounded that tent, every time, with his police force. He drew out of me some hatred with his own love, and his own deeds of love in that community.

God is an incarnational God. He lives his will out through people. So you know I could be heroic, y'all put that in the books, y'all write about that period, but it was people who came alongside me, who embraced my mission. It was always my mission.

CM: Why should you have to forgive those men in that Brandon jail?

JP: It was for my own healing. I'm in the hospital. I want to read the Bible again. I still believe it. And I don't want it convicting me anymore. I don't want it telling me what I'm supposed to do. I still believe it.

CM: So you felt a call to bear witness to the gospel to those men, to your oppressors?

JP: You're making me a hero. Yes, it worked that way, but it isn't that way. [I] am not a hero. What makes a hero is they enter into the pain of the people and they do what they know to at that moment. It wasn't an accident that this pilot [Chesley Sullenberger] landed the plane on the Hudson. You can see he had the integrity and the skills to do that anyway. He became a hero because he did it in the midst of a crisis. So we're not as heroic as we make out—I think it's a matter of us entering into the pain of the people.

See, great leaders for social change enter into the pain of the people who have the pain. And they bear that pain with the people, in the pain. That's

Mahatma Gandhi, that's Martin Luther King, that's César Chávez, that's the apostle Paul, that's Jesus.

And the pain I feel today is for the black community. Seventy percent of the kids today growing up without any father in their life, are committing 60 percent of the crime in our community. This problem is manageable! We can do something about it! Ninety-seven percent of all the black kids in prison come from a family where there's no father. We have done the analysis. The policemen tonight know where the crime is going to take place. It took place there last Saturday night. The church doesn't have the will, and we've also accepted a prosperity theology, and the church is to follow Christ, that he bore our sins in his body; he suffered with us and for us.

Leadership: he called Moses to go back into the pain of the people he led, he called Gandhi to go back into the pain of the people he led, and it was out of that pain that Mandela—twenty-eight years in prison—could come back and come up with a truth and reconciliation [commission] instead of violence for his people, because he had experienced the pain. I want you to know that we are living in a hideous situation. Churches in my urban community are becoming Doctor Dollars, are preaching a prosperity gospel, are becoming T. D. Jakes. It is bringing all the prosperity to individuals, and we haven't made that a collective effort, to deal with the misery that people are suffering from. The highest cause of death in my community is a black person killing another black person. So we got a pain here that the church is not identifying with.

In our society, we're building big buildings, we're buying airplanes, we're buying Bentleys, even, and we're not concerned about the pain. We as blacks are the wealthiest seniors that ever lived on this world. We blacks right now! We might not be that way tomorrow, the next generation might not be, but we retired from Ford, we retired from IBM, we retired as teachers, and most of that money goes to the casinos. So there is no thought pattern—and of course the white church became right-wing, and accommodated these robbers, the Lehman Brothers president making $400 million last year as his salary. If a black woman on welfare had taken too many food stamps, it would have been all over the papers, but the so-called white church has no voice to talk about corporate greed. These robbers put the whole country at risk, and some of the other nations are mad at us, because the greed of America is what brought the whole system down, and you don't hear a word about that in the church. This is a serious situation. It's big enough that our little social welfare isn't going to solve this problem. It's a big problem in our world, and instead of us entering into it, people are now saving more than they saved before this inflation. Our savings have just gone up. And we're talking about 85 percent of our people aren't hurting. They're making the same money they were making before November. But they're not giving it; they're not investing. We're in a crisis, and it's a crisis of faith, a crisis of not having a prophetic witness to our society. All our little charity isn't adequate to the problem. It's going to take the Mark Gornik type; it's going to take the people who are willing to move in and suffer with the people, with the problems in our society.

**CM:** Dr. Perkins, I have just one more question, and then if you don't mind I'd like to open this conversation up to people in the audience. But I just want to note that a former governor and U.S. senator from your home state, and my home state, Mississippi, said often in his political rallies during your childhood and adolescence that this is strictly a white man's country. I'm thinking of old Bilbo. On November 4, 2008, our nation elected Barack Obama as president, the first African American president in our nation's history. I would love it if you would share your feelings and impressions of that historic day.

**JP:** Let me share what I shared, and this will be the end. I was asked that question the Sunday following his election, and I was in Southern California, in Redondo Beach. I'll tell you how I felt that morning. And I began to feel that way when my daughter ran down the steps at 10 o'clock, and said Obama has been elected president. This is what I did that Sunday morning. This is the way I felt; these are the words: "Lift every voice and sing 'till earth and heaven ring, ring with the harmonies of Liberty. Let our rejoicing rise, high as the listening skies, let it resound loud as the rolling sea . . ."

That morning, I wanted to go out into the streets, and if I could have gone out in the streets I would have lifted my voice and sang, "My country 'tis of thee, Sweet land of liberty, of thee I sing. Land where my fathers died, land where all those slaves ploughed, from every mountainside I would say this morning that freedom is ringing." That's the way I felt. I felt what Martin Luther King said, "Free at last." I feel that now; I feel that freedom! Nobody, no white folks need to do nothing else for me! No black need to do nothing else for me! We can join together. We can join together and do something. We're free. Many of us don't know that. We still think we need to be patronized. Barack Obama represents something different than that. He represents a person who is not judged by the color of his skin, but by the content of his character. That's different from patronizing. It's time that we joined together. We're at the place where we could be reconciled. But I'm going to have to get up. I'm going to have to stop bowing down. I'm going to have to give leadership. That's what he's doing. He went to Europe the other week, and he was the leader of the free world. He went to Latin America, and he shook hands with Hugo Chávez. He wasn't afraid of him. Do you understand? I think we're at a whole new day and opportunity. So this is the time we could join together as equals, and do something about it. That's how I feel.

CM: Thank you.

Audience Member: I've been thinking about the fact that it seems like one of the most segregated times of the week is Sunday morning at 10 o'clock. Our churches are really quite segregated, and even very committed Christians seem to worship separately. I wonder if you could say something about that.

JP: Naturally I agree with you, but one of the encouragements I have that you don't have is that in most of the major cities I'm going into, there are new intentional movements; sometimes they're called the Emergent Church. Young folks are rejecting the old, traditional, ritual service, and they have a great love for the Word of God, and there is new music that's coming out to accommodate that.

But they have got to join with the pain. Just to organize a [new] place of worship doesn't identify people with the pain. That's what the megachurches are doing. They've got great personalities, they've got great art and all that is wonderful. And so people almost get satisfied when they go to their church. And so they grow, they grow, but we're not engaging that church with the pain of the people. Now of course there are some exceptions. Next week I do some work with Willow Creek. I'll be carrying them on a Justice Journey where we go down and spend five days in Alabama, where the civil rights movement took place. So there are some hopeful signs that I'm connected with. I see that and that gives me enough hope, but I also see what you see.

Audience Member: I wonder if, for the folks who haven't heard you before, if you could just say a few words about CCDA. We haven't really talked about your more recent work tonight. Could you share a little bit with this group about what you're doing through CCDA?

JP: CCDA is the Christian Community Development Association. And it's unique; it's so unique that people don't believe it, because we organize to give ourselves away. We reverse the pyramid. The basic pyramid of power is sending all the power at the top. We reverse that; we believe that the people with the problem, if supported and nurtured, can solve their own problem. So we really organize CCDA along those lines. It's an association of people coming together once a year, and we do four days of both celebration and teaching in the different cities. We have also developed an On the Road Institute that we do in different cities around the country. If a community wants to have an institute, they get together with two or three other organizations in that town, and then they invite us and we have a curriculum that we use in those neighborhoods and communities. It's hard to believe that there is such a thing as an association that doesn't have some other agenda, outside of helping the people within the community.

We try to equip the church with the great truths and with the practical involvement of being concerned for the poor. We also just read and teach the Bible. That's what I do there: each morning I read and teach the Bible to the people there. So what we're really trying to do is learn how to live out the Bible. The Bible says not they that hear the Word will be blessed, but they that do the Word will be blessed, and so we want to become doers of the Word. Because it says that if you become a hearer and not a doer, then you deceive yourself, and you think hearing is as good as doing, and you come together and we're back at the Sunday morning. We can hear the Word in a black church, we can hear the Word in a white church, so hearing is what it is, but when you begin to do reconciliation, when you begin to *do* those texts, that makes a difference.

We have a slogan in CCDA, that says "go to the people, live among them, love them, learn from them, plan with them, start with what they know, build on what they have, and that the best leaders, when our work is finished, when our task is done, we want the people to say 'We've done it ourselves.'" We believe in the inherent dignity of the people with the problem, and we come along to help them.

They get me out in Seattle to speak sometimes; they want me to solve their problems. Seattle is the most sophisticated city in the world, and they get a third grader to come out there!

I believe they can solve their problems. I think they've got the possibility out there; they've got Microsoft and all those people out there!

You get the idea?

So you've got to believe in the inherent dignity and affirm the people and get them to release the resources within those neighborhoods.

**CM:** Thank you so much.

# APPENDIX B.

## The Four Ministries of the Holy Spirit

### Lowell Noble

I HAVE TRIED TO GET JOHN PERKINS TO ARTICULATE HOW THE HOLY Spirit works in his life and ministry. I have seen John practicing Luke 4:18–19—the Spirit, the poor, the oppressed, and jubilee justice—in a unique and powerful way. I would argue that the church would benefit greatly if John would describe how the Spirit anoints his understanding and practice of incarnating jubilee justice in poor and oppressed communities. He refuses to do so, so that is why I am writing this essay—to describe what I have seen and heard.

John seldom says much about the Holy Spirit in public messages, in part because he feels that too many people too casually say the Holy Spirit said this or the Holy Spirit told me to tell you, and there does not seem to be much substance to their lives. Also, John does not want the Holy Spirit to be blamed for his mistakes. One time on the way to the airport I was pressing him to articulate how the Holy Spirit worked in his life and ministry. I wanted some practical, applied comments. Guess what John did to me; he retreated to a rather lofty theological treatise on the Holy Spirit and the trinity. It was good stuff, but he avoided directly answering my more practical question. John sometimes accuses me of being too academic, too theoretical, and not practical enough. This time John avoided the practical answer that I wanted; possibly it might be better for another person to bear witness to how they see the Spirit at work in John's life. The following are my eyewitness observations and analysis. This essay is based primarily on my extensive personal contact with John Perkins as I have volunteered at the Perkins Center in Jackson, Mississippi, from 1998 to 2011. I have known of him and his ministry for a much longer period of time. I have heard John Perkins speak, teach, and preach a multitude of times. I have read the twelve books that he has authored, coauthored, or edited. We have had numerous one-on-one conversations as I have transported him to the Jackson Airport, possibly a hundred times.

## BACKGROUND

John Perkins's Christian community development ministry began in Mendenhall, Mississippi, in 1960. Mendenhall is the county seat of Simpson County, a poor, rural, racist part of Mississippi. What was the state of Christianity in the heart of the Bible Belt? There was high church attendance in both the black and white communities, with everyone worshipping in segregated churches. At the same time, this Mississippi brand of highly Americanized Christianity left poverty, oppression, and racism largely unchallenged and unchanged. To use the language of Jeremiah 7, biblical "truth had perished" and "deceptive words" abounded, even in the temple, supposedly the house of God. This language seemed to sanction and sanctify the widespread oppression in Judah. Similarly today, to use the words of Lee Harper, who was born and raised in Mississippi: "Injustice ran deep and cloaked itself well among those things that appeared just."[1]

Half the gospel, half-truths, posing as the whole gospel, the whole truth. I suppose one could argue that half a gospel was better than none because the half gospel being preached was the cross and resurrection, so some Mississippians were being born again. On the other hand, leaving out the kingdom of God as justice for the poor and oppressed (Luke 4:18–19), and leaving out the social reconciliation message of Ephesians 2:11–22, produces a disobedient born-again Christian. God does not allow us to pick and choose what parts of the Bible we want to obey. According to Micah 6:8, God requires that we "do justice." Followers of Jesus Christ are not allowed to participate in, tolerate, or even stand idly by when horrible, systematic oppression is dehumanizing a people created in the image of God. Such was the state of Mississippi Christianity and culture when John Perkins arrived in Mendenhall. How does a person bring biblical truth to bear in such a confused and chaotic spiritual situation? A tough assignment indeed faced Perkins in the summer of 1960.

In this essay, I attempt to draw out the four ministries of the Holy Spirit that are evident in Scripture and that I see at work in John Perkins's life and ministry:[2] the Spirit of truth, the relationship of the Holy Spirit and the kingdom of God, the fruit of the Spirit, and the gifts of the Spirit.[3]

## / 1 / SPIRIT OF TRUTH

First, a short historical perspective going back to Mendenhall where John's ministry began. John started out as an evangelist and Bible teacher, in some ways a fundamentalist. Most fundamentalists are strong on evangelism and doctrine, but weak on the social or holistic gospel. Soon, in response to the deep needs of the people, he added Christian community development in order to respond to the lack of decent housing, medical care, legal services, and adequate education. One could almost say John was carrying on three full-time ministries at the same time all wrapped up into one. Certainly his fundamentalist background did not prepare him for such a ministry. John had no human mentor to teach him how to do it. He had not read a book on holistic ministry—probably none existed. But he did have some wise counsel from some older black friends in the community, which John highly valued.

To elaborate, John has been an evangelist, Bible teacher, pastor, reconciler, community developer, civil rights activist, prophet, author, and, as a hobby, John loves to play architect. A running joke about John is that he has never met a porch he did not want to enclose. As I see it, God and John sat down together every morning to plan the ministry for the day and the weeks ahead. It was the Holy Spirit drawing close, guiding John, empowering John, and providing wisdom beyond his own. Yes, John was a diligent student of the Scriptures. Yes, John has a brilliant and quick mind. But it was the Holy Spirit who brought it all together. The people sensed the Holy Spirit at work, not only in John as a person but also in the church and community.

In the midst of massive social evil, deceit, and half gospel, John definitely needed the ministry of the Holy Spirit as the spirit of truth. I believe that the Holy Spirit not only guides us into "spiritual truth" but also gives insight and wisdom in regard to the state and needs of society as well. John reached out to the white pastor Robert Odenwald of the downtown Baptist church; he convinced the pastor that they should work together in ministry in the quarters across the railroad tracks. Reverend Odenwald began to preach a holistic, biblical gospel to his congregation. His congregation was more committed to southern segregated culture than the Bible, so they rejected the pastor's biblical teaching. The pastor was so disillusioned that he committed suicide. Even today in Mississippi, segregation in the churches is the norm, with some notable exceptions and some token integration.

Building upon his understanding of creation and the jubilee/sabbatical laws, John defined justice as an economic issue; justice is also an ownership issue, a stewardship issue. Justice has to do with equal access to the resources of God. If John Perkins had been present at the time of Acts 4:32–35, he would have seen to it that as the rich sold their surplus houses and lands to provide charity for the poor, some of that land would have been donated to the poor so that poor families could grow enough food to feed themselves. John never developed a full, biblical theory of oppression as he did justice, but implied is that oppression creates an economic system that destroys community whereas justice would create an economic system that creates community. His own Mississippi background in and experiences of oppression and poverty enabled John to see these issues more sharply than most middle-class Bible teachers.

Also implied is that justice and oppression are holistic concepts in the sense that they are spiritual/social/economic issues. At its heart, the rich/poor theme that pervades both the Old Testament and the New Testament is understood best when seen through the lens of its oppression/justice teaching or better yet its oppression/justice/ shalom teaching. The Spirit has enabled John to perceive this understanding better than any other American evangelical that I know.[4]

## THE SPIRIT AND THE KINGDOM OF GOD

One of John Perkins's favorite teachings is that the gospel cuts across cultural, social, and economic barriers. To illustrate that the gospel can and must cut across cultural, social, and economic barriers, John often uses the story of Jesus reaching out to the Samaritan woman as found in John 4. I have heard him present this teaching a number of times, but one presentation is particularly memorable.

Just before Christmas in 2002, a SPRINT mission team of Seattle Pacific University (SPU) students came to the Perkins Center in Jackson for a week. In addition to rehabbing a house, the students gathered each morning for a teaching from Perkins. The president of SPU, Dr. Philip Eaton, joined them for two days. One morning John taught from John 4 on how Jesus broke through the division between Jews and Samaritans. Humanly speaking, this barrier was very deep and nearly insurmountable. In a quiet but powerful way, the Holy Spirit rested upon John that morning. Eaton was seated at one end of a long table; Perkins was at the other end. The students sat around the table, and I sat a short distance away where I could observe both Perkins and Eaton. President Eaton was deeply moved by what he heard, as we all were. He sensed he was in the presence of greatness. So the SPU president asked for a meeting to discuss the possibility of establishing a partnership between the Perkins Center and SPU.

Two years later, the John Perkins Center opened at SPU to promote John's ideas on reconciliation and community development. Slowly but surely, John's unique ideas are permeating the curriculum and campus at SPU. Few prestigious Christian universities would see the need for a relationship with a black Mississippian who was a third grade dropout. Only the Holy Spirit, I believe, could orchestrate such a series of events.

One of Perkins's foundational Scriptures is Acts 1:8: "But you will receive power when the Holy Spirit comes on you, and you will be my witnesses in Jerusalem and in all Judea, and Samaria and to the ends of the earth." In New Testament times the Jews tended to see God as their own private God; he was not a God of the Samaritans and the Gentiles (Luke 4:25–30; 9:51–56). Jesus, in Acts 1:8, contradicts this heresy by asserting that the Holy Spirit will anoint the church to take the gospel of the kingdom not only to Israel (Jerusalem and Judea) but also to the despised Samaritans and the unclean, pagan Gentiles.

In Acts 1:3, after his resurrection and before his ascension, Jesus was still teaching incessantly about the kingdom of God. In Acts 1:1–8 there are two interrelated themes: the Holy Spirit and the kingdom of God. Jesus talked so much about the kingdom that it prompted a legitimate but ethnocentric question, "Are you at this time going to restore the kingdom to Israel?" In Acts 1:8 Jesus, in a sense, answered "Yes," but with a huge qualification—the kingdom of God was also for everyone, every ethnos, including—believe it or not—the despised Samaritans and Gentiles. What a blockbuster statement to drop on his followers just as he was leaving them!

And, of course, we know that even the Spirit-filled church only fulfilled this marching order slowly and under some duress. Only persecution drove a few followers to take the gospel into Samaria (Acts 8), and only a supernatural calling brought Paul on the scene to take the gospel to the Gentiles (Acts 9). None of the original Pentecost crowd took the gospel to the Gentiles. Apparently, their ethnocentrism prevented them from obeying Jesus's command to do so (Acts 1:8). That the kingdom of God is central to the gospel is expressed again in Acts 8, 12, and 28:23–31. What was the gospel that was being preached first in Samaria, then in Rome? Philip "preached the good news of the kingdom of God and the name of Jesus Christ" (Acts

8:12). And Paul preached exactly the same message in Rome, first to the Jews, and then to the Gentiles.

The context of the kingdom message is nowhere defined in any detail in the book of Acts, so one has to go to the messianic passages in Isaiah (previously cited). In these passages, which predicted and described the nature of the coming kingdom of God, we find these recurring themes: the Spirit, justice, and the poor. A one-sentence summary: the Holy Spirit will anoint the Messiah King to incarnate the kingdom of God as justice for the oppressed poor.

These same concepts of the Spirit, the poor, the oppressed, and jubilee justice are repeated in Luke 4:18–19, which is a quotation from Isaiah 61. If Isaiah 61 had been written after Pentecost, it might have read like this: "The Holy Spirit has anointed the church to preach good news to the oppressed poor by incarnating jubilee justice in a community." Though the phrase "the kingdom of God" is not found in Luke 4:18–19, I believe that these verses are Jesus's mission statement for the kingdom of God. I sense a similar sentiment in my paraphrase of Romans 14:17: "The kingdom of God is justice, shalom, and joy in the Holy Spirit." *[handwritten: ; righteousness, peace & joy in]*

The church in Acts would have brought this understanding of the kingdom with them to 8:12, 28:23, and 31, in my opinion. If true, their understanding of the relationship of the Spirit and the kingdom would have been, *[handwritten: the Holy Spirit]* to use the language of today, "tight." Acts is clear about what it means to preach Jesus Christ. This good news is about the cross, the resurrection, and the redemption they provide. American evangelicals excel with this part of the gospel, but they are weak on the kingdom as justice part. To summarize, one could say preaching Jesus Christ is the justification by faith gospel; preaching the kingdom is the justice for the oppressed poor gospel. A fully biblical gospel must include this two-pronged gospel. *John Perkins seamlessly wove these two threads together to preach and practice a "holistic gospel,"* one of his favorite phrases.

## ☒ FRUIT OF THE SPIRIT

The third ministry of the Spirit in John Perkins's life and ministry is the fruit of the Spirit. The fruit of the Spirit—love, joy, peace, and so forth (Gal. 5:22–23)—produces Christian character. The fruit should be cultivated before one seeks to exercise the gifts of the Spirit. If not, the gifts may and often do become "spiritual toys" used to promote self-edification rather than church edification. This is the lesson to be learned from 1 Corinthians 12, 13, 14. The gifts of the Spirit were highly prized and aggressively pursued in the Corinthian church. It was almost as though there was a spiritual contest, a spiritual beauty pageant, in which the contestants competed for first place. So Paul wrote the Corinthian church that love must come first, love must control the exercise of the gifts for the good of the church.

A close friend of John Perkins calls him quite often to check up on John's character. This friend wants John to "finish well." This friend has seen far too many Christian leaders fall. Pride, fame, money, and/or sex trip them up. This friend does not want this to happen to John.

John has the intelligence, energy, and charisma so that had he so chosen, I am sure he could have been a sort of cult leader, a TV evangelist, the pastor of a megachurch, or the dictator of a CCDA empire. Instead, he has kept the poor central in his life; he has always lived among the poor in the community where he lived instead of moving to the more comfortable spiritual suburbs. This helped keep his feet on the ground. He has always kept the memory of his mother front and center. His mother—as a dirt-poor black woman from rural Mississippi—died of malnutrition while John was still an infant. This memory inspires, and to a degree, haunts John. John imagines that after he passes and sees his mother in heaven, the first thing she may ask him is "What did you do for my people? Did you remember the poor?" This keeps him on the straight and narrow path.

Christian character must precede and control the exercise of spiritual gifts.

## 4 | GIFTS OF THE SPIRIT

Finally, the gifts of the Spirit. I quite often ask people who have attended at least a workshop or other event with John to give me a one-word description of him. A wide variety of words are used such as "passion," but the most common word is "wisdom." This is first on the list of the gifts in 1 Corinthians 12:8; another list from 12:27–30 highlights teachers.

John's IQ has never been measured to my knowledge, but I would rate him as one of the most intelligent people that I know. As a former college professor, I have been around many smart people. But wisdom is much more than intelligence. His intelligence has been deeply informed by biblical truth and the Spirit's anointing. I would say that John Perkins is the wisest person I have known. John has authored, coauthored, or edited twelve books. They have been well received and widely read, not just because John has a good story to tell. The readers find much wisdom in these books as well.

Perkins is widely known as a reconciler and community developer; however, on his tombstone he would prefer the phrase "Bible teacher." This has been his passion all his life, and he excels in it. His ability to easily quote numerous Scriptures appropriate to his teaching is remarkable. John lives in the Word, and the Spirit enables him to use it as a spiritual sword. I also sense a prophetic streak in John as he, at times, preaches a hard but necessary truth to his listeners. The prophetic message is often required when you are confronting oppression/justice issues.

A final comment on the four ministries of the Holy Spirit: most denominations emphasize one of these ministries, often to the neglect of the other three. Of all the people I have known, John Perkins brings the best balance to these four ministries.

To conclude this essay, I would like to compare the lives, ministries, and gods of two Protestant saints, A. W. Tozer and John Perkins. Both men had long preaching and teaching ministries that influenced evangelical churches in America. Wheaton College recognized their respective contribution when it awarded Tozer an honorary doctorate in 1950 and Perkins his honorary doctorate in 1980.[5]

The point of this comparison is not to defame the deceased Tozer, although to Tozer's disciples, this is likely to be their first reaction. The purpose is to move all American Christians toward doing justice in poor communities. This issue is especially urgent in Jackson, Mississippi, where Perkins lives. The 2010 census data revealed a continuing white flight and a black middle-class flight to the safer and more prosperous suburbs. This exodus leaves the city of Jackson 80 percent black and increasingly poor. I am sure that many of those leaving, white and black, profess to be Christian. Why are they not staying to fulfill the scriptural admonition to "preach good news to the poor" (Luke 4:18)?

Tozer was a person of passionate prayer and intense worship of the glorious and majestic God of the universe, yet strangely, his God may have been too small, too narrowly defined. It appears to me that Tozer's God fit well with the white middle class. Perkins's God includes some of Tozer's God, but Perkins's God was a large God, a more holistic and universal God who included poor blacks as well as middle-class whites. The biblical God—the God of Amos, Isaiah, and Micah—hates oppression, loves justice, and puts the poor at the top of his list. Tozer's God did not hate oppression, love justice, and have a special concern for the poor.

This is a very serious charge! What is the evidence? From Tozer's biographer, we discover the following: Tozer ministered in a Christian Missionary Alliance church located on the south side of Chicago for thirty years. Then the surrounding community slowly changed from white to black. White members started to move out to the safer suburbs. Soon the church board voted unanimously to move as well, and Tozer agreed with the board's decision. In their eyes, the surrounding community had deteriorated irreparably. It was too dangerous to remain in the area.[6] Tozer's God was not big enough, powerful enough, loving enough, just enough, to enable the church to stay in south Chicago and incarnate jubilee justice among the oppressed poor.

The God of John Perkins would have enabled the church to seize the opportunity, stay in the community, and with love and justice begin the process of transforming the community. John Perkins believes in relocating to the area of greatest need. Tozer's God, or maybe the false god of the American trinity (individualism, materialism, and ethnocentrism), relocated the church in the wrong direction, away from the community of deep need.[7]

Remember, the God of Amos, Isaiah, and Micah raged against a spirituality divorced from justice (Amos 5; Isa. 1, 58; Mic. 6:8).

Choose your saint carefully; choose your God wisely. The wrong choice has deadly consequences as the history of the American church indicates. Remember yesterday's slavery and segregation, and today's mass incarceration of young black males.[8]

The right choice will please Jesus the Christ who has charged the Spirit-anointed church to preach good news to the poor, to release the oppressed, to incarnate jubilee justice in the surrounding community (Luke 4:18–19). This is what the kingdom of God here on earth is all about. This biblical message lies at the heart of John Perkins's ministry. Evangelicals urgently need to start producing disciples of God who hate oppression, love justice, and care deeply about the poor.

## NOTES

1. Lee Harper is cofounder of Koinonia Coffee House, which is a center for economic redevelopment in Jackson, Mississippi. http://www.koinoniacoffee.com/. Perkins talks about her ministry in John M. Perkins and Shane Claiborne, *Follow Me to Freedom: Leading and Following as an Ordinary Radical* (Ventura, Calif.: Regal Books, 2009), 162.

2. I have had the advantage of seeing John Perkins up close and personal for many years, but of course many readers will not have had this privilege. So I will try to make explicit what may at times only be implicit in John's life and ministry.

3. The biblical foundation for the four ministries of the Holy Spirit are: First, the Spirit of truth is described by Jesus in John 14–16, as well as in 1 John. Second, the relationship of the Holy Spirit and the kingdom of God is found in the Messianic passages in Isaiah 9:6–7; 11:1–4; 16:5; 28:16–17; 42:1–4; 61:1–4; Luke 4:18–19; Acts 1:1–8; 8:12; 28:23; 31. Third, the fruit of the Spirit in Galatians 5:22–23. And fourth, the gifts of the Spirit in 1 Corinthians 12 and Romans 12.

4. I do not know of a single major article or book written by a white American evangelical on the powerful and extensive biblical teaching on oppression, so I have to turn to two authors writing from a Latin American context: Thomas D. Hanks, *God So Loved the Third World: The Biblical Vocabulary of Oppression*, trans. James C. Dekker (Eugene, Ore.: Wipf & Stock, 2001); and Elsa Tamez, *Bible of the Oppressed* (Maryknoll, N.Y.: Orbis, 1982). See also Nicholas Walterstorff, *Justice: Rights and Wrongs* (Princeton, N.J.: Princeton University Press, 2007); and Joseph Grassi, *Informing the Future: Social Justice in the New Testament* (Mahwah, N.J.: Paulist Press, 2003).

5. Interestingly, Regal Press publishes both Perkins's and Tozer's books.

6. James L. Snyder, *The Life of A. W. Tozer* (Ventura, Calif.: Regal, 2009), 205–206.

7. I coined this phrase "the American trinity." For more on ethnocentrism, see Reginald Horsman, *Race and Manifest Destiny* (Cambridge, Mass.: Harvard University Press, 1981); Richard T. Hughes, *Myths America Lives By* (Urbana: University of Illinois Press, 2004); and Ronald Takaki, *A Different Mirror: A History of Multicultural America* (New York: Back Bay Books, 1993). For more on individualism, see C. Norman Kraus, *The Authentic Witness: Credibility and Authority* (Grand Rapids, Mich.: Eerdmans, 1979); Dennis Hollingers, *Individualism and Social Ethics: An Evangelical Syncretism* (Latham, Md.: University Press of America, 1983); and Charles L. Kammer, *The Kingdom Revisited: An Essay on Christian Social Ethics* (Washington, D.C.: University Press of America, 1981). For materialism, see Jacques Ellul, *Money and Power* (Downers Grove, Ill.: InterVarsity Press, 1984).

8. On the unjust mass incarceration of young black and Hispanic males and how mass incarceration is similar to slavery and segregation as a system of oppression, see Michelle Alexander, *The New Jim Crow: Mass Incarceration in the Age of Colorblindness* (New York: New Press, 2010).

# CONTRIBUTORS

MICHAEL ANDRES is the Marvin and Jerene DeWitt Professor of Religion at Northwestern College, Orange City, Iowa. He teaches courses in systematic theology and philosophical theology. Over the years he has taken many students on Spring Service Projects and to Christian Community Development Association conferences.

MAE ELISE CANNON is an ordained pastor in the Evangelical Covenant Church and currently serves as the senior campaign and policy analyst for Jerusalem/West Bank for World Vision USA. She is the author of *Just Spirituality: How Faith Practices Fuel Social Action* (InterVarsity Press, 2013) and *Social Justice Handbook: Small Steps for a Better World* (InterVarsity Press, 2009). Cannon formerly served as director of development and transformation for extension ministries at Willow Creek Community Church in Barrington, Illinois.

KELLY WEST FIGUEROA-RAY is a Ph.D. candidate at the University of Virginia and research assistant for the Project on Lived Theology. Figueroa-Ray's research focuses on the relationship between Scripture and theology as it is lived out in communities of faith, with a particular interest in multicultural Christian ministries. She is part of the Comparative Scripture, Interpretation, and Practice (SIP) program at the University of Virginia and is a regular contributor to the Huffington Post.

LISA SHARON HARPER is Sojourners director of mobilizing based in Washington, D.C. She was the cofounder and executive director of New York Faith & Justice, a movement of churches, organizations, and individuals dedicated to following Christ, uniting the church, and ending poverty in New York through spiritual formation, education, and direct advocacy. She is a featured op-ed writer for the God's Politics blog and BeliefNet's Progressive Revival blog. She is the author of *Evangelical Does Not Equal Republican . . . Or Democrat* (New Press, 2008), an editor-at-large for the magazine *Sojourners*, and a contributor for *Prism, Urban Faith,* and *Conspire* magazines.

PETER GOODWIN HELTZEL is associate professor of theology and director of the Micah Institute at New York Theological Seminary. He is the author of *Resurrection City: A Theology of Improvisation* (Eerdmans, 2012) and *Jesus and Justice: Evangelicals, Race and American Politics* (Yale University Press, 2009). His edited volumes include *Prophetic Evangelicals: Envisioning a Just and Peaceable Kingdom* (Eerdmans, 2012) with Malinda Elizabeth Berry and Bruce Ellis Benson, *The Chalice Introduction to Theology* (Chalice Press, 2008), *Evangelicals and Empire* (Brazos Press, 2008) with Bruce Ellis Benson, and *Theology in Global Context* (T&T Clark, 2004) with Amos Yong.

CHARLES MARSH is professor of religious and theological studies and director of the Project on Lived Theology at the University of Virginia. Marsh's books include *Reclaiming Dietrich Bonheoffer: The Promise of His Theology* (Oxford University Press, 1994); *God's Long Summer: Stories of Faith and Civil Rights* (Princeton University Press, 1997), which won the 1998 Grawemeyer Award in Religion; *The Beloved Community: How Faith Shapes Social Justice, from the Civil Rights Movement to Today* (Basic Books, 2005); and *Wayward Christian Soldiers: Freeing the Gospel from Political Captivity* (Oxford University Press, 2007). He coauthored a book with John Perkins, *Welcoming Justice: God's Movement toward Beloved Community* (InterVarsity Press, 2009).

PAUL LOUIS METZGER is professor of Christian theology and theology of culture, and director of the Institute for the Theology of Culture: New Wine, New Wineskins at Multnomah School of the Bible. Metzger is the author of *The Gospel of John: When Love Comes to Town* (InterVarsity Press, 2010), *New Wine Tastings: Theological Essays of Cultural Engagement* (Cascade, 2011), *Consuming Jesus: Beyond Race and Class Divisions in a Consumer Church* (Eerdmans, 2007), *Exploring Ecclesiology: An Evangelical and Ecumenical Introduction* (coauthored with Brad Harper; Brazos, 2009), and *The Word of Christ and the World of Culture: Sacred and Secular through the Theology of Karl Barth* (Eerdmans, 2003). He is coeditor of *A World for All?: Global Civil Society in Political Theory and Trinitarian Theology* (with William F. Storrar and Peter J. Casarella; Eerdmans, 2011), and editor of *Trinitarian Soundings in Systematic Theology* (T&T Clark, 2005).

ALBERT G. MILLER is professor of religion at Oberlin College, where he teaches American and African American religious history. He is author of

*Elevating the Race: Theophilus G. Steward and the Making of an African-American Civil Religion, 1865–1924* (University of Tennessee Press, 2003). Miller is senior minister of Oberlin House of the Lord Fellowship.

LOWELL NOBLE is emeritus professor of sociology and anthropology, Spring Arbor University. He has volunteered at the John Perkins Center in Jackson since 1998. Not only has he made a close study of Perkins's teaching, as numerous student groups visiting Jackson can attest, he has enriched the teaching at the center with his understanding of current sociology on race in the United States.

TED OWNBY is the director of the Center for Southern Culture and professor of history and southern studies at the University of Mississippi. A leading scholar in the history of religion and culture in the American South, he is the author of *American Dreams in Mississippi: Consumers, Poverty, and Culture, 1830–1998* (University of North Carolina Press, 1999) and *Subduing Satan: Religion, Recreation and Manhood in the Rural South, 1865–1920* (University of North Carolina Press, 1990), and editor of *Black and White: Cultural Interaction in the Antebellum South* (University Press of Mississippi, 1993).

SOONG-CHAN RAH is the Milton B. Engebretson Assistant Professor of Church Growth and Evangelism, North Park Theological Seminary. He is the author of *The Next Evangelicalism: Freeing the Church from Western Cultural Captivity* (InterVarsity Press, 2009). Rah was the founding senior pastor of the Cambridge Community Fellowship Church, a multiethnic, urban ministry–focused church committed to living out the values of racial reconciliation and social justice in the urban context.

CHRIS RICE is founding codirector of the Duke Divinity School Center for Reconciliation. He coauthored *More Than Equals* (InterVarsity Press, 1993) with Spencer Perkins. It is a book on the importance and possibilities of racial reconciliation rooted in his seventeen years living in Jackson, Mississippi, as part of an intentional interracial community and member of Voice of Calvary. Since working at Duke Divinity School, Rice has written *Grace Matters: A True Story of Race, Friendship, and Faith in the Heart of the South* (Jossey-Bass, 2002) and coauthored *Reconciling All Things* (InterVarsity Press, 2008) with Emmanuel Katongole.

CHERYL J. SANDERS is senior pastor of the Third Street Church of God in Washington, D.C., and professor of Christian ethics at the Howard University School of Divinity. She is the author of over fifty articles and several books, including *Ministry at the Margins: The Prophetic Mission of Women, Youth & the Poor* (InterVarsity Press, 1997), *Saints in Exile: The Holiness-Pentecostal Experience in African American Religion and Culture* (Oxford University Press, 1996), and *Empowerment Ethics for a Liberated People: A Path to African American Social Transformation* (Fortress Press, 1995).

RONALD J. SIDER is the president of Evangelicals for Social Action; professor of theology, holistic ministry, and public policy at Palmer Theological Seminary; and director of the seminary's Sider Center on Ministry & Public Policy. He wrote the influential book *Rich Christians in an Age of Hunger* (InterVarsity Press, 1977). Author of over thirty books, his other titles include *Just Generosity: A New Vision for Overcoming Poverty in America* (Baker Books, 1999) and *Good News and Good Works: A Theology for the Whole Gospel* (Baker Books, 1993). He coauthored with Heidi Rolland Unruh *Saving Souls, Serving Society: Understanding the Faith Factor in Church-Based Social Ministry* (Oxford University Press, 2005).

PETER SLADE is associate professor of the history of Christianity and Christian thought at Ashland University in Ashland, Ohio. He is the author of *Open Friendship in a Closed Society: Mission Mississippi and a Theology of Friendship* (Oxford University Press, 2009).

CHRISTIAN T. COLLINS WINN is assistant professor of historical and systematic theology at Bethel University. He is the author of *"Jesus Is Victor!": The Significance of the Blumhardts for the Theology of Karl Barth* (Pickwick Publications, 2009). He edited *From the Margins: A Celebration of the Theological Work of Donald W. Dayton* (Pickwick Publications, 2007), and coedited *The Pietist Impulse in Christianity* (Pickwick Publications, 2011).

LAUREN F. WINNER is assistant professor of Christian spirituality, Duke Divinity School. Her books include *A Cheerful and Comfortable Faith: Anglican Religious Practice in the Elite Households of Eighteenth-Century Virginia* (Yale University Press, 2010), *Girl Meets God: On the Path to a Spiritual Life* (Algonquin Books, 2002), *Mudhouse Sabbath* (Paraclete Press, 2003), and *Real Sex: The Naked Truth about Chastity* (Brazos Press 2006).

# ACKNOWLEDGMENTS

THE EDITORS OF THIS VOLUME WANT TO THANK ALL THE PARTICIPANTS in the 2009 Spring Institute for Lived Theology, particularly John Perkins for his generous and inspiring presence. We are grateful to Noel Castellanos for enabling us to hold a panel discussion on the legacy of John Perkins at the Christian Community Development Association's annual meeting in Cincinnati that same year. We want to thank Gail Davis and Joe Strife for their work transcribing Charles Marsh's conversation with John Perkins and Cheryl Sanders's conference presentation, and for Kristina Garcia Wade's editorial work on both pieces. Thanks to all the graduate assistants who worked with the Project for Lived Theology during the extended gestation of this book, including A. J. Walton and Kendall Cox. Thanks to Roger Hoover and his skill with Photoshop. Thanks to our editor, Craig Gill, at the University Press of Mississippi, and to the Project on Lived Theology for its support of this project.

# INDEX

*New York Times,* 61
*Newsweek,* 72
Niebuhr, H. Richard, 178
Niebuhr, Reinhold, 62–63

Obama, Barack, 71, 133, 200–201
Odenwald, Robert, 66, 126, 194, 195, 205
"On Being a Good Neighbor" (King), 41
On the Road Institute, 202
"One Father—One Blood" (Trentham), 42
Osteen, John, 93

Pasadena, California, ix
Pelagianism, 93
Perkins, Clyde, 32–33, 113, 161, 191
Perkins, Elizabeth, 91
Perkins, Maggie, 24, 93, 113, 162, 189, 190, 192, 209
Perkins, John M.: African American churches, 4, 6, 9–10, 11, 62, 116–17, 162, 191; alternative calendar, 21; black-on-black crime, 17; Christian brotherhood, 32–34, 50–56; Christmas, 20; church as agent of change, 18–19, 25–26; church as family, 21–25; church leadership, ix, 19; civil rights movement, vii, 12–13, 72–75, 113–14, 163–64, 172, 194, 197; community development, 51, 95, 108, 112, 117, 126–27, 204–5; consumerism, 135, 195, 199; conversion to Christianity, 4, 9, 11, 53, 101, 162–63, 192; corporate greed, 199; decision to leave Mississippi, 33, 162, 191; early life, 4, 7, 24, 32–33, 93, 113, 161, 189–91; economic empowerment, ix; fame, 90–91; Federation of Southern Cooperatives, 114; holistic ministry (or holistic gospel), x, 17, 64, 67–71, 72, 75, 194, 208; indigenous leadership, ix; influence of Apostle Paul, 3, 11, 13, 25, 83, 101, 147; influence of Martin Luther King Jr., 74; influence on white evangelical church, xvi, 3, 60, 68–70, 72–73, 75, 173, 195; jail

beating, 53, 84, 93, 114, 147, 153, 163, 172, 173, 197–98; John M. Perkins Foundation for Reconciliation & Development, 68; love, 166–68, 171, 192; organic soteriology, 95, 96, 105; prayer, 20; prophetic church, 108; prosperity gospel movement, 87, 199; racial reconciliation, 32–33, 51–53, 56, 70, 103, 130, 132, 167, 185, 186, 195, 197; racism in religion, 116; redistribution, 56, 83, 88, 117; religious influences, 10, 114, 118; return to Mississippi, 60–61, 114, 163, 192; Ruby McKnight Williams award, 28; self-help (or self-determination), 4, 10, 12–13, 17, 52; social ministry (or social gospel), vii, xvi; Task Force on Food Assistance, xvi, 16, 18, 27–28; three Rs: relocation, reconciliation, redistribution, viii–ix, xvii, 3, 19–20, 52, 60, 67, 70, 85, 86, 88, 91, 94, 95, 117, 118, 127, 145, 148–50, 154–56, 171, 173–74; use of the term *Holy Spirit,* 192, 203; welfare, ix, xvi, 17–18, 20–21, 23, 25–26, 28

**Works:** *Follow Me to Freedom: Leading and Following as an Ordinary Radical,* 73; *He's My Brother: Former Racial Foes Offer Strategy for Reconciliation,* 32, 33, 53–54, 56; *Let Justice Roll Down,* 33, 50–51, 73, 115, 162, 171, 189–90, 191; *A Quiet Revolution,* 18, 51; "Resurrecting Hope," 116; "Walk Your Talk," 17; *With Justice for All,* 51–52, 55–56, 171
Perkins, Spencer, viii, 11, 147, 153–55, 162, 190, 193
Perkins, Vera Mae, vii, ix, x, xi, 4–5, 7, 9–10, 60–61, 113, 155, 172, 189, 191, 194–95
Perkins Center. *See* Spencer Perkins Center
Pinn, Anthony, 8
Piper, John, 181
pluralism, 66–67, 71–72
Portland, Oregon, 84, 90
"Power and Racism" (Carmichael), 49

## ABOUT THE EDITORS

PETER SLADE is associate professor of religion at Ashland University in Ohio. He is the author of *Open Friendship in a Closed Society: Mission Mississippi and a Theology of Friendship.*

CHARLES MARSH is professor of religious studies and the director of the Project on Lived Theology at the University of Virginia. He is the author of multiple titles including *Reclaiming Dietrich Bonheoffer: The Promise of His Theology.*

PETER GOODWIN HELTZEL is associate professor of theology and the director of the Micah Institute at New York Theological Seminary and an ordained minister in the Christian Church (Disciples of Christ). He is the author of *Jesus and Justice: Evangelicals, Race and American Politics* and *Resurrection City: A Theology of Improvisation.*

CPSIA information can be obtained at www.ICGtesting.com
Printed in the USA
BVOW08s1922080913

330511BV00003B/4/P